Traveler's Language Guides: French

Developed by
Jacqueline Sword

All inquiries should be addressed to:
Barron's Educational Series, Inc.
250 Wireless Boulevard
Hauppauge, NY 11788
http://www.barronseduc.com

ISBN-13: 978-0-7641-3205-6
ISBN-10: 0-7641-3205-9
Library of Congress Control Number 2005921549

Printed in China
9 8 7 6 5 4 3 2 1

Translation: Eric A. Bye, M.A.

Photo Credits
Self-help Association for the Physically Handicapped, Krautheim: 75; Cycleurope, Bergisch-Gladback: 59; Ford, Inc.: 56; H. Geissel, Stuttgard: 15, 81, 115, 125, 137, 143, 177; HB-Publishing, Chr. Böttcher and Th. Tiensch: 9; U. Messelhäuser, Salem: 71; M. Sucha, Prague: 19, 31, 47, 91; Wolpert Photo Design, Stuttgart: 38–39, 100–106, 165
Cover: Tiofoto (Anders Lindh/Kim Naylor/Ulf Sjöstedt)

Pronunciation

Vowel Sounds

In general French vowel sounds are pure and "open," with no slurring or diphthongization.

a as in the English word *father*	mad**a**me, l**a** salle, l**à**
é, -ez, and *–er* as in *day*	caf**é**, mang**er**, regard**ez**
i like the vowel sound in *peel*	**i**l, l'am**i**e, lyc**é**e
o as in *ozone*	p**o**rte, P**au**l, al**o**rs
eu like German ö: a close approximation is the vowel sound in the English word *fur*	un p**eu**, d**eu**x
ou as in *rule*	**ou**, **où**, bonj**ou**r
u: sharper than in English: purse the lips as if to say ***ou*** but instead pronounce *i* [as above]	t**u**, r**u**e, sal**u**t
in, ain, ein: strongly nasalized, without pronouncing the consonant	enf**in**, f**aim**, pl**ein**, b**ien**, **un**
on, om: strongly nasalized, without pronouncing the consonant	b**on**, m**on**tre, il t**om**be
ans, ant, ent: similar to the middle sound in the English word *haunt*, but strongly nasalized, and without pronouncing the consonant	d**ans**, pr**ends**, pend**ant**

Consonants

Most consonant sounds are similar to what we are used to in English. Note the following special points:

s can be like either the first *s* in the English word *season*	**s**oeur, ta**ss**e
s can also be like the second *s* in the English word *sea**s**on*	mai**s**on, chai**s**e
ch as in the familiar terms *papier mâ**ch**é* and ***ch**ablis*	**ch**aise, je **ch**erche
j is softer than in English, as in the familiar expression *Bon voya**g**e!*	**j**e, bon**j**our
gn like the middle consonant sound in *ca**ny**on*	co**gn**ac, il ga**gn**e
r is far more guttural than in English, and comes from farther back in the throat	**r**avi, autou**r**, **r**egarde

Sounds not specifically identified in this brief summary are quite close to their counterparts in English.

The Alphabet

A	a	[ah]	J	j	[zheh]	S	s	[es]
B	b	[beh]	K	k	[ka]	T	t	[teh]
C	c	[seh]	L	l	[el]	U	u	[ue]
D	d	[deh]	M	m	[em]	V	v	[veh]
E	e	[euh]	N	n	[en]	W	w	[doobleh-veh]
F	f	[ef]	O	o	[o]	X	x	[eeks]
G	g	[zheh]	P	p	[peh]	Y	y	[eegreck]
H	h	[ahsch]	Q	q	[kue]	Z	z	[zed]
I	i	[ee]	R	r	[air]			

Common Abbreviations

ACF	Automobile Club de France	French Automobile Club
Av. J.-C	avant Jésus-Christ	BC
CV	curriculum vitae	c.v.
EDF	Electricité de France	Electricity France
HLM	habitation à loyer modéré	Low-rent housing
M.	Monsieur	Mr.
Mlle	Mademoiselle	Miss
Mme	Madame	Mrs.
MM	Messieurs	Gentlemen
p.ex.	par exemple	for example, e.g.
P.R.	poste restante	general delivery
PDG	Président-directeur general	CEO
PetT	Poste et Télécommunications	Post Office and Telecommunications
SA	société anonyme	Inc.
SARL	Société à responsabilité limitée	Limited liability corporation
SNCF	Société Nationale des Chemins de Fer Français	French National Railroad
s.t.p.	s'il te plaît	please (informal)
s.v.p.	s'il vous plaît	please (formal)
TGV	Train à grande vitesse	high speed train
TVA	Taxe à valeur ajoutée	value-added tax

Abbreviations in the Travel Dictionary

	English	French
abst	abstract	abstrait
acoust	acoustics	acoustique
adj	adjective	adjectif
adv	adverb	adverbe
art	article	article
conj	conjunction	conjonction
el	electricity	électricité
f	feminine	feminine
m	masculine	masculine
M.	Mr.	monsieur
med	medicine	médecine
Mlle	Miss	mademoiselle
Mme	Mrs.	madame
nº	number	numéro
pers prn	personal pronoun	pronom personnel
pl	plural	pluriel
poss prn	possessive pronoun	pronom possessif
prep	preposition	préposition
prn	pronoun	pronom
qc	something	quelque chose
qn	someone	quelqu'un
refl	reflexive	réfléchi
rel	religion	religion
sing	singular	singulier
sn	someone	quelqu'un
sth	something	quelque chose
s.t.p.	please (informal)	s'il te plait (informel)
superl	superlative	superlatif
s.v.p.	please (formal)	s'il vous plait (formel)
tele	telephone	téléphone

**Different Lands,
Different Customs**

Cross-cultural Tips

Greetings

In greeting people you say **bonjour** (hello, good day); good friends may greet each other by saying **salut** (hi). People also ask **ça va?** (How's it going?), and the common answer is **ça va**, regardless of how you really feel!
Bonsoir (good evening) is used in the evening, and before going to bed it's common to say **bonne nuit** (good night).
When people part they say **au revoir** (good-bye), **salut** or **tchao** (so long). There is no real equivalent to "Take it easy" or "Take care."

Forms of Direct Address

In France it is impolite to address a person you know only casually by first name. The family name also lends a familiar touch that should be avoided. Thus, it is preferable to say simply, **Bonjour, Madame** or **Bonjour, Monsieur**.
When you say **merci** (thank you) it is more polite to follow it with **Monsieur** or **Madame** instead of leaving it hanging. **Mademoiselle** (miss) is always used in addressing girls or young women, but nowadays people change to **Madame** at a certain age, whether or not the lady in question is married. But there is one interesting exception: Very well-known, highly regarded actresses are addressed as **Mademoiselle**—followed by their family name–at major social events. (Mademoiselle Huppert—mother of three children—is among the few to whom this honor is accorded.) In France people with the title of *doctor* get no special recognition: no one learns of their academic degree because they are addressed simply as **Monsieur** or **Madame** (see p.166 for the only exception).

A Handshake or a Kiss?

People often shake hands when they greet one another. Among family members, friends, and acquaintances, and even colleagues, kisses are very common between women, and even between women and men. Men are more likely to greet one another with a handshake. Whether people kiss two, three, or four times depends on the location: in Paris it's twice, in southern France four times, in neighboring Switzerland three times; these kissing rules are quite flexible and also depend on personal customs.

Thus, even the French often don't know how many times to kiss. You begin with two, and then you get further instructions: "Moi, c'est quatre" (I do four) or "Chez nous c'est trois" (We use three)— and *we* can mean the area as well as the specific family.

Savoir-vivre

The commonly cited **savoir-vivre** doesn't mean that people know how to enjoy life, but rather that they know how to behave in all types of situations. This can involve such simple things as holding the door open for the next person, giving someone flowers on appropriate occasions—in brief, people know how to conduct themselves properly. That also includes making ample use of **merci** (thank you) and **pardon** (excuse me). For example, in France you say **pardon** even when you walk past someone in a doorway.

Using the Telephone

A few years ago the area codes were done away with, or else integrated into the phone numbers themselves. That means that with both long distance and local calls, the area code is always dialed as part of the number, and all phone numbers have ten digits.

A person who answers the phone says **Allô**. Then as the caller you may ask if you have the right number – unless you recognize the voice: **Je suis bien chez …?** (Is this …?) Then the conversation can begin. Company employees answer with the company name. The digits of a telephone number are not spoken individually, but rather in pairs, e.g., 03 21 30 39 91: zero trois, vingt-et-un, trente, trente-neuf, quatre-vingt-onze.

Some important telephone numbers:

Renseignements (Information)	12
SAMU (Emergency medical attention, rescue)	15
Pompiers (Fire Department)	17
Police	18

So-called **numéros verts** (green numbers) are free and begin with 0800.

Telephone Booths and Phone Cards

Every telephone booth can be called with an individual number, which is located at the top right over the telephone. So it's easy to have someone call you at a telephone booth if necessary.

11

Phone cards are available in post offices and in every **café/ bar-tabac**, recognizable by a sign that looks like a small carrot. There are two models to choose from: one with an electronic chip and one with a PIN number that first must be exposed by rubbing. The latter is better for calling other countries if you dial the number provided on the card and give Northern Europe as the preferred destination.

Eating

At midday many French eat an **hors-d'oeuvre** (cold appetizer) such as **crudités** (raw vegetables). With the **plat de résistance** (the main course) you can chose between **viande** (meat) and **poisson** (fish). In addition there are several types of **accompagnements** (side dishes). Then come the **fromage** (cheese) and/or a **dessert**. The evening meal is lighter: a soup, a salad with ham or something similar, and cheese and/or yogurt. In a restaurant, on Sundays and with guests, people begin with an **apéritif**. They toast with **à la vôtre** (Cheers!), **santé** (Health!), and even **tchin-tchin** ("down the hatch" – among friends).

The meal ends with a **café** (espresso) and a **digestif** (liqueur). Working people who can't drive home and must make do with a sandwich go to small restaurants that offer a **plat du jour** (daily special) at midday. Nowadays there are often **formules** (literally, *formulas*): these are possible combinations at advantageous prices, such as appetizer, daily special, and drink; or daily special, dessert, and coffee.

Vegetarian menus are not very common in France.

In a Restaurant

Normally the **déjeuner** (midday meal) is served between 12:30 and 2:00; the **dîner** (evening meal) between 7:30 and 10:00 P.M. **Du pain** (fresh bread) and **une carafe d'eau** (a pitcher of tap water) are already on the table and provided at no additional cost. To call the waiter, it's usual to say, **s'il vous plaît** (Excuse me). After the meal you say **l'addition, s'il vous plaît** (The check, please).The bill that's presented is for the whole table, and it's expected that the diners will divide it among themselves. To pay, you put the cash or the credit card onto the plate provided for the purpose.

Even when the tip is already included in the price, it is still common – at least in the case of courteous service – to leave a small tip behind.

Breakfast

The **petit déjeuner** (breakfast) commonly consists only of **café au lait** (coffee with milk), **thé** (tea), or **chocolat chaud** (hot chocolate) and a baguette or tartines (slices of bread) and butter and/or jelly. **Croissants** are eaten primarily in **cafés** and hotels. At home people eat them mainly on weekends or on vacation.

Hotels

In hotels the prices are posted either outside or in the entrance. Normally these prices are understood to apply per room, not per person. For rooms with two beds the word **twin** is becoming common, at least in Paris. A **chambre double** (double room) almost always contains a double bed. Usually breakfast is not included in the price; this can be a bargaining chip and you may be able to get it at no extra cost (but only occasionally). Frequently a breakfast buffet is offered instead of the modest French breakfast.

Invitations

If people don't know each other very well, or on vacation, if people don't want to do a lot of preparation, you may be invited for an **apéritif** (drink), either at 12–12:30 or in the early evening (7:00 P.M.). There are also **amuse-gueules** (snacks) or **canapés** (appetizers). Usually people stay a good hour and then head home. If you are invited to a midday or evening meal, it's fine to come a quarter-hour late. As in this country, it's common to bring a gift for the host, such as flowers, chocolates, wine, or champagne. Often the bottle you bring will be consumed, or the chocolates will be offered after the meal. So bring along something good, because you may get some of it!

DIFFERENT LANDS, DIFFERENT CUSTOMS

Business Hours

Business hours in France are always very customer-friendly. You can basically count on stores remaining open until 7:00 P.M., some even as late as 7:30. **Hypermarchés** (supermarkets) usually stay open until 10:00 P.M. Stores are open all day long even on Saturdays. On Sundays, you can get everything you need at least until noontime. On Mondays most small shops are closed. The midday break in smaller cities is often strictly observed: starting at 12:00 noon or 12:30 at the latest you will find the door locked. In compensation, the parking between 2:00 and 4:00 P.M. is almost always free (except in Paris).

Odds and Ends

Not only telephone cards, but also postage stamps and bus and metro or streetcar tickets are available in **café/bar-tabacs**. Before you get on, the ticket has to be canceled. Orange-colored automatic machines are provided for the purpose. If you forget, contact the ticket collector to explain the situation at the outset.

It costs money to use the highways; that is, the highways are subdivided into segments, for the use of which you have to pay the **péage** (toll) every time.

Credit cards have been popular for many years. There is scarcely anyplace where they are not accepted. If someone asks you, **Vous payez par carte bleue?** (Are you paying with a blue card?), that refers to the credit card, even if yours happens to be pink.

E DE **COMMERCE** ET **D'INDUSTRIE** DE

Preparations for Travel

If you're going on a trip ...

With a mouse click you can find out the essentials about your destination by doing a simple online search by place name.
In addition to the travel guide information, you will also find online:
- current, daily travel news and interesting reports
- regular specials and contests
- mini-guides that can be printed

Booking a Hotel by E-mail

Madame, Monsieur,
Je voudrais réserver une chambre simple / double / twin pour 2 nuits du 28 au 30 juin. Je vous serais reconnaissant/e de me confirmer cette réservation et de me donner le prix pour les deux nuits, petit-déjeuner inclus. Je vous remercie d'avance.
Meilleures salutations

Dear Sir or Madam,
I would like to book a single / double / twin-bedded room for 2 nights from June 28-30. Would you please confirm this reservation and let me know the price for the 2 nights including breakfast? Thanking you in advance.
Yours faithfully,

Hiring a Car by E-mail

Madame, Monsieur,
Je voudrais louer une petite voiture / voiture de classe moyenne/une berline/ un monospace (pour 7 personnes) du 20 au 27 juillet à l'aéroport de Nice. Je souhaite rendre la voiture à Paris-Charles de Gaulle, puisque je repartirai de là-bas. Pourriez-vous m'informer de vos tarifs et me dire quels papiers il me faudra produire?
Meilleures salutations

Dear Sir / Madam,
I would like to hire a small / mid-range / luxury car / 7-seater people carrier from July 20-27 at Nizza airport. I wish to leave the car at Paris-Charles de Gaulle since I will depart from there. Could you please inform me of your rates and tell me which documents I shall require.
Yours faithfully,

General Questions

I am planning to spend my vacation in your area. Could you send me some information on lodging?
J'ai l'intention de passer mes vacances dans votre région. Pourriez-vous me donner des renseignements sur les possibités de logement?

What area do you recommend for a boating vacation?
Quelle région recommandez-vous pour des vacances en bateau?

What kind of accommodations did you have in mind?
A quel genre de logement avez-vous pensé?

> **A hotel**
> un hôtel
>
> **A boarding house**
> une pension
>
> **A room in a private house**
> une chambre chez l'habitant?
>
> **A rental property**
> une location?

Questions About Accommodations

Hotel—Bed and Breakfast—Private Room

I'm looking for a hotel, but it mustn't be too expensive – something in the medium-price range.
Je cherche un hôtel pas trop cher – quelque chose dans des prix moyens.

I'm looking for a hotel with a swimming pool / golf course / tennis court.
Je cherche un hôtel avec piscine / golf / court de tennis.

Do you know where I could find a nice room in a bed and breakfast?
Vous savez où je pourrais trouver une belle chambre d'hôte?

For how many people?
Pour combien de personnes?

Are dogs allowed?
Les chiens sont-ils autorisés?

How much is that per week?
Quel est le prix pour une semaine?

Vacation Houses / Vacation Rentals

I'm looking for a vacation rental: an apartment or a bungalow.
Je cherche une location pour les vacances: un appartement ou
un bungalow

Could you recommend a farm that offers vacation rentals?
Vous pourriez me recommander une ferme qui loue pour les
vacances?

How much is the deposit and when is it due?
Combien d'arrhes faut-il verser et jusqu'à quelle date?

Where and when can I come and get the keys?
Où et quand puis-je venir chercher les clés?

Camping

**I'm looking for a nice campground on the coast. Could you
recommend something?**
Je cherche un beau terrain de camping sur la côte. Pourriez-
vous me recommander quelque chose?

The Essentials in Brief

Yes.
Oui.

No.
Non.

Please.
S'il vous plaît. / S'il te plaît.;
(in response to "Thank you") De rien! *(It's nothing!)*

Thank you!
Merci!

Pardon me?
Comment?, Pardon?

Of course!
Naturellement!; Bien entendu!

Agreed!
D'accord!

OK!
O.K.

Understood!
Entendu!

Excuse me!
Excusez-moi

Pardon me!
Pardon!

Just a moment, please!
Un instant, s'il vous plaît / s'il te plaît!

That's enough!
Ça suffit maintenant!

20

Help!
Au secours!, A l'aide!

Who?
Qui?

What?
Quoi?

Which? Which one(s)?
Lequel?/Laquelle?/Lesquels?/Lesquelles?

To whom?
A qui?

Whom?
Qui

Where?
Où?

Where is? / Where are?
Où est? / Où sont ...?

Why?
Pourquoi?

What for?
Dans quel but?; Pour quoi faire?

How many?
Combien?

How long?
Combien de temps?

When?
Quand?

At what time?
A quelle heure?

I would like ...
Je voudrais ...; J'aimerais ...

Is there ...?
Il y a ...?; Est-ce qu'il y a ...?

Numbers – Sizes – Weights

0	zéro
1	un
2	deux
3	trois
4	quatre
5	cinq
6	six
7	sept
8	huit
9	neuf
10	dix
11	onze
12	douze
13	treize
14	quatorze
15	quinze
16	seize
17	dix-sept
18	dix-huit
19	dix-neuf
20	vingt
21	vingt et un
22	vingt-deux
23	vingt-trois
24	vingt-quatre
25	vingt-cinq
26	vingt-six
27	vingt-sept
28	vingt-huit
29	vingt-neuf
30	trente
31	trente et un
32	trente-deux
40	quarante
50	cinquante
60	soixante
70	soixante-dix
80	quatre-vingts
90	quatre-vingt-dix

100	cent
101	cent un
200	deux cents
300	trois cents
1000	mille
2000	deux mille
10,000	dix mille
100,000	cent mille
1,000,000	un million
first	premier/première
second	deuxième, second(e)
third	troisième
fourth	quatrième
fifth	cinquième
sixth	sixième
seventh	septième
eighth	huitième
ninth	neuvième
tenth	dixième
one half	un demi
one third	un tiers
one fourth	un quart
three fourths	trois quarts
3.5%	trois virgule cinq pour cent
27°C	vingt-sept degrés
–5°C	moins cinq degrés
1999	mille neuf cent quatre-vingt-dix-neuf
2005	deux mille cinq
millimeter	le millimètre
centimeter	le centimètre
meter	le mètre
kilometer	le kilomètre
square meter	le mètre carré
liter	le litre
gram	le gramme
pound	la livre
kilogram	le kilogramme, le kilo

Telling Time

The Time

What time is it, please?
Quelle heure est-il, s'il vous plaît?

It is (exactly, approximately) …
Il est (exactement/environ) …

Three o'clock.
trois heures.

Five past three.
trois heures cinq.

Ten past three.
trois heures dix.

Quarter past three.
trois heures et quart.

Three-thirty.
trois heures et demie.

Quarter of four.
quatre heures moins le quart.

Five to four.
quatre heures moins cinq.

Twelve noon / midnight.
midi/minuit.

At what time / When?
A quelle heure?/Quand?

At one o'clock.
A une heure.

At two o'clock.
A deux heures.

Around four o'clock.
Vers quatre heures.

In one hour.
Dans une heure.

In two hours.
Dans deux heures.

Not before nine in the morning.
Pas avant neuf heures du matin.

After eight o'clock in the evening.
Après huit heures du soir.

Between three and four o'clock.
Entre trois (heures) et quatre (heures).

The expression *chercher midi à quatorze heures* doesn't mean to "look for noon at two o'clock in the afternoon," but rather to look for problems where there are none. And if it's already *high time*, "five to twelve" becomes even shorter in French: *Il est moins une.* ("It's one minute to.")

How long?
Combien de temps?

Two hours.
Deux heures.

From 10 to 11.
De dix à onze.

Up till five o'clock
Jusqu'à/Avant cinq heures.

Since what time?
Depuis quelle heure?

Since 8:00 in the morning.
Depuis huit heures du matin.

For (= since) a half hour.
Depuis une demi-heure.

For (= since) a week.
Depuis huit jours.

around noon	vers midi
at night	la nuit
at noontime	le midi
at this time	à cette heure-ci
during the day	pendant la journée
earlier	*(sooner)* plus tôt; *(formerly)* autrefois
early	tôt
every day	tous les jours
every hour	toutes les heures
from time to time	de temps en temps
in a week	dans une semaine
in the morning	dans la matinée
in two weeks	dans quinze jours
last Monday morning	lundi dernier au matin
late	tard
later	plus tard

next year	l'année prochaine
now	maintenant
sometimes	quelquefois
soon	bientôt
Sunday	dimanche
ten minutes ago	il y a dix minutes
the afternoon	l'après-midi
the day after tomorrow	après-demain
the day before yesterday	avant-hier
the evening	le soir
the morning	le matin
the other day	l'autre jour
this morning / this evening	ce matin / ce soir
this week	cette semaine
this weekend	ce week-end
today	aujourd'hui
tomorrow	demain
tomorrow morning/ tomorrow evening	demain matin/demain soir
within a week	en une semaine
yesterday	hier

The Days of the Week

Monday	lundi
Tuesday	mardi
Wednesday	mercredi
Thursday	jeudi
Friday	vendredi
Saturday	samedi
Sunday	dimanche

The Months

January	janvier
February	février
March	mars
April	avril
May	mai
June	juin
July	juillet
August	août

September	septembre
October	octobre
November	novembre
December	décembre

The Seasons

Spring	le printemps
Summer	l'été *m*
Fall	l'automne *m*
Winter	l'hiver *m*

Some French Traditions:
- ❏ On January first a custom that probably descends from the Gauls leads people to kiss under the *gui,* or sprig of mistletoe, to enjoy good luck for the whole year.
- ❏ On Epiphany there is a *galette* (a puff pastry cake with almond paste), in which there is hidden a *fève*, a large plastic bean. Whoever finds it becomes king or queen.
- ❏ Crepes are eaten at *la Chandeleur* (Candlemas), on February 2; before eating them, you have to flip them in the air while holding a coin in one hand and the pan in the other.
- ❏ On May 1 people give gifts of lucky Lily of the Valley, which is sold on many street corners. This is the only day of the year that many French people go into the woods: They prefer to pick the Lily of the Valley themselves.
- ❏ The national holiday is celebrated on July 14 with minstrels, fireworks, and dancing in the streets.

Holidays

Ash Wednesday	le mercredi des cendres
Carnival	le carnaval
Easter	Pâques *f*
Easter Monday	le lundi de Pâques
Epiphany	la Fête des Rois, l'Epiphanie
Good Friday	le vendredi saint
Mardi gras	le mardi gras
May first	la Fête du Travail
New Year's Day	le Nouvel An

Workers' Day, the End of the War on May 8, the National Holiday, and the Assumption are practically never called by name, but rather by the date: *le premier mai, le 8 mai, le 14 juillet and le 15 août*. If most French people were asked, they wouldn't know what May 8 and August 15 stand for!

May 8 . . . . le huit mai
Ascension . . . . l'Ascension *f*
Pentecost . . . . la Pentecôte
Pentecost Monday . . . . le lundi de Pentecôte
The Feast of Corpus Christi . la Fête-Dieu
National Holiday (July 14) . . le quatorze juillet
Assumption . . . . l'Assomption *f*
All Saints' Day (Nov. 1) . . . . la Toussaint
Armistice Day . . . . l'Armistice *m*
  (Nov. 11, 1918)
Christmas Eve . . . . la veille de Noël, le réveillon
Christmas . . . . Noël
New Year's Eve . . . . la Saint-Sylvestre

Dates

What's today's date?
On est le combien aujourd'hui?

Today is June 30.
Aujourd'hui, c'est le 30 juin.

Weather

What great/awful weather!
Quel temps superbe/affreux!

It is very cold/hot/humid.
Il fait très froid/chaud/lourd.

It is foggy/windy.
Il y a du brouillard. / Il fait du vent.

The weather will remain nice/bad.
Le temps va rester beau. / Le mauvais temps va persister.

It's going to become warmer/colder.
Le temps va se radoucir / se rafraîchir.

It's going to rain/snow.
Il va pleuvoir/neiger.

The roads are slippery.
Les routes sont verglacées.

Visibility is only 20 m / less than 50 m.
La visibilité n'est que de vingt mètres / est de moins de cinquante mètres.

Chains are required.
Il va falloir mettre des chaînes.

air	l'air *m*
calm	le calme
cloud	le nuage
cloudy	nuageux
cold	froid
damp	humide
fog	le brouillard
frost	le gel
gust of wind	la rafale
heat	la chaleur
heat wave	la canicule, la vague de chaleur
high tide	la marée haute
hot	très chaud
humid	lourd
ice	la glace, le verglas
lightning	l'éclair *m*
low tide	la marée basse
rain	la pluie
rainstorm	l'averse *f*
rainy	pluvieux
snow	la neige
storm	l'orage *m*, la tempête
sun	le soleil
sunny	ensoleillé
temperature	la température
thunder	le tonnerre
variable	variable

warm	chaud
weather forecast	les prévisions *f* météo(rologiques)
weather report	le bulletin météo(rologique), la météo
wind	le vent
wind speed	la force du vent

Colors

beige	beige
black	noir
blue	bleu
brown	marron
colored	de couleur
dark blue/dark green	bleu/vert foncé
gold	doré
gray	gris
green	vert
light blue/light green	bleu/vert clair
orange	orange
pink	rose
purple	lilas, mauve
red	rouge
silver	argenté
turquoise	turquoise
violet	violet
white	blanc
yellow	jaune

A handshake or a kiss? In France, it's not just politicians and the President who like to shake hands; people generally shake hands when they greet each other. Among family members, friends, and colleagues kisses are common when people meet— especially two women, or a man and a woman. Whether people kiss two, three, or even four times depends on the location and personal customs. Incidentally, you needn't take the trouble to greet your vacation neighbors by name. In France it is impolite to address someone you know only casually by their last name. So be content with *Bonjour Monsieur, Bonjour Madame.*

Saying Hello and Good-bye

Saying Hello

Good morning!
Bonjour!

Hello!
Bonjour!

Good evening!
Bonsoir!

Hi!
Salut!

What is your name?
Comment vous appelez-vous?

What is your name?
Comment tu t'appelles?

My name is …
Je m'appelle …

How are you?
Comment allez-vous?

How's it going?
(Comment) Ça va?

Fine, thanks. You?
Bien, merci. Et vous-même / toi?

Introductions

May I introduce people? This is …
Puis-je faire les présentations? C'est …

  Mrs. X.
  Madame X.

Miss X.
Mademoiselle X.

Mr. X.
Monsieur X.

my husband. / my wife.
mon mari. / ma femme.

my son. / my daughter.
mon fils. / ma fille.

my friend. / my (girl) friend.
mon ami. / mon amie.

Saying Good-bye

Good-bye!
Au revoir!

See you later!
A tout à l'heure!

See you tomorrow!
A demain!

See you soon!
A bientôt!

Good night!
Bonne nuit!

So long!
Salut!

Have a good trip!
Bon voyage!

Courtesy

Please and Thank You

Usually people don't say anything in response to *merci*. They probably find it hard spending their entire life answering "Thank you" with "You're welcome."

Please.
S'il vous plaît. / S'il te plaît.; De rien!

Yes, please.
Oui, je veux bien.

No, thanks!
Non, merci!

May I?
Vous permettez?

Excuse the interruption.
Excusez-moi de vous déranger.

Pardon me, may I ask you something?
Excusez-moi, je pourrais vous demander quelque chose?

Could you tell me …?
Pourriez-vous me dire, …?

Could you please help me?
Vous pouvez m'aider, s'il vous plaît?

May I / Could I ask you a favor?
Je peux / je pourrais vous demander un service?

Would you be so kind as to …?
Auriez-vous l'amabilité de …?

Thanks very much. You have helped me a lot.
Merci beaucoup. Vous m'avez bien aidé.

Thank you!
Merci!

Thank you, gladly!
Merci, bien volontiers!

Thank you, you are very kind.
Vous êtes bien aimable, merci.

You're welcome. Don't mention it.
Je vous en prie. / De rien.

Apologies

Excuse me!
Excusez-moi / Excuse-moi.

I'm very sorry!
Je suis vraiment désolé/e!

That's not what I meant.
Ce n'est pas ce que je voulais dire.

Don't mention it / It's nothing.
Je vous en prie / Ça ne fait rien!

Unfortunately that's not possible.
C'est malheureusement impossible.

Wishes

Congratulations!
Toutes mes félicitations!

Happy birthday!
Bon anniversaire!

Good luck!
Bonne chance!

I'm keeping my fingers crossed for you.
Je croise les doigts pour vous!

Bless you! (after a sneeze)
A vos souhaits!

Get better soon!
Je vous / Je te souhaite un prompt rétablissement.

Opinions and Feelings

Agreement and Keeping a Conversation Going

Good.
Bon/Bien.

Right.
Tout à fait.

Agreed!
D'accord!

That's fine!
C'est bon!

OK!
OK!

Precisely.
Exactement.

Ah!
Ah!

I see!
Ah bon!

Really?
Vraiment?

Interesting!
Intéressant!

Great!
Très bien!

35

I understand.
Je comprends

That's the way it is.
C'est comme ça.

I agree entirely. That's right.
Tout à fait de votre avis. C'est bien ça.

I think that's (just) fine.
Je trouve ça (très) bien.

Gladly.
Avec plaisir!

Declining

I have no time.
Je n'ai pas le temps.

I don't feel like it.
Je n'en ai pas envie.

I don't agree with that.
Là, je ne suis pas d'accord.

That's out of the question!
Il n'en est pas question!

No way!
En aucun cas!

Not with me!
Sans moi!

I don't like that at all.
Ça ne me plaît pas du tout.

Preferences

I like that. / I don't like that.
Ça me plaît / Ça ne me plaît pas.

I would rather ...
J'aimerais mieux / Je préférerais ...

What I would like best would be ...
Ce qui me plairait le plus, ce serait de ...

I would really like to know more about it.
J'aimerais bien en savoir plus.

Saying You Don't Know

I don't know
Je ne sais pas

No idea
Aucune idée

Indecision

It's all the same to me.
Ça m'est égal.

I don't know yet.
Je ne sais pas encore.

Maybe.
Peut-être.

Probably.
Probablement.

Happines—Enthusiasm

If you suddenly hear *le pied!* in some context, don't be
alarmed: in French that can be used to express enthusiasm!

Great!
Formidable!

Perfect!
Parfait!

Neat!
Génial!

Great!
Super!

Wild!
Fou!

Satisfaction

I am totally satisfied.
Je suis tout à fait satisfait/e!

I can't complain.
Je ne peux pas me plaindre!

That turned out really great!
Ça a vraiment très bien marché!

Boredom

How boring! What a bore!
Qu'est-ce que c'est ennuyeux!

How dreary!
La galère!

Body Language

Well, I never!

We'll talk by phone.

I don't know.

I've had it!

Shall we go?

It went right by me.

My eye.

Let's eat!

Smart!

Let's get a drink!

Outstanding! (combined with a click of the tongue)

Don't give me any baloney!

Surprise – Astonishment

I see!
Ah bon?!

Really?
Vraiment?

Amazing!
C'est pas croyable!

Unbelievable!
Incroyable!

Relief

Fortunately, …
Heureusement que …!

Thank God!
Dieu merci!

Finally!
Enfin!

Composure

Don't panic / Take it easy!
Pas de panique!

Don't worry.
Ne vous faites pas de soucis!

Annoyance

What a bother!
Ça, c'est embêtant!

Darn!
Mince alors!

That's enough!
Ça suffit maintenant!

That's a bother!
Ça m'énerve.

What nerve!
Quel culot!

That can't be true!
Mais c'est pas vrai!

Rebuke

What are you thinking of!
Qu'est-ce qui vous prend!

That's far enough!
N'allez pas trop loin!

That's out of the question!
Il n'en est pas question.

Regret – Disappointment

Nuts!
Zut!

I'm sorry.
Je suis navrée/désolée.

I'm very sorry about …
Je suis vraiment désolé/e pour …

Too bad!
Dommage!

Compliments

Great!
Très bien!

That's wonderful!
C'est formidable!

That's very kind of you!
C'est très gentil de votre/ta part!

I think you are very nice!
Je vous trouve très sympathique!

The meal was excellent!
Le repas était excellent!

We have rarely eaten as well as at your house.
Nous avons rarement aussi bien mangé que chez vous.

Things are really great here!
C'est vraiment fantastique ici!

You speak very good English
Vous parlez très bien l'anglais.

That looks good!
Ça a l'air bien / bon!

This dress fits you well.
Cette robe te/vous va bien.

beautiful	beau
delicious	délicieux
excellent	excellent

INTERPERSONAL MATTERS

41

friendly	aimable
impressive	impressionnant
likeable	aimable
nice	sympa
pleasant	agréable
pretty	joli
splendid	splendide

Small Talk

Personal Details

How old are you?
Quel âge avez-vous? / Tu as quel âge?

I am 39.
J'ai 39 ans.

What kind of work do you do?
Qu'est-ce que vous faites / tu fais dans la vie?

I am ...
Je suis ...

I work for ...
Je travaille chez ...

I am retired.
Je suis retraité/e.

I'm still in school.
Je vais encore à l'école.

I am a student.
Je suis étudiant/étudiante.

Origin and Residence

Where are you from?
D'où êtes-vous? / Tu es d'où?

I am from Minneapolis.
Je suis de Minneapolis.

Have you been in ... for a long time?
Vous êtes / Tu es à ... depuis longtemps?

I have been here since ...
Je suis là depuis ...

How long are you staying?
Vous restez / Tu restes combien de temps?

Is this your first time here?
C'est la première fois que vous venez / que tu viens ici?

Do you like it?
Ça vous / te plaît?

Are you married?
Vous êtes marié/e?

Do you have children?
Vous avez des enfants?

Yes, but they are already grown.
Oui, mais ils sont déjà adultes.

How old are your children?
Quel âge ont vos enfants?

My daughter is eight (years old) and my son is five (years old).
Ma fille a 8 ans et mon fils 5 ans.

Hobbies ➤ also Active and Creative Vacations

Do you have a hobby?
Vous avez/Tu as un hobby?

I spend a lot of time with my children.
Je passe beaucoup de temps avec mes enfants.

I really enjoy reading.
J'aime beaucoup lire.

I surf the internet a lot.
Je navigue beaucoup dans Internet.

I like working in the garden.
J'aime bien jardiner.

I paint a little.
Je peins un peu.

I collect stamps / antiques.
Je collectionne les timbres / les antiquités.

What are you interested in?
Vous vous intéressez à quoi?

I am interested in ...
Je m'intéresse à .../au ...

I belong to a(n) ...
Je fais partie d'un/d'une ...

INTERPERSONAL MATTERS

to cook	faire la cuisine
to do handcrafts	bricoler
to do pottery	faire de la poterie
to draw	dessiner
to learn languages	apprendre des langues
to listen to music	écouter de la musique
to paint	peindre
to play music	faire de la musique
to read	lire
to relax	se détendre
to travel	voyager

Fitness ➢ also Active Vacations

How do you stay in shape?
Comment vous maintenez-vous en forme?

I jog / swim / cycle.
Je fais du jogging / de la natation / du vélo.

I play tennis / volleyball once a week.
Je joue une fois par semaine au tennis/volley-ball.

I regularly go to the gym.
Je vais régulièrement dans un centre de gym.

What sport do you do?
Quel sport est-ce que vous pratiquez?

I play ...
Je fais du / de la ...

I'm a fan of ...
Je suis un/e passionné/e de ...

I like to go ...
J'aime bien aller ...

Appointments

The word *rendez-vous* has no double meaning in French:
Business people have a *rendez-vous* with one another, and I
have a *rendez-vous* with my brother or with a girlfriend.

Do you have any plans for tomorrow evening?
Vous avez / Tu as quelque chose de prévu pour demain soir?

We can go together if you wish.
On peut y aller ensemble, si vous voulez / si tu veux.

May I invite you to dinner tomorrow evening?
Est-ce que je peux vous inviter / t'inviter à manger demain soir?

When shall we meet?
On se voit à quelle heure?

Let's meet at 9:00 in front of … / at the …
On se retrouve à 9 h devant …/au …

I'll pick you up.
Je viens vous/te chercher.

May I see you again?
Est-ce que je peux vous/te revoir?

This was really a nice evening!
C'était vraiment une soirée sympa!

Flirting

You have beautiful eyes.
Tu as des yeux magnifiques.

I like the way you laugh.
J'aime bien quand tu ris.

I like you.
Tu me plais.

I think you're great!
Je te trouve absolument super!

I love you!
Je t'aime.

Do you have a boyfriend / girlfriend?
Tu as un petit copain / une petite copine?

Are you married?
Tu es marié/e?

I am divorced.
Je suis divorcé/e.

I'm separated.
Je suis séparé/e.

Will you come to my place?
Tu viens chez moi?

No, not so soon!
Non, ça va trop vite!

We can cuddle.
On peut se faire des câlins.

Scram!
Va-t-en maintenant!

Leave me alone, please.
Laissez-moi tranquille, je vous en prie.; Foutez-moi la paix!

Stop that right now!
Arrêtez tout de suite!

Communication Difficulties

Pardon me?
Comment?; Pardon?

I don't understand.
Je ne comprends pas.

Would you please repeat?
Vous pouvez répéter, s'il vous plaît?

Could you please speak more slowly?
Vous pourriez parler un peu plus lentement, s'il vous plaît?

Yes, I understand.
Oui, je comprends.

Do you speak ...
Vous parlez/ Tu parles ...

German?
allemand?
English?
anglais?
French?
français?

I speak only a little ...
Je parle un tout petit peu ...

Could you write that down for me, please?
Vous pourriez me l'écrire, s'il vous plaît?

On the Move

Car or Train?

If you want to get somewhere fast, it's a good idea to take the train in France. The High Speed Train *TGV* (*Train à grande vitesse*) makes it possible to go from Paris to Marseille (526 miles/863 km) in three hours and ten minutes at a speed of up to 180 miles (300 km) per hour. You need a reservation, but you can get one up to five minutes before departure. People who prefer to drive have to stick to the highway speed limit of 80 mph (130 km/h) or else reach deep into their pockets. Even if you pay attention to the speed limit it's not cheap to use the highways in France, for there are tolls nearly everywhere. There is ample warning, however, and it's possible to get off the highways. The magic word is *péage* (toll). If you see a sign with the notices *péage* and *sortie* (exit) together, you can still continue your trip on regional and local roads.

Asking for Directions

Which way?

across from	en face de
behind	derrière
beside	à côté de
close	près
curve	le virage
far	loin
here	ici
in front of	devant
intersection	le carrefour
left	à gauche
right	à droite
straight ahead	tout droit
street	la rue
street corner	le coin de la rue
there	là, là-bas
to, toward, in the direction of	à, vers, en direction de
traffic light	le feu (de circulation)

Giving Directions

Excuse me, how do I get to …?
Excusez-moi, pour aller à …, s'il vous plaît?

Straight ahead until …
Toujours tout droit jusqu'à …

Then turn left/right at the traffic light.
Ensuite, vous tournez à gauche / à droite, au feu.

Follow the signs.
Suivez les panneaux.

The sign *Toutes directions* (All Directions) sometimes causes foreigners to smirk. But it often works wonders and gets people where they are headed!

Is that far from here?
C'est loin d'ici?

It's quite close to here.
C'est tout près d'ici.

Pardon me sir, miss, madame, is this the road to …?
Pardon Mme/Mlle/M., je suis bien sur la route de …?

Excuse me sir, miss, madame, would you please tell me where … is?
Pardon Mme/Mlle/M., où se trouve …, s'il vous plaît?

I'm sorry, I don't know.
Je suis désolé, je ne sais pas.

I'm not from here.
Je ne suis pas d'ici.

Go straight ahead / turn left / right.
Vous allez tout droit. / Vous prenez à gauche / à droite.

The first / second road to the left / right.
La première/deuxième rue à gauche / à droite.

Cross…
Vous traversez …

  the bridge.
  le pont.
  the square.
  la place.
  the street.
  la rue.

It's best to take bus number …
Le mieux, c'est de prendre le bus n°…

49

Passport Inspection

Your passport, please!
Votre passeport, s'il vous plaît.

Do you have a visa?
Vous avez un visa?

Can I get the visa here?
Est-ce que je peux obtenir le visa ici?

Customs Inspection

Do you have anything to declare?
Vous avez quelque chose à déclarer?

Please go to the right / left!
Rangez-vous sur la droite / la gauche, s'il vous plaît!

Please open up the trunk / this suitcase!
Ouvrez votre coffre / cette valise, s'il vous plaît!

Do I need to declare that?
Il faut déclarer ça?

Particulars

Date of birth	la date de naissance
Family name	le nom de famille
First name	le prénom
Identity	l'identité f
Maiden name	le nom de jeune fille
Marital status	la situation de famille
married	marié
single	célibataire
widow	veuve
widower	veuf
Nationality	la nationalité
Place of birth	le lieu de naissance
Residence	le domicile

Border

American/Canadian citizen .	le citoyen des États-Unis/du Canada
border	la frontière
border crossing	le poste frontière
citizen of the European Union	le citoyen européen
country sticker	la plaque de nationalité
customs	la douane
customs duties	les droits de douane
departure, exit	la sortie
driver's license	le permis de conduire
duty free	exempt de droits de douane
entry	l'entrée f
green (insurance) card	la carte verte
ID card	la carte d'identité
international vaccination . .	le carnet international de vaccination
record	
license plate	la plaque d'immatriculation
passport	le passeport
passport inspection	le contrôle des passeports
subject to customs duties . .	soumis aux droits de douane
valid	valable
visa	le visa

Car and Motorcycle

It is well known—and yet still puzzling: Driving in France is different, and some rules that are strictly enforced in other places are not as important in France. For example, drivers rarely stop for people in crosswalks, even for old people and small children. No French person expects that, so the system works fine. The French wait at the edge of the crosswalk until there are no more cars, and if a car stops unexpectedly, people are grateful.

At traffic lights sometimes the opposite behavior is observed: when the walk light is red, pedestrians dash right across the street. And the drivers are fairly tolerant in such situations. This habit is best left to the natives if you hope to enjoy your stay in France right to the end. Still, if there is no car anywhere in sight, everyone will wonder why you bother waiting at a red pedestrian light.

Travel Routes and Regulations

entrance	l'entrée f
exit	la sortie (d'autoroute)
fast lane	la voie rapide
fine	l'amende f
highway	l'autoroute f
hitchhiker	l'auto-stoppeur / l'auto-stoppeuse
legal alcohol limit	le taux d'alcoolémie maximal
main road	la rue principale
on / off ramp	la bretelle
radar control	le contrôle radar
rest area	l'aire f de repos, l'aire f de service
road use fee	le péage
secondary road	la route secondaire, la route départementale
service area	le restoroute
side street	la rue adjacente
signpost	le poteau indicateur
to hitchhike	faire de l'auto-stop
toll	le péage
traffic jam	l'embouteillage m

At the Gas Station ➤ also Repair Shop

Where is the nearest gas station, please?
Où est la station-service la plus proche, s'il vous plaît?

I would like ... liters.
Je voudrais ... litres, s'il vous plaît.

Gas (unleaded)
Du (sans plomb) 95 (octanes).

Super (unleaded)
Du (sans plomb) 98 (octanes).

High octane
Du super.
Diesel
Du gazole/gasoil.

In France high octane gas is not unleaded. If you want lead-free super, choose *du 98*.

Thirty euros of super, please!
Du 98, s'il vous plaît, pour 30 euros.

Fill it up, please!
Le plein, s'il vous plaît!

I would like a road map of this area, please.
Je voudrais une carte routière de la région, s'il vous plaît.

Notices and Information

Arrêt interdit	No stopping
Attention	Caution
Chantier	Construction
Chaussée déformée	Uneven Road Surface
Danger	Danger
Dérapage	Danger of Skidding
Descente dangereuse	Steep Downhill
Déviation	Detour
Ecole	School
Entrée interdite	No Entry
Fin d'interdiction de stationner	End of No Parking
Gravillons	Loose Gravel
Haute tension	High Voltage
Hôpital	Hospital
Péage	Toll
Poids lourds	Trucks
Priorité à droite	Right of Way on Right
Prudence	Caution
Ralentir	Slow Down
Rappel	Reminder of previous sign
Secours routier français	Breakdown Assistance
Serrer à droite (à gauche)	Squeeze Right (Left)
Sortie d'autoroute	Exit
Sortie de véhicules	Do Not Block Exit
Stationnement interdit	No Parking
Trous en formation	Bad Road Surface
Virage dangereux	Dangerous Curve
Zone à stationnement réglementé	Short-term Parking

Parking at meters between noon and 2:00 P.M. is often free. But first check to see if you need to put money in! This nice custom is not observed in Paris!

Excuse me, is there any parking near here?
Excusez-moi, est-ce qu'il y a un parking près d'ici, s'il vous plaît?

Is the parking lot supervised?
Est-ce que le parking est gardé?

How much does it cost per hour?
Quel est le tarif pour une heure?

Is the parking open all night?
Est-ce que le parking est ouvert toute la nuit?

A Breakdown

I've had a breakdown.
Je suis en panne.

Is there a repair shop in the area?
Pardon Mme/Mlle/M., est-ce qu'il y a un garage près d'ici, s'il vous plaît?

Could you please call roadside service for me?
Vous pourriez téléphoner pour moi à un service de dépannage, s'il vous plaît?

Could you give me a little gas, please?
Vous pourriez me donner un peu d'essence, s'il vous plaît?

Could you please help me change the tire?
Vous pourriez m'aider à changer la roue, s'il vous plaît?

Could you give me a ride to the nearest garage?
Est-ce que vous pouvez m'emmener jusqu'au prochain garage?

breakdown	la panne
breakdown service	le service de dépannage
emergency flashers	les feux de détresse
emergency telephone	le téléphone de secours
flat tire	le pneu crevé
gas can	le bidon d'essence
jack	le cric
jumper cable	le câble de démarrage
spare tire	la roue de secours
tools	les outils m
to tow	remorquer
towing cable	le câble de remorquage
warning triangle	le triangle de présignalisation
wrecker, tow truck	la dépanneuse

At the Repair Shop

My car doesn't start.
Ma voiture ne démarre pas.

Something is wrong with the motor.
J'ai des ennuis de moteur.

... isn't / aren't working.
... est/sont défectueux/défectueuse(s).

There is an oil leak.
Il y a une fuite d'huile.

There is a strange noise on the right side.
Il y a un drôle de bruit à droite.

Can you please take a look?
Vous pouvez jeter un coup d'œil, s'il vous plaît?

When will my car / my motorcycle be ready?
Quand est-ce que ma voiture / ma moto sera prête?

About how much will it cost?
Ça va coûter combien à peu près?

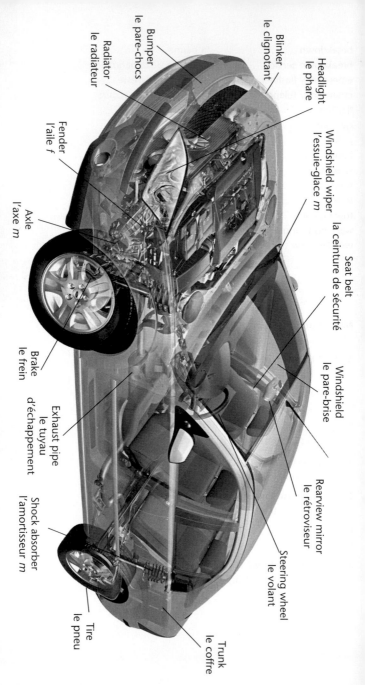

Blinker
le clignotant

Bumper
le pare-chocs

Radiator
le radiateur

Headlight
le phare

Windshield wiper
l'essuie-glace m

Seat belt
la ceinture de sécurité

Fender
l'aile f

Axle
l'axe m

Brake
le frein

Exhaust pipe
le tuyau
d'échappement

Windshield
le pare-brise

Rearview mirror
le rétroviseur

Windshield
le pare-brise

Steering wheel
le volant

Shock absorber
l'amortisseur m

Tire
le pneu

Trunk
le coffre

56

air filter	le filtre à air
alarm system	le système d'alarme
alternator	la dynamo
antifreeze	l'antigel *m*
automatic transmission	la boîte automatique
backup lights	les feux *m* arrière
blinker	le clignotant
bolt	la vis
brake	le frein
brake fluid	le liquide de frein
brake lights	les stops *m*
bumper	le pare-chocs
clutch	l'embrayage *m*
coolant	l'eau *f* de refroidissement
damage	le dommage
defect	le défaut
drive belt	la courroie de transmission
electronic start protection	l'antidémarrage *m* électronique
emergency brake	le frein à main
emergency flashers	les feux *m* de détresse
exhaust pipe	le tuyau d'échappement
gas pedal	l'accélérateur *m*
gas pump	la pompe à essence
gas tank	le réservoir
headlight	le phare
high beams	les feux *m* de route
hood	le capot
horn	le klaxon
ignition	l'allumage *m*
low beams	les codes *m*
motor	le moteur
oil	l'huile *f*
oil change	la vidange
parking lights	les feux *m* de position
radiator	le radiateur
rearview mirror	le rétroviseur
repair shop	le garage
seat belt	la ceinture de sécurité
short circuit	le court-circuit
snow tires	le pneu neige
spark plug	la bougie
speed	la vitesse
first	la première
neutral	le point mort
reverse	la marche arrière

starter	le démarreur
tachometer	le compteur
tire	le pneu
transmission	la boîte de vitesses
trunk	le coffre
wheel	la roue
windshield	le pare-brise
windshield washer	l'essuie-glace *m*

Accidents

There has been an accident.
Il y a eu un accident.

Please call ... quickly!
Appelez vite ...

an ambulance
une ambulance!

the police
la police!

the fire station
les pompiers!

Do you have a first-aid kit?
Vous avez une trousse de secours?

You didn't ...
Vous ...

yield the right of way.
n'avez pas respecté la priorité.

signal.
n'avez pas mis votre clignotant.

You ...
Vous ...

were driving too fast.
rouliez trop vite.

went through a red light.
avez brûlé un feu rouge.

Give me your name and address, please.
Donnez-moi votre nom et votre adresse, s'il vous plaît.

Thanks a lot for your help!
Je vous remercie beaucoup de votre aide!

Gear lever
le dérailleur

Handlebar
le guidon

Saddle
la selle

Air pump
la pompe à air

Headlight
les phares *m*

Tail light
les feux *m*
arrière

Brake
le frein

Inner tube
la chambre
à air

Tire
le pneu

Chain
le chaîne

Pedal
la pédale

Wheel
la roue

Spoke
le rayon

Hub
le moyeu

I would like to rent ... for two days / a week.

Je voudrais louer pour deux jours / une semaine ...

a four-wheel drive car
une voiture tout terrain / un 4x4.

a motorcycle
une moto.

a motor scooter
un scooter.

a moped
un cyclomoteur.

a bicycle
un vélo.

How much is that per day / week?
Quel est le tarif à la journée/semaine?

With unlimited mileage?
C'est avec kilométrage illimité?

What's the cost per kilometer?
Quel est le prix au kilomètre?

Is it possible to return the vehicle in ...?
Est-ce qu'il est possible de rendre le véhicule à ...?

ON THE MOVE

child seat	le siège-enfants
deposit	la caution
driver's license	le permis de conduire
green insurance card	la carte verte
helmet	le casque de moto
ignition key	la clé de contact
kidney belt	la ceinture de moto
to leave	déposer
papers	les papiers *m*
sunroof	le toit ouvrant
third-party insurance	l'assurance *f* au tiers
weekend rate	le forfait-weekend

Airplanes

Booking a Flight

Could you please tell me when the next flight to ... is?
Vous pouvez me dire quand part le prochain avion pour ..., s'il vous plaît?

Are there still seats available?
Est-ce qu'il y a encore des places?

I would like a one-way plane ticket to ...
Je voudrais un billet d'avion pour ... en aller simple.

I would like a round-trip plane ticket to ...
Je voudrais un billet d'avion pour ... en aller retour.

How much is the flight for tourist / business class?
Combien coûte le vol en classe économique/affaires?

Smoking or non-smoking?
Fumeur ou non-fumeur?

I would like ...
Je voudrais ...

a window seat.
une place à la fenêtre, s'il vous plaît.

an aisle seat.
une place sur l'allée, s'il vous plaît.

I would like to change this flight.
Je voudrais changer ce vol.

At the Airport

Where is the desk for ... Airlines, please?
Où se trouve le guichet de la compagnie ... s'il vous plaît?

May I see your ticket, please?
Je pourrais voir votre billet, s'il vous plaît?

Can I take this on as hand baggage?
Je peux prendre ça comme bagage à mains?

On Board

Could you please bring me a glass of water?
Vous pourriez m'apporter un verre d'eau, s'il vous plaît?

Could I please have another pillow / a blanket?
Je pourrais avoir encore un coussin / une couverture, s'il vous plaît?

Would you mind changing places with me?
Ça vous ennuierait d'échanger votre place avec moi?

Arrival ➢ also Lost and Found

My baggage has been lost.
Mes bagages ont été égarés.

My suitcase is damaged.
Ma valise est abîmée.

Where does the bus to ... leave from?
D'où part le bus pour ...?

➢ also Rail Travel

airline	la compagnie aérienne
airport	l'aéroport *m*
airport bus	le bus pour l'aéroport
airport taxes	les taxes *m* d'aéroport
arrival	l'arrivée *f*
arrival time	l'heure *f* d'arrivée
baggage	les bagages *m*
baggage cart	le chariot
baggage check-in	l'enregistrement *m* des bagages
baggage pick-up	l'arrivée *f* des bagages
boarding pass	la carte d'embarquement

61

to cancel	annuler
to change	changer
to check in	faire les formalités *f* d'embarquement
connection	la correspondance
delay	le retard
departure, takeoff	le départ, le décollage
domestic flight	le vol intérieur
duty-free shop	la boutique hors-taxes
emergency exit	la sortie de secours
emergency landing	l'atterrissage *m* forcé
evacuation slide	le toboggan d'évacuation
excess baggage	l'excédent *m* de bagages
flight	le vol
gate	la porte *f* d'embarquement
international flight	le vol international
landing	l'atterrissage *m*
life vest	le gilet de sauvetage
pilot	le pilote
security check	le contrôle de sécurité
security tax	la taxe de sécurité
steward / stewardess	le steward / l'hôtesse *f* de l'air
stopover	l'escale *f*
terminal	le terminal

Taking the Train

On every platform or in smaller railroad stations before the platforms, you will find orange-colored machines for canceling the tickets. Anyone caught with an uncancelled ticket, even by mistake, is considered a fare dodger and has to pay a fine. Foreign travelers are no exception ...

Buying Tickets

Two one-way tickets to ..., please.
Deux allers simples pour ...
  tourist class / first class
  deuxième/première classe

non-smoking / smoking
Non-fumeur/ Fumeur

A round-trip ticket to ..., please.
Un aller-retour pour... s'il vous plaît.

Are there any discounts for children / students / senior citizens?
Est-ce qu'il y a des réductions pour les enfants / les étudiants / les personnes du troisième âge?

I would like to reserve two non-smoking seats, please:
Je voudrais réserver deux places non-fumeur:

in the TGV to...
dans le TGV pour ...

on ... at ... o'clock
le ... à ....heures

in the couchette car
dans la voiture-couchette

in the sleeper car
dans le wagon-lits

Is there a ... motorail train?
Est-ce qu'il y a ...

(night) un train autos-couchette?
(daytime) un service auto-express?

What time is my connection for ... in ...?
A quelle heure est-ce que j'ai une correspondance à ... pour ...?

How many times do I have to change?
Combien de fois est-ce que je dois changer?

In the Railroad Station

I would like to send my suitcase as registered luggage.
Je voudrais faire enregistrer ma valise en bagage accompagné.

Where can I register my bicycle?
Où est-ce que je peux faire enregistrer mon vélo?

Excuse me, what platform does the train to ... leave from?
Excusez-moi, le train pour ... part de quelle voie, s'il vous plaît?

The inter-city train from ... is ten minutes behind schedule.
Le train Corail en provenance de ... a 10 minutes de retard.

On the Train

Is this seat taken?
Cette place est encore libre?

May I please open / close the window?
Est-ce que je peux ouvrir/fermer la fenêtre, s'il vous plaît?

Excuse me, I think that's my seat. Here is my reservation.
Excusez-moi, je crois que c'est ma place. Voilà ma réservation.

➤ also Airplane

to arrive	arriver
compartment	le compartiment
departure	le départ
departure time	l'heure *f* de départ
to get out	descendre
stop	l'arrêt *m*

Notices and Information

L'accès aux quais	To the platforms
Arrivée	Arrival
Buffet	Refreshments / snacks
Consigne	Baggage locker
Dames	Ladies
Eau non potable	Non-potable water
Fumeurs	Smoking
Horaire des trains	Itinerary
Lavabo	Washroom
Libre	Unoccupied
Messieurs	Men
Non-fumeurs	Non-smoking
Occupé	Occupied
Passage souterrain	Underpass
Passerelle	Overpass
Quai	Platform
Renseignements	Information
Salle d'attente	Waiting room
Signal d'alarme	Emergency brake
Sortie	Exit
Toilettes	Toilets
Voie	Track
Voiture-couchettes	Couchette car
W.-C.	Toilet
Wagon-lit	Sleeper car
Wagon-restaurant	Dining car

aisle	le couloir
baggage	les bagages *m*
baggage check-in	la consigne
baggage locker	la consigne automatique
baggage window	le guichet des bagages
buffet car	la voiture-bar
to cancel	composter
car number	le numéro de la voiture
chief steward	le chef de bord
child's ticket	le billet enfants
companion	l'accompaganteur/trice
compartment	Compartiment
conductor	le contrôleur/la contrôleuse
couchette	la couchette
departure	Départ
dining car	le wagon-restaurant
discount	la réduction
EC (EuroCity)	le Corail
to get off / out	descendre
to get on / in	monter (dans le train)
handicapped person	le/la handicapé/e
IC/ (InterCity)	le TGV
ICE (InterCityExpress)	le TGV
information	Informations
interrail	Interrail
itinerary	l'horaire *m* (de chemin de fer)
main railway station	la gare principale
mini-bar	la vente ambulante
motorail train (*night*)	le train autos-couchettes,
(*daytime*)	le service auto-express
non-smoking section	le compartiment non-fumeurs
open car	le wagon sans compartiments
person in a wheelchair	la personne en fauteuil roulant
rail card	la carte Escapades
railroad station	la gare
reservation	la réservation
round-trip ticket	le billet aller-retour
seat reservation	la réservation
smoking section	le compartiment fumeurs
stop	Séjour
surcharge	le supplément
ticket	le billet
ticket control	le contrôle des billets
ticket price	le prix du billet
ticket window	le guichet

track	la voie
train	le train
waiting room	la salle d'attente
window seat	le coin-fenêtre
workday	le jour ouvrable

Boat Travel

Information

Could you please tell me when the next boat / ferry leaves?
Pourriez-vous me dire quand part le prochain bateau /
le prochain ferry pour ...?

How long does the crossing take?
La traversée dure combien de temps?

When do we arrive in ...?
Quand est-ce qu'on arrive à ...?

How long is the stopover?
L'escale à ... dure combien de temps?

I would like ...
Je voudrais ...

  a ticket for ...
  un billet pour ...

  first class
  en première classe

  tourist class
  en classe touristes

  a private cabin
  une cabine pour une personne

  a cabin for two people
  une cabine pour deux personnes

I would like a ticket for a ... o'clock departure, please.
Je voudrais un billet pour le départ de ... heures, s'il vous plaît.

On Board

Where is the dining room / the lounge, please?
Où est la salle à manger / le salon s'il vous plaît?

I don't feel well.
Je ne me sens pas très bien.

Would you please call the doctor on board?
Pourriez-vous appeler le médecin de bord, s'il vous plaît.

Could you please give me some medicine for seasickness?
Pourriez-vous me donner un médicament contre le mal de mer, s'il vous plaît.

cabin	la cabine
captain	le capitaine
coast	la côte
cruise	la croisière
deck	le pont
dock	le quai
ferry	*(river)* le bac, *(ocean)* le ferry
hovercraft	l'hovercraft *m*, l'aéroglisseur *m*
hydrofoil	l'hydroglisseur *m*
land excursion	l'excursion *f* à terre
life vest	le gilet de sauvetage
lifeboat	le canot de sauvetage
lifesaver	la bouée de sauvetage
mainland	la terre ferme, le continent
port, harbor	le port
reservation	la réservation
sea conditions	l'état *m* de la mer
to be seasick	avoir le mal de mer
steamer	le vapeur
to have a stopover in	faire escale à
ticket	le billet
tour	le circuit

Even though the Metro and buses in Paris are inexpensive, it's often worth it to get a day ticket (*une Carte Mobilis*). These tickets are also available for several days. The *Paris Visite* ticket serves the same purpose, but is more expensive, since it also provides for price reductions in museums and other attractions. Check to see which is best for you.

Where is the nearest ..., please?
Où se trouve ...

bus stop
l'arrêt de bus le plus proche?

Paris is a good city to discover by bus. For example, take Bus 42 from the *Gare du Nord* towards *Parc André-Citroën*. It goes by the Opera, the *Madeleine*, the *Assemblée Nationale,* the *Place de la Concorde*, the *Pont de l'Alma,* the *Avenue Montaigne* (with its many designer shops), and the *Eiffel Tower.* You can hardly get a cheaper tour of the city ...

streetcar stop
l'arrêt de tram le plus proche?

metro station
la station de métro la plus proche?

Which line goes to ..., please?
C'est quelle ligne pour ..., s'il vous plaît?

When does the first / last metro leave for ...?
Le premier/dernier métro pour ... est à quelle heure?

Excuse me, is this the bus to ...?
Excusez-moi, c'est bien le bus pour ...?

How many stops are there between here and ...?
Il y a combien d'arrêts d'ici à ...?

Pardon me, where do I have to get off / change?
Excusez-moi, à quel arrêt est-ce que je dois descendre/changer?

Would you please let me know when I have to get off?
Vous pourriez me dire quand je dois descendre, s'il vous plaît?

One ticket to ..., please.
Un billet pour ..., s'il vous plaît.

The ticket machine is out of order.
Le distributeur de billets ne marche pas.

The ticket machine doesn't accept bills.
Le distributeur n'accepte pas les billets.

automatic ticket machine . .	le distributeur de billets
booklet of tickets	le carnet de tickets
bus	le bus
bus station	la gare routière
to cancel	composter
coach	le car
cog railway	le chemin de fer à crémaillère
conductor	le contrôleur
day ticket	le billet pour une journée
departure	le départ
direction	la direction
to get on / in	monter
itinerary	l'horaire *m* (des bus / du métro / des trolleys)
local train	le train de banlieue
metro	le métro
stop, station	l'arrêt *m*, la station
streetcar	le tram
subway	le métro
terminal	le terminus
ticket	le billet
ticket inspector	le contrôleur
ticket price	le prix du billet
ticket puncher	le composteur
trolley	le trolley
weekly ticket	la carte hebdomadaire

Excuse me, where is the nearest taxi stand?
Excusez-moi, où est la station de taxis la plus proche, s'il vous plaît?

To the railroad station, please.
A la gare, s'il vous plaît.

To the ... Hotel, please.
A l'hôtel ..., s'il vous plaît.

... Street, please.
Rue ..., s'il vous plaît.

To ..., please.
A ..., s'il vous plaît.

How much does it cost to get to ...?
Il faut compter combien pour aller à ...?

Would you please stop here?
Vous pourriez arrêter ici, s'il vous plaît?

Would you give me a receipt, please?
Vous pourriez me donner un reçu, s'il vous plaît?

Keep the change.
Gardez la monnaie.

Gardez la monnaie means "Keep the change." That's something you should say only if the change is worth mentioning—not just a couple of cents.

to fasten the seatbelt	mettre la ceinture
flat rate	le prix forfaitaire
house number	le numéro de la maison / de l'immeuble
price per kilometer	le prix au kilomètre
receipt	le reçu
seatbelt	la ceinture de sécurité
to stop	arrêter
taxi driver (m. and f.)	le chauffeur/la chauffeuse de taxi
taxi stand	la station de taxis
tip	le pourboire

Traveling with Children

A Good Arrangement
During school vacations many seaside vacation resorts offer vacation clubs for children (*clubs de vacances, clubs Mickey, and others*). Also, the tourist information office can surely suggest some activities for children.

Useful Questions

Is there a child-care facility here?
Est-ce qu'il y a une garderie ici?

Starting with what age?
A partir de quel âge?

Do you know anyone who could babysit at our place?
Vous connaissez quelqu'un qui pourrait faire du baby-sitting chez nous?

Do you have an intercom for the baby?
Vous avez un interphone pour bébés?

Are there discounts for children?
Il y a aussi des réductions pour les enfants?

On the Move

Children up to age four ride free on trains and the Metro. After that they pay half-price—up to age ten on the Metro and age twelve on trains.

We are traveling with an infant. Could we get seats near the front?
Nous voyageons avec un enfant en bas-âge. Pourrions-nous avoir des places sur le devant?

Do you have a child's seatbelt?
Vous avez une ceinture de sécurité pour enfants?

Would you have any crayons and paper / a coloring book?
Vous avez peut-être des crayons et du papier / un album à colorier?

Do you rent car seats for children?
Vous louez des sièges-enfants pour les voitures?

Important: Be sure to instruct your children that in France people in crosswalks don't necessarily have the right of way. The French are not unpredictable; they simply follow different customs.

In a Restaurant

Would you please bring us a child's seat?
Vous pourriez nous apporter une chaise d'enfants, s'il vous plaît?

Is there a menu for children?
Vous avez des menus-enfants?

Could you please warm up this bottle for me?
Vous pourriez me réchauffer le biberon?

Is there a nursery here?
Vous avez une nursery?

baby bathtub	le bassin pour enfants
baby bottle	le biberon
baby food	la nourriture pour bébés
baby intercom	l'interphone *m*
babysitter	le baby-sitter
booster seat *(for car)*	le réhausseur
bottle	la gourde
bottle warmer	le chauffe-biberon
cap	la casquette
changing table	la table à langer
child's bed	le lit d'enfant
child's discount	la réduction-enfants
child's seat	le siège-enfants
childcare	la garderie
children's clothing	les habits *m* pour enfants
coloring book	l'album *m* à colorier
diapers	les couches *f*
flotation ring	la bouée
infant seat *(for car)*	le siège-bébés
nipple	la tétine
pacifier	la sucette (de caoutchouc)
to play	jouer
playground	l'aire *f* de jeux
sunscreen	la protection solaire
toys	les jouets *m*
wading pool	la pataugeoire
water wings	les bracelets *m*

Can you please tell me if there is a children's doctor here?
Vous pourriez me dire s'il y a un pédiatre ici, s'il vous plaît?

My son / daughter has ...
Mon fils / Ma fille a ...

Is he / she allergic to ...?
Il/Elle est allergique à ...

He / she threw up.
Il/Elle a vomi.

He / she has diarrhea.
Il/Elle a la diarrhée.

He / she has been stung.
Il/Elle a été piqué/e.

allergy	l'allergie f
bug bite	la piqûre d'insecte
chickenpox	la varicelle
childhood disease	la maladie infantile
children's hospital	l'hôpital m pour enfants
cold (illness)	le rhume
electrolyte solution	la solution de réhydratation
fever	la fièvre, la température
German measles	la rubéole
head cold	le rhume de cervean
inner ear infection	l'otite f
measles	la rougeole
mumps	les oreillons m
mycosis	la mycose
rash	les rougeurs f
scarlet fever	la scarlatine
a tick	la tique
vaccination record	le carnet de vaccinations
whooping cough	la coqueluche

Travel for the Handicapped

Fending for Yourself

❑ The French railway system publishes a brochure to help handicapped people prepare for their trip: *Le Mémento du Voyageur a mobilité réduite* (*Handbook for Handicapped Travelers*). Here are a couple of excerpts from it:

"You can travel in your wheelchair in the fast- and very high-speed trains. An aisle is set aside for you in a first class car. A reservation is required no later than 48 hours in advance, excluding Saturday, Sunday, and holidays. There is no extra charge for riding in first class.

Upon demand we will make available to you a small wheelchair that will make it easier for you to access the toilet and get around inside the train. If you need special help in the train stations or the trains (getting to the trains, getting in and out, and so forth), please request this in advance at the station of departure."

This brochure, which is also available in Braille, is available from Mission Voyageurs Handicapés SNCF, 209/211rue de Bercy, 75585 *Paris Cedex 12.*

❑ There is a toll-free number available to all handicapped people to help them get ready for their travel: 0800 15 47 53.

❑ Information on hotels, museums, and transportation for handicapped people in Paris and the surrounding area is contained in a guide in English and French that is published by the CNRH under the title *Paris et Ile de France pour tous.* This guide is also available online at *www.handitel.org.*

❑ The *Fédération des Gîtes de France* (French Federation of Country Lodging, 59 rue Saint-Lazare, 75439 Paris Cedex 09) also has published an informational guide for handicapped people (title: *Gîtes accessibles aux personnes handicapées*).

I am...
Je suis ...

   physically handicapped.
   handicapé physique.

   visually impaired.
   mal-voyant.

I have...
J'ai ...

   difficulty walking.
   des difficultés à marcher.

   multiple sclerosis.
   de la sclérose en plaques.

In most fairly large cities in France there are buses for people in wheelchairs. Generally they come on request and cost no more than the regular municipal buses.

Can I take my (folding) wheelchair on the plane?
Je peux emporter mon fauteuil roulant (pliant) dans l'avion?

Is there a wheelchair available on departure from / arrival at the airport?
Il y a un fauteuil roulant de prévu au départ / à l'arrivée à l'aéroport?

Could I get a seat on the aisle?
Je pourrais avoir une place sur l'allée?

Are there handicap toilets?
Il y a des toilettes aménagées pour handicapés?

Is there a washroom for handicapped people?
Il y a une salle d'eau pour handicapés?

Could someone help me change trains?
Est-ce que quelqu'un pourrait m'aider à changer de train?

Is the entryway to the cars at ground level?
Est-ce que la montée dans les voitures est au niveau du sol?

Are there kneeling buses for the handicapped?
Il y a des bus à marche surbaissée?

Are there access ramps on the platforms for people in wheelchairs?
Il y a des rampes d'accès aux quais pour personnes en fauteuil (roulant)?

Are there cars with hand controls for handicapped people?
Vous avez des voitures avec commandes à mains pour handicapés?

Do you rent trailers for handicapped people (in wheelchairs)?
Vous louez des caravanes équipées pour handicapés (en fauteuil)?

Is it possible to rent bicycles for handicapped people around here?
Peut-on louer ici quelque part des bicyclettes pour handicapés?

TRAVEL FOR THE HANDICAPPED

Accommodations

Could you please send me information on the hotels in ... that are set up for handicapped people?
Pourriez-vous m'envoyer des informations sur les hôtels de ... qui sont équipés pour handicapés?

Which hotels and campgrounds are set up for handicapped people?
Quels sont les hôtels et campings qui sont aménagés pour handicapés?

What kind of floor covering does the room have?
La pièce a un sol recouvert de quel revêtement?

Museums, Tourist Sights, Theater ...

Is the exhibition accessible by elevator for handicapped people?
L'exposition est-elle accessible aux handicapés par des ascenceurs?

Are there special tours for handicapped people / city tours for the hearing impaired?
Il y a des visites guidées spécialement pour handicapés / des visites de la ville pour les sourds?

Is it possible to plug in the magnetic loop for the hearing impaired?
Est-ce que vous pouvez brancher la boucle magnétique pour les malentendants?

Are there museum tours / theatrical presentations for the hearing impaired / sight impaired?
Il y a des visites du musée / des représentations théâtrales pour les malentendants / les non-voyants?

access ramp	la rampe d'accès
access without steps	l'accès *m* sans marche
accessibility	l'accessibilité *f*
aisle width	la largeur du couloir
assistance service	le service d'assistance
association for handicapped people	l'association *f* de handicapés
automatic door	la porte automatique
automatic door opener	l'ouverture *f* automatique des portes
banister, hand rail	la rampe
barrier-free	sans obstacle
bathroom facilities	les installations *f* sanitaires

bedridden	grabataire
blind	aveugle
blind person	l'aveugle *m/f* ; le/la non-voyant/e
braille	le braille
cabin set up for people . . . confined to a wheelchair (ship)	la cabine équipée pour handicapés
cane (of blind person)	la canne d'aveugle
car set up for handicapped . people (train)	le wagon aménagé pour handicapés
crutch	la béquille
deaf	sourd
deaf mute	sourd-muet
deaf person	le sourd / la sourde
deaf-mute person	le/la sourd/e-muet/te
door width	la largeur de la porte
elevator platform, lift	la plate-forme, l'élévateur
epilepsy	l'épilepsie *f*
escort (m. and f.)	l'accompagnateur *m* / l'accompagnatrice *f*
at ground level	au niveau du sol, surbaissé
hand controls (car)	les commandes *f* manuelles
handhold	la poignée
handicap ID	la carte d'invalidité
handicap toilet	les toilettes *f* pour handicapés
handicapped person in . . . a wheelchair	le handicapé en fauteuil roulant
handrail, banister	la rampe
headset, headphones	les écouteurs *m*
health and advice center . . .	le centre social de soins
hearing-impaired	malentendant
height	la hauteur
magnetic loop	la boucle magnétique
mentally handicapped	handicapé mental
Minitel dialogue	le minitel-dialogue
mobile medical station	le centre de soins
mute	muet
paraplegic	paraplégique
parking place for . . . . handicapped people	la place de stationnement pour handicapés
person with reduced mobility	la personne à mobilité réduite
physical handicap	le handicap physique
seated shower	la douche assise
seeing-eye dog	le chien d'aveugle
set up for handicapped . . . . people	aménagé/équipé pour handicapés

severely handicapped person	le/la grand/e handicapé/e
sight-impaired	malvoyant
sight-impaired person	le/la malvoyant/e
sign language	la langue des signes
slope	la pente
social services	les services *m* d'aide sociale
steering wheel knob (car) . .	le volant mobile
step	la marche
step (of bus, train, etc.)	le marche-pied
threshold	le seuil
transportation service	le service de transport
(for the handicapped)	(pour handicapés)
walker	le déambulateur
wheelchair	le fauteuil roulant
electric wheelchair	le fauteuil roulant électrique
folding wheelchair	le fauteuil roulant pliant
onboard wheelchair	le fauteuil transport
width	la largeur

Lodging

Dreaming French
Before you decide to stay in one of the usual hotel chains that always have the same setup, maybe you should keep an eye peeled for a hotel with a little more character. *Logis de France* is an amalgamation of hotels with a French flair in all categories. They are located throughout France. For evaluating them the usual stars are replaced by chimneys. A hotel guide with a list of these hotels is published regularly and is available in bookstores. People who prefer to stay in private accommodations should investigate the *chambres d'hôte* and get the addresses from the appropriate tourist offices.

Information

Could you please recommend ...
Vous pourriez m'indiquer ..., s'il vous plaît?

a good hotel
un bon hôtel

a modest hotel
un hôtel pas trop cher

a guest house
une pension de famille

Is it in the center / in a quiet area / near the beach?
Est-ce qu'il/qu'elle est dans le centre / dans un quartier tranquille / près de la plage?

Is there also ... here?
Est-ce qu'il y a aussi ... ici?

a campground
un terrain de camping

a youth hostel
une auberge de jeunesse

Hotel—Guest House—Private Room

Reception

I have a room reserved. My name is ...
J'ai réservé une chambre. Je m'appelle ...

Do you still have rooms available?
Est-ce que vous avez encore des chambres de libres?

... for one night
... pour une nuit

... for two nights
... pour deux jours

... for a week
... pour une semaine

No, I'm afraid not.
Non, désolé.

Yes, what kind of room do you want?
Oui, qu'est-ce que vous désirez comme chambre?

I would like ...
Je voudrais ...

a single room
une chambre pour une personne

a double room
une chambre double

a room with twin beds
une chambre à deux lits/une twin

a quiet room
une chambre calme

with a shower
avec douche

with a bath
avec salle de bains

with a view of the ocean
avec vue sur la mer

May I see the room?
Est-ce que je peux voir la chambre?

Can you put in a third bed / a child's bed?
Est-ce que vous pouvez installer un troisième lit / un lit pour enfant?

How much is the room, including ...
Quel est le prix de la chambre avec, ...

breakfast?
petit déjeuner compris?

half-board?
en demi-pension?

full board?
en pension complète?

Where can I park my car?
Où est-ce que je peux garer ma voiture?

In our garage.
Dans notre garage.

In our parking lot.
Sur notre parking.

When does breakfast begin?
Le petit déjeuner est à partir de quelle heure?

What times are meals served?
Quelles sont les heures des repas?

Where is the dining room?
Où est la salle à manger?

Where is the breakfast room?
Où est la salle de petit-déjeuner?

Can you wake me up at 7:00 tomorrow morning, please?
Vous pouvez me réveiller demain matin à 7 heures, s'il vous plaît?

Could you please bring me ...
Vous pourriez m'apporter

  a bath towel
  une serviette de bains

  another blanket
  encore une couverture

How does ... work?
Comment fonctionne ...?

Number 11, please.
La 11, s'il vous plaît.

Is there any mail for me?
Il y a du courrier pour moi?

Where can I ...
Où est-ce que je peux...

  get something to drink here?
  boire quelque chose ici?

  rent a car?
  louer une voiture

  make a phone call?
  téléphoner?

Can I leave my valuables in your safe?
Est-ce que je peux déposer mes objets de valeur dans le coffre?

Can I leave my baggage here?
Est-ce que je peux laisser mes bagages ici?

Complaints

My room has not been cleaned today.
Ma chambre n'a pas été nettoyée aujourd'hui.

The air conditioning doesn't work.
L'air conditionné ne fonctionne pas.

The faucet drips.
Le robinet goutte.

There is no (warm) water.
Il n'y a pas d'eau (chaude).

The toilet / the sink is plugged up.
Les W.-C. sont bouchés / Le lavabo est bouché.

I would like another room, please.
J'aimerais une autre chambre, s'il vous plait.

Departure

I am leaving this evening / tomorrow at ... o'clock.
Je pars ce soir / demain à ... heures.

Could you prepare the bill for me, please?
Vous pouvez préparer la note, s'il vous plaît?

Do you accept credit cards?
Vous prenez les cartes de crédit?

Could you please call a taxi for me?
Vous pourriez m'appeler un taxi, s'il vous plaît?

Thanks for everything! Good-bye!
Merci pour tout! Au revoir!

air conditioning	l'air *m* conditionné
armchair	le fauteuil
ashtray	le cendrier
balcony	le balcon
bath towel	la serviette de bains
bathroom	la salle de bains
bathtub	la baignoire
bed	le lit
bidet	le bidet
blanket	la couverture

breakfast	le petit déjeuner
breakfast buffet	le buffet (de petit déjeuner)
breakfast room	la salle de petit déjeuner
chair	la chaise
change of linen	le changement de linge
to clean	nettoyer
cleaning lady	la femme de chambre
cup	la tasse
cupboard / wardrobe	l'armoire f
dining room	la salle à manger
dinner	le dîner
elevator	l'ascenseur m
extended week	la semaine supplémentaire
faucet	le robinet
floor/story	l'étage m
full board	la pension complète
garage	le garage
glass	le verre
guest house	la pension (de famille)
half-board	la demi-pension
hand towel	la serviette de toilette
hanger	le cintre
heating	le chauffage
key	la clé
lamp	la lampe
light	la lumière
light bulb	l'ampoule f
light switch	l'interrupteur m
living room	le salon
lunch	le déjeuner
mattress	le matelas
mini-bar	le minibar
motel	le motel
multi-plug adapter	la prise multiple
night lamp	la lampe de chevet
night table	la table de nuit
night's stay	la nuit
notepad	le bloc-notes
off-season	l'arrière-saison f
parking space	la place de stationnement
peak season	la pleine saison
pillow	l'oreiller m

plug	la fiche
porter, concierge (m. and f.)	le portier, le/la concierge
pre-season	l'avant-saison *f*
price list	la liste des prix
(*e.g., for the mini-bar*)	
radio	la radio
reception	la réception
reception hall	le hall
to repair	réparer
reservation	la réservation
room	la chambre
room telephone	le téléphone (de la chambre)
safe	le coffre-fort
sheets, bed linens	les draps *m*
shoe-shine kit	le nécessaire à cirage
shower	la douche
shower attachment	la douchette
shower curtain / sliding door	le rideau/la porte coulissante
shower head	la pomme de douche
shuttle bus	la navette
sink	le lavabo
stationery	le papier à lettres
swimming pool	la piscine
table	la table
table setting	le couvert
television	le téléviseur
terrace	la terrasse
toilet	les toilettes *f*
toilet paper	le papier hygiénique
TV room	la salle de télévision
ventilator	le ventilateur
wall socket/ plug	la prise de courant
wastebasket	la poubelle
water	l'eau *f*
cold water	l'eau froide
hot water	l'eau chaude
water glass	le verre à eau
window	la fenêtre
wool blanket	la couverture de laine

Vacation Houses and Vacation Rentals

Are water and electricity included in the rent?
Est-ce que l'eau et l'électricité sont comprises dans le loyer?

Are pets allowed?
Est-ce que les animaux domestiques sont admis?

Do we have to do the final cleaning ourselves?
Est-ce que nous devons faire nous-mêmes le nettoyage de fin de séjour?

> also Hotel – Guest House – Private Room

arrival day	le jour de l'arrivée
bedroom	la chambre à coucher
bungalow	le bungalow
bunk bed	le lit à étages
charges	les charges f
coffee maker	la machine à café
dishes	la vaisselle
dishtowel	le torchon
electrical current	le courant (électrique)
farm	la ferme
final cleaning	le nettoyage de fin de séjour
key return	la remise des clés
kitchen	la cuisine
kitchenette	le coin-cuisine
living room	la salle de séjour
owner	le propriétaire (de la maison)
pets	les animaux m domestiques
refrigerator	le réfrigérateur, le frigo
rent	le loyer
to rent	louer
sleeper couch	la banquette-lit
stove	la cuisinière
studio	le studio
studio apartment	le studio
trash/garbage	les ordures f
vacation village	le village de vacances
vacation/country home	la maison de vacances / de campagne
voltage	le voltage
washing machine	la machine à laver
water consumption	la consommation d'eau

Camping

Could you tell me if there is a campground near here?
Vous pourriez me dire s'il y a un terrain de camping par ici?

Do you have a spot for a trailer / tent?
Vous avez encore de la place pour une caravane / une tente?

What is the charge per day and per person?
Quel est le tarif par jour et par personne?

How much is it for ...
Quel est le tarif pour ...

  the car?
  les voitures?

  the trailer?
  les caravanes?

  the camper?
  les camping-cars?

  the tent?
  les tentes?

Do you rent camping trailers?
Vous louez des caravanes?

We are staying ... days/weeks.
Nous restons ... jours/semaines.

Where are ...
Où sont ...

  the toilets?
  les toilettes?

  the washrooms?
  les lavabos?

  the showers?
  les douches?

to camp	camper
campground	le (terrain de) camping
camping	le camping
camping guide	le guide de camping-caravaning
camping permit	la licence camping
camping trailer	la caravane
camping vehicle	le camping-car
drinking water	l'eau *f* potable
electrical current	le courant (électrique)
gas cartridge	la cartouche de gaz
gas cylinder	la bouteille de gaz
gas stove	le réchaud à gaz
kerosene lamp	la lampe à pétrole

LODGING

plug	la fiche
propane	le propane
reservation	la réservation
sink	le lavabo pour la vaisselle
stove	le réchaud
tent	la tente
wall plug	la prise de courant
washroom	les lavabos *m*
water	l'eau *f*
water can	le bidon d'eau

Gastronomy

Shall We Eat? – On Va Manger?

❑ A **café** serves primarily drinks, but also *croissants* or *baguettes, sandwichs,* and other small items for moderate hunger. In a **café-tabac**, tobacco products, newspapers and magazines, stamps, phone cards, and bus tickets are also sold.
❑ You can get complete hot meals in a **café-restaurant**.
❑ *Bistro* is the general term for the café on the corner and for all small places; but a bistro can also be a small restaurant in the old tradition, that is, with red and white checked tablecloths and generally good, economical menus.
❑ A **brasserie** was originally a beer hall. But recently it has come to mean a large café-restaurant, sometimes with Alsatian specialties. In a **brasserie** you can also make do with a single course without being looked at askance.
❑ In a **restaurant**, on the other hand, it is often expected that you order several courses plus wine.
❑ A **salon de thé** is the equivalent of a café in other countries, and the term **crêperie** has been part of everyone's vocabulary for a long time.

Going Out to Eat

Could you suggest ...
Vous pourriez m'indiquer ...

a good restaurant?
un bon restaurant?

a reasonably priced restaurant?
un restaurant pas trop cher?

In the Restaurant

I would like to reserve a table for four people for this evening.
Je voudrais retenir une table pour ce soir, pour quatre personnes.

Is this table available, please?
Est-ce que cette table est libre, s'il vous plaît?

I would like a table for two / three people.
Je voudrais une table pour deux/trois personnes.

Where are the restrooms, please?
Où sont les toilettes, s'il vous plaît?

May I smoke?
Je peux fumer?

Waiter / Waitress,
Monsieur / Madame (Mademoiselle),

a menu, please.
la carte, s'il vous plaît.

the beverage list, please.
la carte des boissons, s'il vous plaît.

What do you recommend?
Qu'est-ce que vous me conseillez?

Are there half-portions for children?
Vous faites des demi-portions pour les enfants?

Have you decided?
Vous avez choisi?

I'll have …
Je prends …

As an appetizer / main course / dessert, I'll have …
Comme entrée / plat principal / dessert, je prends …

I don't want an appetizer, thank you.
Je ne veux pas d'entrée, merci.

Could I have … instead of …?
Est-ce qu'à la place de … je pourrais avoir …?

How do you want your steak cooked?
Comment voulez-vous votre bifteck?

well done
bien cuit

medium
à point

rare
saignant

What would you like to drink?
Qu'est-ce que vous voudriez boire?

A glass of …, please.
Un verre de …, s'il vous plaît.

A bottle / a half-bottle of …, please.
Une bouteille / Une demi-bouteille de …, s'il vous plaît.

Enjoy your meal!
Bon appétit!

GASTRONOMY

93

Here's to your health!
A votre santé / A la vôtre.

Would you like anything else?
Vous désirez encore quelque chose?

Please bring us ...
Apportez-nous ..., s'il vous plaît.

Could you please bring us some more bread / water / wine?
Est-ce que vous pourriez nous apporter encore un peu de pain / d'eau / de vin, s'il vous plaît?

Complaints

If you need to complain about something, preface your complaint with *Excusez-moi;* for example, *Excusez-moi, mais je n'ai pas de ....* With a second complaint in the same restaurant, you may dispense with the *Excusez-moi.*

I don't have a ...
Je n'ai pas de ...

Are you remembering my ...?
Vous pensez à mon/ma/mes ...?

This is not what I ordered.
Ce n'est pas ce que j'ai commandé.

The soup is cold / too salty.
Le potage est froid / trop salé.

This meat is tough / too fatty.
Cette viande est dure / trop grasse.

The fish is not fresh.
Le poisson n'est pas frais.

Please take this back.
Vous pouvez le remporter, s'il vous plaît?

Please get the manager.
Allez chercher le patron, je vous prie.

The check, please.
L'addition, s'il vous plaît.

All together.
Je paie le tout.

Is service included?
Le service est compris?

I think there is an error in addition.
Je crois qu'il y a une erreur dans l'addition.

Here are a couple of tips on French customs in *cafés* and *restaurants*:
❑ If several people are dining "Dutch treat," they first get the overall bill, pay it, and then settle up.
❑ People usually leave the tip casually on the table or in the saucer left for the purpose. Even though this brings the donor no personal thank-you, it's no reason to leave a smaller tip.
❑ Check the bill carefully.

I didn't have ... I had ...
Je n'ai pas pris de ... J'ai pris ...

Did you like it?
Ça a été?, Ça vous a plu?

The meal was excellent.
Le repas était excellent.

This is for you.
Voilà pour vous.

That's fine.
C'est bien comme ça.

Café

No matter how full a *café* is, nobody sits down at a stranger's table.

What would you like to drink?
Qu'est-ce que vous buvez?

I would like a coffee, please.
Je voudrais un café, s'il vous plaît.

   ... a black coffee
   ... un café noir

   ... an espresso
   ... un café express

   ... a coffee with milk
   ... un café au lait

   ... a coffee with cream
   ... un café crème

Coffee culture in France is not nearly as developed as in Italy, but you should be aware of a few nuances. People often order
- *un grand crème = un grand café au lait*
- *un petit crème = un petit café au lait*
- *un grand noir = un grand café noir*
- *un petit noir* or *un express*
- *une noisette* (a nut) is a black coffee with a little milk.

The designations and their meanings may vary slightly according to location.

A freshly squeezed lemonade.
Un citron pressé.

A lemonade with peppermint syrup.
Un diabolo menthe.

I would like plain tea / with milk / with lemon.
J'aimerais un thé nature / au lait / au citron.

A beer from the tap, please.
Une (bière) pression, s'il vous plaît.

This is my round.
C'est ma tournée.

Another of the same, please!
La même chose, s'il vous plaît.

What do you have to eat?
Qu'est-ce que vous avez à manger?

We have omelets, cold cuts, our own pâté, or a toasted ham and cheese sandwich.
Nous avons des omelettes, de la charcuterie, du pâté maison ou des croque-monsieur.

> also Food

alcohol-free	sans alcool
appetizer	l'entrée *f*
artificial sweetener	les sucrettes *f*
ashtray	le cendrier
bone	l'os *m*
breakfast	le petit déjeuner
child's portion	le menu enfants
cook (m. and f.)	le cuisinier / la cuisinière
corkscrew	le tire-bouchon
course	le plat
cup	la tasse
saucer	la soucoupe
daily special	le plat du jour
dessert	le dessert
diabetic	le diabétique
dinner	le dîner
dish	le plat
drink	la boisson, la consommation
dry *(wine)*	sec
fishbone	l'arête *f*
fork	la fourchette
from the tap	pression
glass	le verre
water glass	le verre à eau
wine glass	le verre à vin
grill	le gril
homemade	(fait) maison
hot	très chaud
to be hungry	avoir faim
ketchup	le ketchup
knife	le couteau
lunch	le déjeuner
main course	le plat principal
mayonnaise	la mayonnaise
mellow / smooth (wine) . . .	doux/moelleux

menu	la carte, le menu
mustard	la moutarde
napkin	la serviette
oil	l'huile *f*
order	la commande
pepper	le poivre
pepper shaker	la poivrière
pitcher	la carafe
place setting(s)	le couvert, les couverts *m*
plate	l'assiette *f*
portion	la portion
salad bar	le buffet de salades
salt	le sel
saltshaker	la salière
sauce	la sauce
to season	assaisonner
seasoning	l'assaisonnement *m*
slice	la tranche
soup	la soupe, le potage
soup bowl	l'assiette *f* creuse
special diet	la cuisine diététique
specialty	la spécialité
spice	l'épice *f*
spoon	la cuillère
teaspoon	la cuillère à café
spot	la tache
stir-fry	le plat fait à la poêle
straw	la paille
sugar	le sucre
tablecloth	la nappe
tip	le pourboire
toothpick	le cure-dents
tough	dur
vegetarian	végétarien
vinegar	le vinaigre
waiter	le garçon; *(direct address)* Monsieur!
waitress	la serveuse
water	l'eau *f*

Preparation

au gratin	gratiné
boiled	bouilli
braised	à l'étuvée
browned *(potatoes)*	rissolées
casserole	en daube
fried	frit
juicy	juteux
lean	maigre
medium	à point
raw	cru
roast	rôti
on a spit	à la broche
from the grill	sur le gril
in a frying pan	à la poêle
smoked	fumé
sour	aigre
spicy	épicé
steamed	à l'étouffée
stuffed	farci
sweet	doux/douce
tender	tendre
tough	coriace
well done	bien cuit

boiled
bouilli

simmered
mijoté

steamed
à l'étouffée

in a double boiler
au bain-marie

fried
à la poêle

deep fried
frit

grilled
grillé

101

Ginger le gingembre

Garlic
l'ail *m*

Onion
l'oignon *m*

Dill
l'aneth *m*

Bay leaf
le laurier

Rosemary
le romarin

Majoram/Oregano
la marjolaine/
l'origan *m*

Coriander
le coriandre

Parsley
le persil

Basil
le basilic

Nutmeg la muscade

Chili pepper
le piment

Hot pepper
le piment

Chives
la civette

Sage
la sauge

Chervil
le cerfeuil

Thyme
le thym

Savory
la sarriette

Lovage
bot livèche

103

Petit-déjeuner   Breakfast

café noir	black coffee
café au lait	coffee with milk
café décaféiné	decaffeinated coffee
thé au lait/citron	tea with milk / lemon
infusion	herbal tea
chocolat	chocolate
jus de fruits	fruit juice
œuf à la coque	boiled egg
œufs brouillés	scrambled eggs
œufs au bacon	eggs and bacon
pain / petit pain / toast	bread / roll / toast
croissant	croissant
beurre	butter
fromage	cheese
saucisson	sausage
jambon	ham
confiture	jelly / jam
miel	honey
muesli	cereal
yaourt	yogurt
fruit	fruit

Potages et soupes   Soups

bisque d'écrevisses	crawfish soup
bouillabaisse	bouillabaisse
consommé de poulet	chicken soup
potage au cresson	cress soup
potage de légumes	vegetable soup
soupe à l'oignon	onion soup
soupe de poisson	fish soup
velouté d'asperges	cream of asparagus soup

Entrées   Appetizers

asperges à la crème	asparagus in cream
assiette de charcuterie	cold cuts plate
avocat aux crevettes	avocado with shrimp
bouchée à la reine	vol-au-vent

GASTRONOMY

107

cœurs d'artichauts	artichoke hearts
crudités variées	assorted raw vegetables
escargots à la bourguignonne	escargots in garlic butter
feuilleté de chèvre chaud	warm goat cheese in dough
foie gras avec toast	goose liver on toast
hors d'oeuvre variés	assorted hors d'oeuvres
jambon de Bayonne	raw ham from Bayonne
jambon fumé	smoked ham
melon au porto	melon with port wine
œufs à la russe	Russian style eggs
pâté de campagne	country pâté
pâté de foie	liver pâté
pissenlits au lard	dandelion greens with bacon
quiche lorraine	quiche Lorraine
rillettes	potted pork
salade niçoise	salade niçoise (green beans, potatoes, tomatoes, egg, cheese, olives, and tuna or anchovies)
saumon fumé	smoked salmon
terrine de canard	duck terrine
terrine de saumon	salmon terrine
tripes	tripe

Crustacés et coquillages	Shellfish and Mussels
coquilles Saint-Jacques	scallops
crabes	crabs
crevettes	shrimp
écrevisse	crawfish
homard	lobster
huîtres	oysters
langouste	spiny lobster
langoustine	langoustine
moules	mussels
plateau de fruits de mer	assorted seafood

Poissons	Fish
Poissons de mer	**Ocean Fish**
aiglefin	haddock
cabillaud	cod
calmar	squid

colin	pollack
daurade	bream
hareng	herring
lotte	monkfish
maquereau	mackerel
morue	cod
rouget	red mullet
sole	sole
turbot	turbot
Poissons d'eau douce	**Freshwater Fish**
anguille	eel
brochet	pike
carpe	carp
perche	perch
petite friture	small fry
quenelles de brochet	pike dumplings
sandre	pikeperch
truite meunière	trout meuniere

Viandes	Meats
agneau	lamb
bœuf	beef
mouton	mutton
porc	pork
veau	veal
bifteck	steak
blanquette de veau	blanquette of veal
bœuf bourguignon	roasted beef in Burgundy wine
cassoulet	white beans with various meats *(Specialty of Toulouse)*
choucroute	sauerkraut with various meats *(Alsace)*
cochon de lait	suckling pig
côte de bœuf	beef rib steak
entrecôte	beef entrecôte
épaule	shoulder
escalope de veau	veal cutlet
escalope panée	breaded veal cutlet
filet de bœuf	fillet of beef
foie	liver
gigot d'agneau	leg of lamb
grillades	grilled meat
jarret de veau	veal knuckle
langue	tongue

pieds de cochon	pig's feet
paupiettes	stuffed escalope of veal
ris de veau	calves' sweetbreads
rognons	kidneys
rôti	roast
sauté de veau	sautéed lamb/veal
steak au poivre	pepper steak
steak tartare	steak tartare

Volailles et gibier — Poultry and Wild Game

canard à l'orange	duck à l'orange
civet de lièvre	jugged hare
coq au vin	chicken stew with red wine
cuissot de chevreuil	venison haunch
dinde truffée	turkey with truffles
faisan	pheasant
lapin chasseur	rabbit hunter-style
oie aux marrons	goose with chestnut stuffing
perdrix	partridge
pigeons	pigeons
pintade	guinea fowl
poulet rôti	roast chicken
sanglier	wild boar

Why not try some North African specialties some time? *Couscous* has been a favorite dish among the French for many years, along with *steak-frites* and *gigot* (leg of lamb). *Couscous* is a dish containing vegetables such as zucchini, carrots, and chickpeas that are cooked with lamb, beef, or chicken and commonly seasoned with *harissa*, a spicy sauce from North Africa. People also eat special steamed semolina. Two other North African specialties you should try are *taboulé*, a salad made from couscous-semolina with tomatoes, pickles, onions, parsley, lemon juice, and peppermint leaves, which is an ideal summer salad because it is very light, and *merguez*, a very spicy sausage.

Légumes	Vegetables
aubergine	eggplant
chou	cabbage
chou-fleur	cauliflower
courgette	zucchini
endives braisés	braised chicory
épinards en branches	leaf spinach
fenouil	fennel
flageolets	flageolets
jardinière de légumes	mixed vegetables
petits pois	peas
pommes de terre sautées	fried potatoes
pommes mousseline	mashed potatoes
pommes nature,	boiled potatoes
pommes anglaises	
frites	french fries
pommes allumettes	thin french fries
ratatouille niçoise	mixed vegetables containing tomatoes, peppers, eggplant, and zucchini
salsifis	salsify
tomates farcies	stuffed tomatoes

Pâtes et riz	Pasta and Rice
macaronis	macaroni
nouilles	noodles
riz	rice

Fromages	Cheese
assortiment de fromages	assortment of cheeses
fromage blanc	white cheese
fromage de brebis	sheep's milk cheese
fromage de chèvre	goat cheese
gruyère	Gruyere
petit suisse	Petit-suisse
roquefort	Roquefort, green mold cheese

Desserts

Desserts	Desserts
baba au rhum	rum baba
beignets aux pommes	apple doughnuts
charlotte	charlotte; made from ladyfingers with fruits and vanilla-flavored cream
crème caramel	caramel custard
crème Sabayon	zabaglione cream
gâteau	cake
mousse au chocolat	chocolate mousse
omelette norvégienne	baked Alaska
profiteroles	profiteroles, small creampuffs
tarte aux fraises	strawberry tart
tarte Tatin	apple tart with caramel topping

Fruits

Fruits	Fruits
abricots	apricots
cerises	cherries
macédoine de fruits	fruit salad
pêches	peaches
poires	pears
pommes	apples
prunes	plums
raisins	grapes

Glaces / Ice Cream

Glaces	Ice Cream
au café	coffee ice cream
au chocolat	chocolate ice cream
à la fraise	strawberry ice cream
à la pistache	pistachio ice cream
à la vanille	vanilla ice cream
café liégeois	iced coffee topped with whipped cream
coupe maison	dish of ice cream house style
dame blanche	vanilla ice cream with chocolate sauce
poire Belle-Hélène	pear with ice cream and chocolate sauce
sorbet au citron	lemon sherbet

Liste des Consommations / Beverage List

Vin rouge / vin blanc — Red Wine / White Wine

un (verre de vin) rouge . . .	a glass of red wine
1 quart de vin blanc	a quarter-liter (approx. 8.5 fl. oz) of white wine
1 pichet de rosé	pitcher of rosé (approx. 7–17 fl. oz. / 20–50 cl.)

In small restaurants it is always worthwhile to try the house wine. On the beverage list you will find it under *Vin de la maison / Vin en carafe / Vin en pichet / Cuvée du patron / Cuvée* + the name of the restaurant. Otherwise you can ask, *"Vous avez du vin en carafe?"*—"Do you sell wine by the carafe?"

Appellation contrôlée	appellation contrôlée (branded wine)
Beaujolais	Beaujolais: fresh, fruity red wine
Bordeaux *(rouge)*	Bordeaux: fresh, balanced red wine
(blanc)	dry or liqueur-like white wine
Bourgogne	Burgundy (strong red wine)
Champagne	champagne
Côtes-de-Provence	light red or rosé wine
Côtes-du-Rhône	full-bodied red wine

Bière — Beer

(bière) pression	draft beer
demi	general term for a beer (corresponds to a small beer)
bière en bouteille	bottled beer
bière blanche	light, fizzy beer

Apéritifs — Aperitifs

Byrrh, Dubonnet	aperitifs with orange peel
Muscat (Rivesaltes, Frontignan)	aperitif wines
Pastis (Pernod, Ricard)	aperitifs with a taste of anise
Suze	aperitif with a taste of gentian

Alcools et liqueurs	Brandies and Liqueurs
Armagnac	Armagnac, wine brandy
Calvados	Calvados, apple brandy
Cognac	Cognac, wine brandy
Chartreuse	Chartreuse, liqueur made with spices
Framboise	raspberry brandy
Marc	liqueur made from grape marc
Mirabelle	plum brandy
Rhum	rum

Cidre	**Cider / apple wine**
Jus de fruits	**Fruit juices**

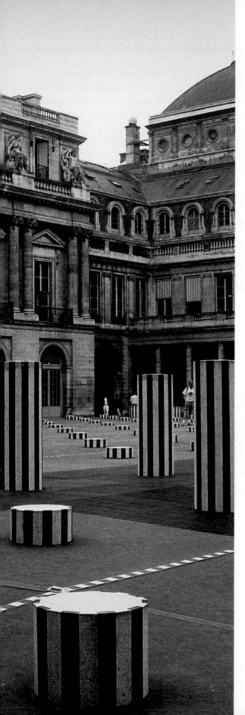

Sightseeing and Tours

Another Side of Paris

The city of Paris has over eighty museums. The *Louvre* and the *Musée d'Orsay* are known to nearly everybody, but perhaps on your next trip you will want to discover some unusual museums. The first three – characteristically French? – deal with perfume, love, and wine:

❏ *Le Musée du parfum* (39 Boulevard des Capucines, Métro Opéra)

❏ *Le Musée de l'érotisme (*72 Boulevard de Clichy, Métro Blanche)

❏ *Le Musée du vin* (Rue des Eaux, 5 Square Charles Dickens, Métro Passy)

The next three span the range from beautiful utensils to magic:

❏ *Le Musée du stylo et de l'écriture* – the museum of writing implements

(3 rue de Maupassant, Métro rue de la Pompe)

❏ *Le Musée de la contrefaçon* – the museum of counterfeiting

(16 rue de la Faisanderie, Métro Pte Dauphine)

❏ *Le Musée de la curiosité et de la magie* – The Museum of Curiosities and Magic (11 rue St-Paul, Métro St-Paul) And since all good things come in threes, here are three more tips:

❏ There is even a children's museum in Paris: *Le Musée en herbe* (rough translation: The little museum) (Jardin d'acclimatation, Bois de Bologne, Métro Sablons).

❏ In case you have spent too much money in Paris, you can visit the *Louvre* and some other museums free of charge on the first Sunday of each month.

❏ If you want to fortify yourself for further undertakings and enjoy a view of Paris, then you can go to the *Institut du monde arabe* with its *Salon de thé* on the ninth floor, where you get a broad view over the Seine and the islands *La Cité* and *Saint-Louis*. In the art-deco coffeehouse *La Samaritaine* you can enjoy the view from the fifth floor over lunch, dinner, or tea, or a wide angle view of Paris from the panorama restaurant and bar with a cold buffet on the tenth floor.

In the Tourist Office

I would like a map of ...
Je voudrais un plan de ...

Do you have an events calendar for this week?
Vous avez le programme des manifestations de cette semaine?

Are there guided bus tours of the city?
Est-ce qu'il y a des visites guidées de la ville en car?

How much is the tour, please?
Quel est le prix du tour, s'il vous plaît?

Sightseeing – Museums

Hours of Operation, Guided Tours, Tickets

Could you please tell me which monuments to see here?
Pouvez-vous me dire quels sont les monuments à voir ici, s'il
vous plaît?

You absolutely must visit ...
Il faut absolument visiter ...

When is the museum open?
Quelles sont les heures d'ouverture du musée?

For many French midday is a sacred time—unfortunately also
for the attractions and the tourist offices that should be
promoting them. So it's better not to plan on any visits
between noon and two o'clock, or you may be disappointed.
This restriction doesn't apply to Paris, though.

When does the next guided tour begin?
Quand commence la prochaine visite guidée?

Is there also a guided tour in English?
Est-ce qu'il y a une visite guidée en anglais?

Is photography allowed?
Est-ce qu'on peut prendre des photos?

117

Two tickets, please.
Deux billets, s'il vous plaît.

Two adults and one child.
Deux adultes et un enfant.

Is there a discount for ...
Est-ce qu'il y a des réductions pour ...

... children?
les enfants?

... students?
les étudiants?

... senior citizens?
les personnes du troisième âge?

... groups?
les groupes?

Is there a catalog for the exposition?
Est-ce qu'il y a un catalogue de l'exposition?

What? When? Where?

Is this ...
C'est ...?

When was this building constructed /restored?
Quand est-ce que ce bâtiment a été construit/restauré?

Who painted this picture?
Qui a peint ce tableau?

General Information

alley	la ruelle
archeological remains	les vestiges *m* archéologiques
art	l'art *m*
attractions	les curiosités *f*
birth city	la ville natale
changing of the guard	la relève de la garde
downtown	le centre-ville
emblem	l'emblème *m*
emperor / empress	l'empereur *m* / l'impératrice *f*
guide	le/la guide
guided city tour	la visite guidée de la ville
history	l'histoire *f*
hours of operation	les heures *f* d'ouverture
house	la maison
king / queen	le roi / la reine
market	le marché

monument protection	la protection des monuments
museum	le musée
museum of folk art	le musée d'art populaire
outskirts, suburb	la (ville de) banlieue
park, public garden	le parc, le jardin public
pedestrian zone	la zone piétonne
precinct	le quartier
to reconstruct	reconstituer
religion	la religion
remains	les vestiges *m*, les restes *m*
to restore	restaurer
street	la rue
tourist office	l'office *m* de tourisme, le syndicat d'initiative
visit / tour	la visite

Architecture

abbey	l'abbaye *f*
altar	l'autel *m*
amphitheater	l'amphithéâtre *m*
arcades	les arcades *f*
arch	l'arc *m*
arch of triumph	l'arc *m* de triomphe
archeology	l'archéologie *f*
architect	l'architecte *m/f*
architecture	l'architecture *f*
arena	l'arène *f*
bridge	le pont
building	le bâtiment *m*, l'édifice *m*
castle	le château
catacombs	les catacombes *f*
cathedral	la cathédrale
ceiling	le plafond
cemetery	le cimetière
chapel	la chapelle
château	le château
church	*(Cath.)* l'église *f* ; *(Prot.)* le temple
church tower	le clocher
city walls	les murs *m* de la ville
cloister	le cloître
column	la colonne
crypt	la crypte

cupola / dome	la coupole, le dôme
door	la porte
excavations	les fouilles *f*
façade	la façade
fortress	la forteresse
fountain	la fontaine ; le jet d'eau
grave	la tombe
inner courtyard	la cour intérieur
inscription	l'inscription *f*
marketplace	les halles *f*
mausoleum	le mausolée
memorial	le mémorial
menhir	le menhir
monastery / convent	le monastère, le couvent
monument	le monument
obelisk	l'obélisque *m*
old city	la vieille ville
opera	l'opéra *m*
palace	le palais
pediment	le fronton
pilgrimage museum	l'église *f* de pèlerinage
place	la place
portal	le portail
pulpit	la chaire
to reconstruct	reconstruire
roof	le toit
ruin	la ruine
temple	le temple
theater	le théâtre
tomb	le tombeau
tower	la tour
town hall	*(government)* la mairie ; *(historical buildings)* l'hôtel *m* de ville
treasure chamber	la salle du trésor
university	l'université *f*
vault	la voûte
wall	le mur
window	la fenêtre
wing	l'aile *f*

Fine Arts

bronze	le bronze
ceramics	la céramique
copy	la copie
cross	la croix
crucifix	le crucifix
decorative arts	les arts *m* décoratifs
design	le dessin
display piece	la pièce exposée
etching	(la gravure à) l'eau-forte
exposition	l'exposition *f*
gallery	la galerie (de peinture)
goldsmith's art	l'orfèvrerie *f*
graphic art	l'art *m* graphique
lithography	la lithographie
model	le modèle
mosaic	la mosaïque
nude	le nu
original	l'original *m*
painter	le peintre
painting	la peinture, le tableau
painting on glass	la peinture sur verre
photograph	la photographie
porcelain	la porcelaine
portrait	le portrait
poster	l'affiche *f*
pottery	la poterie
sculptor	le sculpteur
sculpture	la sculpture
silkscreen	la sérigraphie
statue	la statue
still life	la nature morte
terra cotta	la terre cuite
torso	le torse
vase	le vase
watercolor	l'aquarelle *f*
wood carving	la sculpture sur bois
wood engraving	la gravure sur bois

Styles and Eras

antique	antique
Art nouveau	l'Art nouveau
baroque	le baroque
Bronze Age	l'âge *m* de bronze
Byzantine	byzantin
Celtic	celte
century	le siècle
Christianity	le christianisme
Cistercians	les cisterciens
Classicism	le classicisme
Cubism	le cubisme
dynasty	la dynastie
epoch	l'époque *f*
Expressionism	l'expressionnisme *m*
Gothic	le gothique
Greek	grec
high point	l'apogée *m*
Impressionism	l'impressionnisme *m*
Mannerism	le maniérisme
Middle Ages	le Moyen Age
Modern	moderne
Norman	normand
pagan	païen
prehistoric	préhistorique
Renaissance	la Renaissance
Rococo	le rococo
Romanesque Art	l'art *m* roman
Romanticism	le romantisme
Stone age	l'âge *m* de pierre
style	le style
Surrealism	le surréalisme
Vikings	les Vikings *m*

Tours

When shall we meet?
A quelle heure est le rendez-vous?

Where do we meet?
Où est le point de rendez-vous?

Will we go by the ...?
Est-ce que nous allons passer devant le/la ...?

Will we also visit the ...?
Est-ce qu'on va visiter également ...?

amusement park	le parc de loisirs
backcountry	l'arrière-pays m
bird sanctuary	le parc ornithologique
botanical garden	le jardin botanique
cave	la caverne
cave with stalactites and stalagmites	la grotte (à stalactites et à stalagmites)
cliff	la falaise
countryside	le paysage
day trip	l'excursion f pour une journée
dike	la digue
field	la lande
fishing village	le village de pêcheurs
forest	la forêt
forest fire	l'incendie m de forêt
gorge	la gorge
grotto	la grotte
island tour	le tour de l'île
lake (ocean)	le lac; la mer
lava	la lave
lighthouse	le phare
market	le marché
mountain(s)	la montagne
mountain pass	le col
mountain town	le village de montagne
museum village	le village-musée
national park	le parc national
nature preserve	la réserve naturelle
observatory	l'observatoire m
open-air museum	le musée en plein air
overlook	le point de vue
pilgrimage site	le lieu de pèlerinage
river	la rivière
round trip	le circuit
spring	la source
summit	le sommet

surroundings . . . . les environs *m*
swamp . . . . le marais
tour, excursion . . . . l'excursion *f*
valley . . . . la vallée
volcano . . . . le volcan
waterfall . . . . la cascade
wildlife park . . . . le parc animalier
zoo . . . . le zoo

Swimming, Active, and
Creative Vacations

France: Vacation Destination for French and Non-French
With approximately sixty million foreign tourists per year, France is one of the most frequently visited countries in the world. During your visit it may strike you as peculiar that 80% of French people spend their vacation in their own country. Since nearly everyone takes their vacation in July (13 million) or August (20 million), you might want to avoid these months when you plan yours. But if you want to experience Paris (nearly) without Parisians, the weekend around August 15 is a good choice; success is assured!

Swimming Vacation

Excuse me, is there a … here?
Excusez-moi, est-ce qu'il y a … ici?

swimming pool
une piscine

an outdoor pool
une piscine en plein air

an indoor pool
une piscine couverte

One ticket, please!
Un billet, s'il vous plaît!

Could you tell me where the … are?
Pourriez-vous me dire où sont les … ?

showers
douches

changing rooms
cabines

Grand bain	For Swimmers Only
Plongeons interdits!	No Diving!
Baignade interdite!	No Swimming!
Courant dangereux	Dangerous Current

Is the beach …
C'est une plage …

sandy?
de sable?

rocky?
de galets?

Are there sea urchins / jellyfish / Is there seaweed?
Est-ce qu'il y a des oursins / des méduses / des algues?

Is the current strong?
Est-ce qu'il y a un fort courant?

Can you tell me if it's dangerous for children?
Vous pouvez me dire si c'est dangereux pour les enfants?

When is low tide / high tide?
La marée basse/haute, c'est quand?

I would like to rent ...
Je voudrais louer ...

a beach chair.
un transat / une chaise-longue.

an umbrella.
un parasol.

a boat.
un canot.

a pair of water skis.
des skis nautiques.

How much is it per hour / per day?
Quel est le tarif à l'heure / à la journée?

air mattress	le matelas pneumatique
beach volleyball	le volley-ball de plage
flippers	les palmes *f*
jet ski	le jet ski, le scooter des mers
kiddy pool	le bassin pour enfants
lawn	la pelouse
lifeguard, pool attendant	le maître-nageur
nudist beach	la plage de nudistes
pedal boat	le pédalo
to swim	nager
swimmer	le nageur
wading pool	la pataugeoire
water skiing	le ski nautique
to go water skiing	faire du ski nautique
water wings	les bracelets *m*
wind shield	le pare-vent

Active Vacations and Sports

What kinds of sports are available here?
Qu'est-ce qu'on peut pratiquer comme sports ici?

> Why not learn a new type of sport?
> People do beach sailing (*faire du char à voile*) on the long beaches of the Opal coast (from Le Touquet to Dunkirk) in northern France. You certainly won't get wet if you try it – unless it rains!

Is there ... here?
Est-ce qu'il y a ... ici?

  a golf course
  un terrain de golf

  a tennis court
  un court de tennis

Where can one ...
Où est-ce qu'on peut ...

  go fishing?
  pêcher?

  take some good hikes?
  faire des belles randonnées?

Where can I rent ...
Où est-ce que je peux louer ...?

I would like to take a beginning / advanced course in ...
Je voudrais prendre des cours de ... pour débutants/avancés.

Water Sports

boating permit	le permis-bateau
canoe, kayak	le canoë, le kayak
to go canoeing / kayaking	faire du canoë / du kayak
canyoning	le canyoning
house boat	la péniche
inflatable boat	le canot pneumatique
motorboat	le canot automobile
oar	la rame
rafting	le rafting
regatta	les régates *f*

riverboat (*houseboat*)	la croisière fluviale
to row	(faire de) l'aviron *m*
rowboat	la barque le canot (à rames)
sailboat	le bateau à voiles
to sail	(faire de) la voile
sailing trip	la croisière à la voile
to surf	faire du surf
surfboard	le surf
transport	le convoyage
wind direction	la direction du vent
to wind surf, windsurfing	(faire de) la planche à voile

Diving

deep-sea diving	la plongée sous-marine
to dive	faire de la plongée
diving equipment	l'équipement *m* de plongée
diving goggles / face mask	les lunettes *f* de plongée
harpoon	le harpon
oxygen tank	la bouteille d'oxygène
snorkel	le tuba
to go snorkeling	faire de la nage sous-marine
wet suit	la combinaison de plongée

Fishing

closed season	la période de fermeture de la pêche
deep-sea fishing	la pêche au gros
to go fishing	pêcher
fishing license	le permis (de pêche)
fishing rod	la canne à pêche
harbor master	la capitainerie du port

Ball Games

ball (*small, like tennis ball*)	la balle
(*larger, like soccer ball*)	le ballon
basketball	le basket-ball
goal (*shot*)	le but *m*
(*goalpost*)	le poteau des buts
goalie	le gardien de buts
halftime	la mi-temps
handball	le hand-ball

net	le filet
rugby	le rugby
soccer	le football
soccer match	le match de football
soccer stadium	le terrain de football
team	l'équipe *f*
volleyball	le volley-ball

Tennis and Badminton

badminton	le badminton
double	le double
racket	la raquette
shuttlecock	le volant
single	le simple
squash	le squash
table tennis / ping pong	le ping-pong
tennis	le tennis
tennis court	le court de tennis
tennis racket	la raquette de tennis

Fitness and Strength Training

aerobics	l'aérobic *m*
bodybuilding	la musculation
conditioning	l'entretien *m* de la forme
fitness center	le fitness
gymnastics	la gymnastique
jazzercise	le modern jazz
jogging	le jogging
to go jogging	faire du jogging
physical therapy exercises	la gymnastique corrective
stretching	le stretching

Wellness

massage	le massage
sauna	le sauna
solarium	le solarium
steam bath	le bain de vapeurs
swimming pool	la piscine
whirlpool	le bassin bouillonnant

Cycling

bicycle	le vélo, la bicyclette
bicycle route	la piste cyclable
bicycle tour	la randonnée cycliste
bike helmet	le casque de protection
to go bike riding	faire du vélo
cycling	le cyclisme
inner tube	la chambre à air
mountain bike	le V.T.T. (vélo tout terrain)
pump	la pompe
racing bicycle	le vélo de course
rollers	les rollers
tire repair kit	le kit de réparation des pneus
touring bike	le V.T.C. (vélo tout chemin)

Hiking and Mountain Climbing

I would like to take a hike in the mountains.
Je voudrais faire une randonnée en montagne.

Can you show me an interesting route on the map?
Vous pouvez m'indiquer un itinéraire intéressant sur la carte?

day trip	la randonnée (pour la journée)
duration of the hike	la durée de la marche
free climbing	la varape
hiking	la randonnée pédestre
to go hiking	faire de la randonnée
hiking trail	le chemin de randonnée
itinerary	l'itinéraire *m*
major trail	le chemin de grande randonnée
mountain climbing	l'alpinisme *m*
rappelling rope	la corde de rappel
shelter	le refuge
trail map	la carte de randonnées
trekking	le trekking

Horseback Riding

horse	le cheval
polo	le polo
ride	la promenade à cheval
to ride	faire du cheval
riding school	l'école *f* d'équitation
riding vacation	les vacances *f* équestres

Golf

clubhouse	le châlet, la clubhouse
course	le parcours
eighteen-hole course	le golf 18 trous
golf	le golf
golf club (implement)	la crosse de golf
golf club (organization)	le club de golf
greens fee	le greenfee
to hit the ball	frapper la balle

Flying

circumnavigating the globe	le tour de la terre
climb	la montée
gliding	le vol à voile
hang-gliding	le deltaplane
hot air balloon	la montgolfière
paraglider, ...	le parapente
paragliding	
parascending (on beach) . .	le parachute ascencionnel
sky-diving	le parachutisme

Winter Vacation

A day pass.
Un pass pour la journée.

How many points does this lift cost?
Combien de points coûte ce remonte-pentes?

What time is the last trip up / down?
La dernière remontée/descente, c'est à quelle heure?

alpine skiing	le ski alpin
cable car	le téléphérique
chairlift	le télésiège
cross-country ski track	la piste de ski de fond
cross-country skiing	le ski de fond
curling	le curling
daily lift ticket	le forfait-journée
halfway stop on ski lift	l'arrêt m intermédiaire du téléski
ice hockey	le hockey sur glace
ice skates	les patins m à glace

kiddy tow	le remonte-pentes pour enfants
lift loading area	le point de départ du téléski
powder snow	la (neige) poudreuse
to skate	faire du patin à glace
skating	le patinage
skating rink	la patinoire
to ski	skier, faire du ski
ski binding	la fixation
ski goggles	les lunettes f de ski
ski instructor (m. and f.)	le moniteur/la monitrice de ski
ski lessons	les cours m/leçons f de ski
ski poles	les bâtons m
ski tow	le téléski, le remonte-pente

A ski tow is called a *téléski* or a *remonte-pente*, but the third designation—and the most common one—is perhaps the most picturesque: *un tire-fesses* (a butt puller).

skiing	le ski
sled	la luge
to go sledding	faire de la luge
snowboard	le surf des neiges
top of the lift	le point d'arrivée du téléski
week's pass	le forfait-semaine

Other Sports

boules	le jeu de boules, la pétanque
bowling	le bowling
bungee jumping	le saut à l'élastique
inline skate	le roller
to do inline skating	faire du roller
miniature golf	le minigolf
ninepins	le jeu de quilles
roller skate	le patin à roulette
to roller skate	faire du patin à roulette
skateboard	la planche à roulettes
to skateboard	faire de la planche à roulettes
track and field	l'athlétisme m

Could you tell me what kinds of sporting events there are here?
Vous pourriez me dire quelles manifestations sportives il y a ici?

I would like to attend the soccer game.
Je voudrais assister au match de football.

When / where does it take place?
Quand/Où est-ce qu'il a lieu?

How much does it cost to get in?
Combien coûte l'entrée?

What's the score?
Quel est le score?

Two to one.
Deux à un.

One to one.
Un partout.

Foul!
Faute!

Good shot!
Beau tir!

Goal!
But!

athlete (m. and f.)	le sportif / la sportive
bicycle race	la course cycliste
cash register	la caisse
championship	le championnat
competition	la compétition
cross	le tir au centre
free shot	le coup franc
game	le match
kickoff	le coup d'envoi
to lose	perdre
loss	la défaite
offside	hors-jeu
pass	la passe
penalty	le pénalty
penalty area	la surface de réparation
playing field	le terrain de sport
program	le programme

race	la course
referee	l'arbitre *m*
stadium	le stade
ticket	le billet
tie	match nul
to win	gagner
win	la victoire

Creative Vacations

I would like to take …
J'aimerais suivre …

pottery lessons.
un cours de poterie.

a French course.
un cours de français.

for beginners
pour débutants

for advanced students
pour avancés

How many hours per day is it?
Combien y a-t-il d'heures par jour?

Is enrollment limited?
Est-ce que le nombre de participants est limité?

Is any experience required?
Est-ce qu'il faut des connaissances de base?

What's the registration deadline?
Jusque quand faut-il s'inscrire?

Are the materials costs included?
Les frais de matériel sont-ils inclus?

What do we have to bring?
Qu'est-ce qu'il faut apporter?

belly dancing	la danse du ventre
cooking	la cuisine
course	le cours
dance theater	le théâtre de la danse
drama group	le groupe théâtral
drawing from a model	le dessin sur modèle
drumming	le tam-tam
goldsmith's art	l'orfèvrerie *f*
language course	le cours de langue

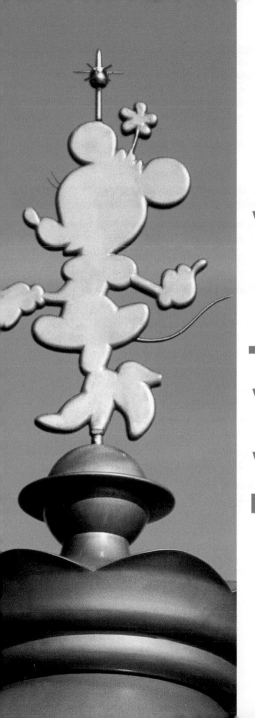

Entertainment

> **Festivals:** The most famous French festivals are probably the *Festival de Cannes* for movies and the *Festival d'Avignon* for theater. But there are all kinds of small *festivals* and *fêtes* nearly everywhere in the summer. Before your trip write (fax or mail) to the tourist office of the area you will visit and ask for a *calendrier des fêtes et des festivals de la région.*

Theater—Concerts—Movies

Could you tell me what play is being presented tonight?
Pourriez-vous me dire quelle pièce on joue ce soir au théâtre?

What's playing tomorrow evening at the movie?
Qu'est-ce qu'on joue demain soir au cinéma?

Are concerts performed in the cathedral?
Est-ce qu'il y a des concerts d'organisés dans la cathédrale?

Can you recommend a play?
Vous pouvez me recommander une pièce de théâtre?

At what time does the performance start?
A quelle heure commence la représentation?

Where does one get tickets?
Où est-ce qu'on peut prendre les billets?

Two tickets for this evening, please.
Deux billets pour ce soir, s'il vous plaît.

Two ... euro seats, please.
Deux places à ... euros, s'il vous plaît.

May I have a program, please?
Un programme, s'il vous plaît.

cloakroom	le vestiaire
festival	le festival
intermission	l'entracte *m*
performance *(theater)*	la représentation
program *(booklet)*	le programme
reservation	la location, la réservation
sales desk	la caisse
screening *(movie)*	la séance
ticket	le billet

Theater

act	l'acte m
actor / actress	l'acteur / l'actrice, le comédien / la comédienne
balcony	le balcon
ballet	le ballet
box	la loge
cabaret	le cabaret
cabaret artist	le chansonnier m
comedy	la comédie
dancer (m. and f.)	le danseur / la danseuse
direction	la mise en scène
drama	le drame
folkloric play	la pièce populaire
musical comedy	la comédie musicale
opera	l'opéra m
operetta	l'opérette f
orchestra (*seating*)	le parterre
outdoor theater	le théâtre en plein air
performance	le spectacle
play	la pièce de théâtre
premiere	la première
presentation	la représentation
program	le programme
theater	le théâtre
theater café	le café-théâtre
tragedy	la tragédie
vaudeville theater	les variétés f

Concerts

blues	le blues
choir	le chœur
classical music	la musique classique
composer (m. and f.)	le compositeur / la compositrice
concert	le concert
classical music concert	le concert de musique classique
church concert	le concert en église
symphony orchestra concert	le concert symphonique
folk	le folk
folk music	la musique folklorique
jazz	le jazz
orchestra	l'orchestre m
orchestra conductor	le/la chef d'orchestre
pop	le pop

rap	le rap
reggae	le reggae
rock	le rock
singer (m. and f.)	le chanteur / la chanteuse (la cantatrice)
soloist (m. and f.)	le/la soliste
soul	le soul
techno	la techno

Movies

direction	la mise en scène
film	le film
action film	le film d'action
animated film	le dessin animé
black and white film	le film en noir et blanc
classic	le classique
comedy	la comédie
documentary	le documentaire
drama	le drame
science fiction film	le film de science-fiction
short feature	le court-métrage
thriller	le film policier
western	le western
leading role	le rôle principal
movie	le cinéma
movie club	le ciné-club
outdoor movie	le cinéma en plein air
movie actor / actress	l'acteur/l'actrice de cinéma
original version	la version originale (la v.o.)
subtitles	les sous-titres m

Even though new movie theaters don't use them, there are still lots of movie theaters in which you are shown to your seat by an usher or *ouvreuse* (literally an *opener*). The usher will guide you to a seat even in a deserted, well lighted theater… and expect a tip, for this tip is part of the person's pay.

Nightlife

What is there to do around here in the evening?
Qu'est-ce qu'on peut faire ici le soir?

Is there a pleasant bar around here?
Est-ce qu'il y a un bistrot sympa dans le coin?

Where can you go dancing around here?
Où est-ce qu'on peut aller danser ici?

Shall we dance (again)?
On danse (encore une fois)?

band	le groupe
bar	le bar, le bistrot
casino	le casino
to dance	danser
dance band	l'orchestre m de danse
discotheque	la discothèque
evening attire	les vêtements m habillés
folk dance evening	la soirée de danse folklorique
folklore	le folklore
game of chance	le jeu de hasard
to go out	sortir
live music	la musique en direct
nightclub	la boîte de nuit
party	la soirée, la fête
show	le show

ENTERTAINMENT

Festivals and Functions

Could you tell when the ... festival takes place?
Pourriez-vous me dire quand a lieu le festival de/du ...?

from the ... to the ...
du ... au ...

every year in August
tous les ans au mois d'août

every two years
tous les deux ans

Can everyone participate?
Tout le monde peut y participer?

carnival	le carnaval
circus	le cirque
fair	la kermesse
fanfare	la fanfare
festival	le festival
fireworks	le feu d'artifice
flea market	la foire à la brocante, le marché aux puces
funfair	le fête foraine
Olympic games	les jeux *m* olympiques
parade	le cortège
procession	la procession
Roland Garros Tennis Tournament (French Open)	le tournoi de Roland Garros
Tour de France	le Tour de France

Shopping

Big Shopping at a Reasonable Price
You will find fewer fairly small supermarkets (*supermarchés*)
in France than at home. Often the huge supermarkets
(*hypermarchés*) determine the landscape on the edge of
cities. Except for charm, they offer everything your heart
may desire – especially special offers (*promotions*). If you are
interested in bargains, you should at least watch for the sign
Soldes (Sales) in the store windows in January and July.

Questions

I'm looking for ...

Is someone helping you?
On vous sert?

I would like ...
Je voudrais ... / J'aimerais ...

Thanks, I'm just looking.
Merci, je regarde.

I'm looking for ...
Je cherche ...

Do you have ...?
Vous avez ...?

Will there be anything else?
Il vous faut autre chose?

Haggling and Buying

How much is that?
Combien ça coûte?

That's expensive!
C'est cher!

In France it's possible to haggle only in flea markets. In certain
situations it may also happen that a small discount is
appropriate. You might then ask:

Do you give any discounts?
Vous faites une réduction?

Alright, I'll take it.
Bon, alors je le prends.

Do you accept ...
Vous prenez ...
  credit cards?
  les cartes de crédit?

Stores

In France you can generally count on stores remaining open until 7:00 P.M. (many are open until 7:30 P.M.); *hypermarchés* are usually open until 10:00 P.M. On Sundays you can get everything you need until noon. And if you are in France on Christmas Eve, you will be able to go shopping in many *hypermarchés* until midnight.

Pardon me, where can I get ...?
Excusez-moi, où est-ce qu'on peut acheter ...?

Business hours—Horaires d'ouverture

Ouvert	**Open**
Fermé	**Closed**
Vacances jusqu'au	**On vacation until ...**

antique shop	le magasin d'antiquités
art dealer	le marchand d'objets d'art
bakery	la boulangerie
bookstore	la librairie
boutique	la boutique
butcher shop	la boucherie
camera shop	le magasin de photos
confectioner's shop	la confiserie
delicatessen	
(caterer)	le traiteur
(international specialties) .	l'épicerie *f* fine
department store	le grand magasin
drugstore	la droguerie
dry cleaner's	la teinturerie

electrical appliances store . .	le magasin d'électro-ménager
fish market	la poissonnerie
flea market	le marché aux puces
florist	le/la fleuriste
fruit and vegetable shop . . .	le magasin de fruits et légumes
grocery store	l'épicerie f
hair stylist's	le salon de coiffure
hardware store	la quincaillerie
health food shop	le magasin de produits diététiques
jewelry store	la bijouterie
laundromat	la laverie
leather goods	la maroquinerie
liquor store	le magasin de (vins et) spiritueux
market	le marché
natural products shops	le magasin de produits naturels
newspaper seller	le marchand de journaux
optician	l'opticien m
pastry shop	la pâtisserie
perfume shop	la parfumerie
pharmacy	la pharmacie
pork butcher's	la charcuterie
second-hand dealer	le brocanteur
shoe store	le magasin de chaussures
shoemaker	le cordonnier
souvenir shop	le magasin de souvenirs
sporting goods store	le magasin (d'articles) de sport
stationery store	la papeterie
supermarket	le supermarché
tailor / seamstress	le tailleur / la couturière
tobacco shop	le bureau de tabac
toy shop	le magasin de jouets
travel agency	l'agence f de voyages
watchmaker	l'horloger m
wine shop	le magasin de vins

Books, Periodicals, and Writing Materials

I would like …
Je voudrais …

an English newspaper.
un journal anglais.

a magazine.
un magazine.

a visitors' guide.
un guide touristique.

a hiking map of the area.
une carte des randonnées de la région.

Books, Periodicals, and Newspapers

book	le livre
comic book	la bande dessinée
cookbook	le livre de cuisine
daily newspaper	le quotidien
detective novel	le roman policier
magazine	le magazine
map	la carte (géographique)
map of the city	le plan (de la ville)
newspaper	le journal
novel	le roman
pocket book	le livre de poche
roadmap	la carte routière
visitors' guide	le guide touristique
women's magazine	le magazine féminin

Writing Materials

ballpoint pen	le stylo à bille
colored pencil	le crayon de couleur
coloring book	l'album *m* à colorier
envelope	l'enveloppe *f*
notepad	le bloc-notes
paper	le papier
pen	le stylo
pencil	le crayon
postcard	la carte postale
stationery	les articles *m* de papeterie
writing paper	le papier à lettres

CDs and Cassettes

➢ also Electrical Items and Concerts

Do you have CDs / cassettes by ...?
Vous avez des CD / des cassettes de ...?

I would like a CD of typically French music.
Je voudrais un CD avec de la musique française typique.

Can I listen to it, please?
Je peux écouter, s'il vous plaît ?

cassette	la cassette
CD (compact disk)	le CD / le (disque) compact
CD player	le lecteur de CD
CD recorder	magnétophone à CD
DVD	le DVD
headphones	les écouteurs *m*
speaker	le haut-parleur
(*stereo component*)	le baffle

Drugstore Items

after-shave lotion	la lotion après-rasage
band-aid	le sparadrap
brush	la brosse
cloth	le torchon
comb	le peigne
condom	le préservatif
cotton pad	le coton hydrophile
cotton swab	le coton-tige
cream	la crème
dental floss	le fil dentaire
deodorant	le déodorant
dish soap	le produit pour laver la vaisselle
dishwashing brush	la brosse pour la vaisselle
elastic	l'élastique *m*
hair gel	le gel pour les cheveux
hair setting lotion	le fixateur
hairpins	les épingles *f* à cheveux
laundry detergent	la lessive
lip balm	le baume pour lèvres

lipstick	le rouge à lèvres
mascara	le mascara
mirror	le miroir
moisturizing cream	la crème hydratante
nail clippers	les ciseaux *m* à ongles
nail polish	le vernis à ongles
nail polish remover	le dissolvant
night cream	la crème de nuit
panty liners	les protège-slips *m*
paper tissues	les mouchoirs *m* en papier
perfume	le parfum
powder	la poudre
protection index (SPF)	l'indice *m* de protection
razor	le rasoir
razor blades	les lames f de rasoir
sanitary napkins	les serviettes *f* hygiéniques
shampoo	le shampooing
shaving brush	le blaireau
shaving cream	la mousse à raser
shower gel	la mousse gel
soap	le savon
sunscreen	la crème solaire
suntan lotion	le lait solaire
suntan oil	l'huile *f* solaire
tampons	les tampons *m*
mini / regular / super / super plus	mini/normal/super/super plus
tea tree oil	l'huile d'arbre à thé
toilet paper	le papier hygiénique
toothbrush	la brosse à dents
toothpaste	le dentifrice
toothpick	le cure-dent
tweezers	la pince à épiler
washcloth	le gant de toilette

Electrical Items

> ➢ also Photo Items and CDs and Cassettes

adapter	l'adaptateur *m*
alarm clock	le réveil
battery	la pile
calculator	la calculatrice
extension cord	la rallonge

hair dryer	le sèche-cheveux
light bulb	l'ampoule *f*
notebook (electronic)	le portable
organizer	l'organizer *m*
pager	le bip
plug	la fiche
recharger	le rechargeur

Photo Items

> ➢ also Film and Photography

I would like ...
Je voudrais ...

  a roll of film for this camera.
  une pellicule pour cet appareil.

  a roll of color film.
  une pellicule couleur.

  a roll of slide film.
  une pellicule pour diapos.

... is not working.
... ne fonctionne plus.

This is broken. Can you please repair it?
C'est cassé. Vous pouvez réparer ça, s'il vous plaît?

automatic shutter	le déclencheur automatique
black and white film	le film en noir et blanc
camcorder	le caméscope
digital camera	l'appareil *m* photo digital
DVD	le DVD
film speed	la sensibilité
flash	le flash
lens	la lentille
light meter	le photomètre, le posemètre
objective	l'objectif *m*
Polaroid	le polaroïd
shutter release	le déclencheur
telephoto lens	le téléobjectif
tripod	le pied
video camera	la caméra vidéo
video film	le film vidéo
video recorder	le magnétoscope
videocassette	la vidéocassette
viewfinder	le viseur

SHOPPING

151

At the Hairstylist's

Shampoo and blow dry, please.
Shampooing et brushing, s'il vous plaît.

A haircut with / without shampoo, please.
Une coupe avec/sans shampooing, s'il vous plaît.

I would like ...
Je voudrais ...

Just a trim.
Les pointes seulement.

Not too short / quite short / a little shorter, please.
Pas trop courts / Très courts / Un peu plus courts, s'il vous plaît.

A shave, please.
Un rasage, s'il vous plaît.

Trim my mustache / beard, please.
Vous me taillez la moustache / la barbe, s'il vous plaît.

Thanks a lot. It's fine.
Merci beaucoup. C'est très bien.

bangs	la frange
beard	la barbe
blond	blond
to blow dry	faire un brushing
to color	faire une coloration
to comb	peigner
curls	les boucles f
dandruff	les pellicules f
to do one's hair	coiffer
hair	les cheveux
hair curler	les bigoudis m
hair style	la coiffure, la coupe de cheveux
hairpiece	le postiche
layer cut	la coupe en dégradé
mustache	la moustache
part	la raie
permanent	la permanente
to set	faire une mise en plis
shampoo	le shampooing
sideburns	les pattes f
strands	les mèches
tint	faire un rinçage
wig	la perruque

Household Goods

As in every language, French uses some words other than the "official" terms in everyday speech. One example: a freezer packet used to keep lunch boxes cold is correctly termed *un accumulateur de froid*, but in slang it is referred to as a *pain de glace* (ice bread).

aluminum foil	le papier (d')alu
bottle opener	l'ouvre-bouteilles *m*
can opener	l'ouvre-boîtes *m*
candles	les bougies *f*
charcoal	le charbon de bois
charcoal lighter	l'allume-barbecue *m*
clothesline	la corde à linge
clothespins	les pinces *f* à linge
corkscrew	le tire-bouchon
denatured alcohol	l'alcool *m* à brûler
fork	la fourchette
freezer packet	le pain de glace
glass	le verre
grill	le gril
household goods	les articles *m* ménagers
insulated bag	la glacière
knife	le couteau
needle	l'aiguille *f*
paper napkins	les serviettes f en papier
petroleum	le pétrole
plastic bag	le sac en plastique
plastic cup	le gobelet en plastique
plastic wrap	le film alimentaire
pocket knife	le couteau de poche
safety pin	l'épingle *f* de sûreté
scissors	les ciseaux *m*
spoon	la cuillère
string	la ficelle
thermos bottle	la (bouteille) thermos
trash bag	le sac-poubelle
wire	le fil de fer

SHOPPING

153

Groceries

What would you like?
Vous désirez?

Please give me ..., please?
Donnez-moi ..., s'il vous plaît.

  one kilo ...
  un kilo de ...

  ten slices of ...
  dix tranches de ...

  a piece of ...
  un morceau de ...

  a package of ...
  un paquet de ...

  a glass of ...
  un verre de ...

  a can of ...
  une boîte de ...

  a bottle of ...
  une bouteille de ...

  a plastic bag
  un sac en plastique

That was a bit too much. Would it be all right?
Ça fait un peu plus. C'est bien?

Will there be anything else?
Et avec ça?

May I have a taste?
Est-ce que je peux goûter?

No, thanks, that's all.
Non, merci. C'est tout.

Fruits	Les fruits
almonds	les amandes f
apples	les pommes f
apricots	les abricots m
bananas	les bananes f
blackberries	les mûres f
cherries	les cerises f
coconut	la noix de coco
dates	les dattes f
figs	les figues f
fruits	les fruits m
grapefruit	le pamplemousse
grapes	les raisins m

lemons	les citrons *m*
melon	*(honeydew melon)* le melon; *(watermelon)* la pastèque
nuts	les noix *f*
oranges	les oranges *f*
peaches	les pêches *f*
pears	les poires *f*
pineapple	l'ananas *m*
plums	les prunes *f*
strawberries	les fraises *f*
tangerines	les mandarines *f*

Vegetables **Légumes**

artichokes	les artichauts *m*
asparagus	l'asperge *f*
avocado	l'avocat *m*
beans	les haricots *m*
green beans	les haricots *m* verts
white beans	les haricots *m* blancs
cabbage	le chou
carrots	les carottes *f*
cauliflower	le chou-fleur
celery	le céleri
chickpeas	les pois *m* chiches
corn	le maïs
cucumber	le concombre; *(pickle)* le cornichon
eggplants	les aubergines *f*
endive	l'endive *f*
fennel	le fenouil
garlic	l'ail *m*
leek	le poireau
lentils	les lentilles *f*
lettuce	la laitue
olives	les olives *f*
onions	les oignons *m*
parsley	le persil
peas	les petits pois *m*
potatoes	les pommes *f* de terre
pumpkin	le potiron
salad	la salade
spinach	les épinards *m*
sweet pepper	le poivron
tomatoes	les tomates *f*
vegetables	les légumes *m*

SHOPPING

Baked Goods, Sweets ...   Pain, Patisserie, Confiserie ...

bread	le pain
black bread	le pain noir
brown bread	le pain bis
white bread	le pain blanc
cake	le gâteau
candy	les bonbons *m*
chocolate	le chocolat
chocolate bar	la barre de chocolat
cookies	les biscuits *m*
honey	le miel
ice cream	la glace
jam	la confiture
muesli	le musli
oatmeal	les flocons *m* d'avoine
pastries	les pâtisseries *f*
roll	le petit pain
sandwich	le sandwich
sweets	les friandises *f*
toast	le toast

Eggs and Milk Products   Œufs et Produits laitiers

butter	le beurre
buttermilk	le babeurre
cheese	le fromage
goat cheese	le fromage de chèvre
sheep's milk cheese	le fromage de brebis
soft cheese	le fromage à pâte molle
cottage cheese	le fromage blanc
cream	la crème
sour cream	la crème aigre
whipping cream	la crème chantilly
eggs	les œufs *m*
milk	le lait
skim milk	le lait écrémé
yogurt	le yaourt

Meats and Sausages

Viandes et Charcuterie

beef	le bœuf
chicken	le poulet
cold cuts	les tranches f de charcuterie / de viande froide
cooked pork	la charcuterie
cutlet	la côtelette
goulash	le/la goulasch
ham	le jambon
cooked ham	le jambon cuit / blanc / de Paris
uncooked ham	le jambon cru
hamburger	la viande hachée
lamb	l'agneau m
meat	la viande
mutton	le mouton
pâté	le pâté de foie
pork	le porc
rabbit	le lapin
salami	le salami
sausage	la saucisse
veal	le veau

Fish and Seafood

Poissons et Fruits de mer

clams	les palourdes f
crab	le crabe
cuttlefish	la seiche
eel	l'anguille f
fish	le poisson
herring	le hareng
mackerel	le maquereau
mussels	les moules f
oysters	les huîtres f
perch	la perche
prawns	les crevettes f roses
sea bream	la dorade
shellfish	les coquillages f
shrimp	les crevettes f
sole	la sole
swordfish	l'espadon m
tuna	le thon

Seasonings	Aromates
basil	le basilic
bay leaf	le laurier
chervil	le cerfeuil
clove	les clous *m* de girofle
coriander	le coriandre
cumin	le cumin
dill	l'aneth *m*
garlic	l'ail *m*
ginger	le gingembre
herbs	les herbes *f*
hot pepper	le piment
marjoram	la marjolaine
mint	la menthe
nutmeg	la muscade, la noix de muscade
onion	l'oignon *m*
oregano	l'origan *m*
paprika	le paprika,
hot pepper	le piment
parsley	le persil
pepper	le poivre
rosemary	le romarin
saffron	le safran
sage	la sauge
savory	la sarriette
tarragon	l'estragon *m*
thyme	le thym

This and That	Ceci cela
bouillon cube	le bouillon-cube
butter	le beurre
flour	la farine
margarine	la margarine
mayonnaise	la mayonnaise
mustard	la moutarde
noodles	les nouilles *f*
oil	l'huile *f*
olive oil	l'huile *f* d'olive
rice	le riz
salt	le sel
sugar	le sucre
vinegar	le vinaigre

158

Drinks   Boissons

Drinks	Boissons
apple juice	le jus de pommes
beer	la bière
non-alcoholic beer	la bière sans alcool
champagne	le champagne
coffee	le café
decaffeinated coffee	décaféiné
lemonade	la limonade
mineral water	l'eau *f* minérale
carbonated	gazéifiée
orange juice	le jus d'orange
tea	le thé
black tea	le thé noir
chamomile tea	la tisane à la camomille
fruit tea	le thé aux fruits
green tea	le thé vert
herbal tea	la tisane
lime blossom tea	le tilleul
mint tea	le thé à la menthe
teabag	le sachet de thé
wine	le vin
red	le (vin) rouge
rosé	le (vin) rosé
white	le (vin) blanc

If you want to bring home a good wine, look for two notices: *Appellation d'origine contrôlée* (regulated designation of origin) and *Mis en bouteille au château* (bottled at production site).

Fashion

> also Colors

Clothing

Could you please show me ...?
Est-ce que vous pouvez me montrer ..., s'il vous plaît?

May I try it on?
Je peux l'essayer?

What size do you take?
Quelle taille faites-vous?

> If you find something that you like, don't worry if you notice that your size is different than at home. You haven't gained weight; it's just that the sizing is different, and a U.S. ladies' blouse size 36 is a 42 in France.

It is too ... for me
Il est trop ... pour moi.

narrow / wide
étroit/large

short / long
court/long

small / large
petit/grand

This fits me. I'll take it.
Ça me va. Je le prends.

This is not exactly what I wanted.
Ce n'est pas tout à fait ce que je voulais.

bathing cap	le bonnet de bain
beach robe	le peignoir de bain
bikini	le bikini
blazer	le blazer
blouse	le chemisier
body	le body
bow tie	le nœud papillon
bra	le soutien-gorge
cap	la casquette
clothing	les vêtements *m*
coat	le manteau; *(men)* le pardessus
cotton	le coton
dress	la robe
gloves	les gants *m*
hat	le chapeau
sun hat	le chapeau de soleil
headscarf	le foulard
jacket	la veste
jeans	le jean
jogging pants	le pantalon de jogging
jogging suit	le jogging
leggings	le caleçon
linen	le lin, la toile
necktie	la cravate
pants	le pantalon

pantyhose	les collants *m*
parka	l'anorak *m*
pullover	le pull-over
raincoat	l'imperméable *m*
scarf	l'écharpe *f*
shirt	la chemise
shorts	le short
silk	la soie
ski pants	le pantalon de ski
skirt	la jupe
sleeve	la manche
sockettes	les socquettes *f*
socks	les chaussettes *f*
stockings	les bas *m*, les chaussettes *f*
suit	le costume
suit (woman's)	le tailleur
swimsuit	le maillot de bain
swimsuit (one-piece)	le maillot une pièce
T-shirt	le t(ee)-shirt
umbrella	le parapluie
underpants	le slip
undershirt	le maillot de corps
underwear	les sous-vêtements *m*
wool	la laine
wool jacket	la veste de laine

Cleaning

I would like to have these things cleaned / washed.
Je voudrais faire nettoyer/laver ces affaires.

When will they be ready?
Quand est-ce qu'elles seront prêtes?

dry cleaning	nettoyer (à sec)
laundry (to be washed)	la lessive
to iron	repasser

Optician

Would you please repair these glasses / frames?
Vous pouvez me réparer ces lunettes / la monture.

I am nearsighted / farsighted.
Je suis myope/hypermétrope.

161

How is your vision?
Comment est votre vue?

right eye ..., left eye ...
œil droit ..., œil gauche ...

When can I pick up my glasses?
Quand est-ce que je peux venir chercher mes lunettes?

I need ...
Il me faudrait ...

  contact lens soaking solution
  du liquide de conservation

  cleaning solution
  du liquide de nettoyage

  for hard / soft contact lenses.
  pour lentilles dures/molles.

I'm looking for ...
Je cherche ...

  sunglasses.
  des lunettes de soleil.

  a pair of binoculars.
  des jumelles.

Shoes and Leather Goods

I would like a pair of shoes.
Je voudrais une paire de chaussures.

My size is ...
Je chausse du ...

These are too narrow.
Elles sont trop étroites.

They are too big.
Elles sont trop grandes.

athletic shoes	les tennis *f*; *(high-tops)* les baskets *m*
backpack	le sac à dos
bag	le sac
bathing shoes	les chaussures *f* en plastique (pour la baignade)
beach shoes	les chaussures *f* de plage
belt	la ceinture
boots	les bottes *f*
fanny pack	la banane
handbag	le sac à main
heel	le talon
lace	le lacet

leather coat	le manteau de cuir
leather jacket	la veste de cuir
leather pants	le pantalon de cuir
pocket (on clothing)	la poche
rubber boots	les bottes f en caoutchouc
sandals	les sandales f
school bag	la sacoche
shoe	la chaussure
shoe brush	la brosse à chaussures
shoe polish	le cirage
ski boots	les chaussures f de ski
sole	la semelle
straps	les courroies f
suitcase	la valise
travel bag	le sac de voyage
wheeled suitcase	la valise à roulettes

Souvenirs

I would like …
Je voudrais …

a nice souvenir.
un joli souvenir.

a souvenir typical of the area.
un souvenir typique de la région.

I would like something not too expensive.
Je voudrais quelque chose de pas trop cher.

Oh, that's nice.
Tiens, ça c'est joli.

Thanks, but I haven't found anything (that I like).
Merci, je n'ai rien trouvé (à mon goût).

authentic	authentique
ceramic	la céramique
embroidery	la broderie
folk doll	la poupée folklorique
handmade	fait-main
jewelry	les bijoux m
kitschy	kitsch
music box	la boîte à musique
pottery	la poterie
regional product / specialty	le produit régional / la spécialité régionale
souvenir	le souvenir
souvenir shop	le magasin de souvenirs

Tobacco Products

A package / a carton of ...
Un paquet / Une cartouche de ...
with / without filter, please.
filtre / sans filtre, s'il vous plaît.

Ten cigars, / cigarillos, please.
Dix cigares / cigarillos, s'il vous plaît.

A pack / a package of tobacco for cigarettes / pipe.
Un paquet / Une boîte de tabac pour cigarettes / pipe.

ashtray	le cendrier
cigar	le cigare
cigarette	la cigarette
cigarillo	le cigarillo
lighter	le briquet
matches	les allumettes
pipe	la pipe

Watches and Jewelry

bracelet	le bracelet
brooch	la broche
costume jewelry	les bijoux *m* fantaisie
crystal	le cristal
earrings	les boucles *f* d'oreilles
gold	l'or *m*
jewelry	les bijoux *m*
necklace	le collier
pearl	la perle
pendant	le pendentif
ring	la bague
silver	l'argent *m*
wristwatch	la montre-bracelet
for women / for men	pour femmes/hommes

Health

In the Drugstore

Could you please tell me where the nearest drugstore (with on-call service) is located?
Pourriez-vous me dire où est la pharmacie (de garde) la plus proche, s'il vous plaît?

Could you please give me something for ...?
Pourriez-vous me donner quelque chose contre ..., s'il vous plaît?

➢ also A Vist to the Doctor

analgesic pills	les cachets *m* contre la douleur
antiseptic	l'antiseptique *m*
aspirin	l'aspirine *f*
band-aid	le sparadrap
bug bite medication	le produit contre les piqûres d'insecte *m*
burn ointment	la pommade contre les brûlures
condom	le préservatif
contraceptive	le contraceptif
cough syrup	le sirop contre la toux
drops	les gouttes *f*
ear drops	les gouttes *f* pour les oreilles
elastic band	la bande élastique
eye drops	le collyre
gauze	la gaze
insulin	l'insuline *f*
laxative	le laxatif
medication for the circulation	le médicament pour la circulation
medicine	le médicament
pills for a headache	les cachets *m* contre les maux de tête
powder	la poudre

prescription	l'ordonnance *f*
remedy	le remède
salve	la pommade
sedative	le tranquillisant
sleeping pills	les somnifères *m*
sunburn cream	la pommade contre les coups de soleil
suppositories	les suppositoires *m*
tablet	le comprimé, le cachet
thermometer	le thermomètre
throat tablets	les pastilles *f* contre le mal de gorge
tincture of chamomile	l'essence *f* de camomille
tincture of iodine	la teinture d'iode
vitamin	la vitamine

Notice	**Instruction Leaflet**
Composition	Composition
Indications	Indications
Contre-indications	Counter-indications
Effets secondaires	Side effects
Autres effets possibles	Further possible effects
Posologie:	**Dispensing Instructions:**
Prendre ... une fois / plusieurs fois par jour	Take ... once / several times a day
un cachet	1 tablet
20 gouttes	20 drops
une mesure	1 measure
avant les repas	before eating
après les repas	after eating
à jeun	on an empty stomach
avaler avec un peu d'eau	swallow with a little water
dissoudre dans un peu d'eau	dissolve in a little water
laisser fondre dans la bouche	let dissolve in the mouth
externe	external
appliquer une fine couche sur la peau et masser	apply a thin layer onto the skin and rub in
les nourrissons	infants
les enfants en bas-âge (jusqu'à ... ans)	toddlers (up to the age of ...)
les jeunes enfants	small children
les grands enfants	youth
les adultes	adults
Ne pas laisser à la portée des enfants.	Keep out of the reach of children.

167

A Visit to the Doctor

> also Traveling with Children

Convenience is for the doctors … Whenever a person, insured or not, goes to the doctor in France, payment is required in advance.

Could you recommend a good …?
Vous pourriez m'indiquer un bon … s'il vous plaît?

doctor (m. and f.)
médecin

eye doctor
oculiste

gynecologist
gynéco(logue)

eye-ear-nose-throat doctor
oto-rhino(-laryngologiste)

dermatologist
dermato(logue)

children's doctor
pédiatre

general practitioner
généraliste

urologist
urologue

dentist
dentiste

Where is his/her office, please?
Où se trouve son cabinet, s'il vous plaît?

Symptoms

In dealing with complaints, there are some country-specific differences: Germans, for example, usually blame their circulation; the French, on the other hand, point to the liver. Of course, that is no reason for you to drink less. No, the French take the precaution of eating fewer eggs!

What's wrong?
Qu'est-ce qui ne va pas?

I have a fever.
J'ai de la fièvre.

I often feel sick.
J'ai souvent mal au cœur.

I frequently feel dizzy.
J'ai souvent des vertiges.

I passed out.
Je me suis évanoui.

I have a bad cold.
Je suis très enrhumé.

I have a headache / sore throat.
J'ai mal à la tête / à la gorge.

I have a cough.
Je tousse.

I have been stung / bitten.
J'ai été piqué/mordu.

I have indigestion.
J'ai une indigestion.

I have diarrhea.
J'ai la diarrhée.

I am constipated.
Je suis constipé.

I have an upset stomach. / I can't stand the heat.
Je digère mal. / Je ne supporte pas la chaleur.

I hurt myself.
Je me suis blessé.

I fell.
Je suis tombé.

Can you please give me / prescribe something for ...?
Vous pouvez me donner / me prescrire quelque chose contre ...,
s'il vous plaît?

Normally I take ...
Normalement je prends ...

My blood pressure is high / low.
Je fais de l'hypertension / de l'hypotension.

I am diabetic.
Je suis diabétique.

I am pregnant.
J'attends un enfant / Je suis enceinte.

Where does it hurt?
Où est-ce que vous avez mal?

I have a pain here.
J'ai des douleurs ici.

Please undress / roll up your sleeve.
Déshabillez-vous / Retroussez votre manche, s'il vous plaît.

Take a deep breath. Hold your breath.
Inspirez profondément. Retenez votre respiration.

I need a blood / urine sample.
J'ai besoin d'une prise de sang / d'un échantillon d'urine.

You should stay in bed for a couple of days.
Vous devriez garder le lit pendant quelques jours.

Do you have a vaccination record?
Vous avez un certificat de vaccination?

I have been vaccinated for ...
Je suis vacciné contre ...

In the Hospital

How long do I have to stay here?
Combien de temps est-ce que je vais devoir rester ici?

Give me ... please.
Donnez-moi ..., s'il vous plaît.

 a glass of water
 un verre d'eau

 a pain pill
 un cachet contre la douleur

 a sleeping pill
 un somnifère

 a hot water bottle
 une bouillotte

I can't go to sleep.
Je n'arrive pas à m'endormir.

When can I get up?
Quand est-ce que je peux me lever?

170

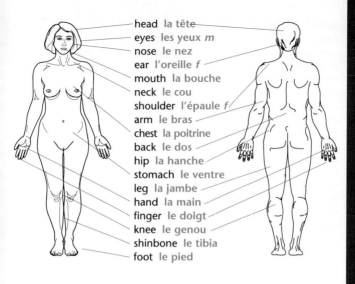

head	la tête
eyes	les yeux *m*
nose	le nez
ear	l'oreille *f*
mouth	la bouche
neck	le cou
shoulder	l'épaule *f*
arm	le bras
chest	la poitrine
back	le dos
hip	la hanche
stomach	le ventre
leg	la jambe
hand	la main
finger	le doigt
knee	le genou
shinbone	le tibia
foot	le pied

Illnesses and Ailments

abscess	l'abcès *m*
AIDS	le sida
to be allergic to ...	être allergique à ...
allergy	l'allergie *f*
angina	l'angine *f*
antibiotic	l'antibiotique *m*
appendicitis	l'appendicite *f*
asthma	l'asthme *m*
attack	l'attaque *f*
back pain	les douleurs *f* au dos
bleeding	le saignement
bloody nose	les saignements *m* de nez
break	*(bones)* la fracture; *(groin)* la rupture
broken	cassé
bronchitis	la bronchite
burn	la brûlure
cancer	le cancer
cardiac deficiency	la déficience cardiaque
cholera	le choléra
circulatory problems	les troubles *m* de la circulation

cold	le rhume
colic	la colique
concussion	la commotion cérébrale
constipation	la constipation
contagious	contagieux
contusion	la contusion
cramp	la crampe
cut	la coupure
diabetes	le diabète
diarrhea	la diarrhée
digestive trouble	les troubles *m* digestifs
diphtheria	la diphtérie
fainting fit	l'évanouissement *m*, la syncope
fever	la fièvre, la température
flatulence	les vents *m*
food poisoning	l'intoxication *f* alimentaire
fracture	la fracture
grippe	la grippe
hay fever	le rhume des foins
headaches	les maux *m* de tête
heart attack	la crise cardiaque
heart trouble	les troubles *m* cardiaques
heartburn	les aigreurs *f* d'estomac
hemorrhoids	les hémorroïdes *f*
hernia	la hernie
hoarse	enroué
hypertension	l'hypertension *f*
illness	la maladie
impaired balance	les troubles *m* de l'équilibre
infarction	l'infarctus *m*
infection	l'infection *f*
inflammation	l'inflammation *f*
to injure	blesser, faire mal
injury	la blessure
inner ear infection	l'otite *f*
insomnia	l'insomnie *f*
to itch, scratch	démanger, gratter
jaundice	la jaunisse
kidney inflammation	la néphrite
kidney stone	le calcul rénal
lumbago	le tour de reins, le lumbago
malaria	la malaria
migraine	la migraine

miscarriage	la fausse-couche
nausea	la nausée
pain in the side	le point de côté
pains	les douleurs *f*
paralysis	la paralysie
pill (contraceptive)	la pillule (anticonceptionnelle)
pneumonia	la pneumonie
poisoning	l'empoisonnement *m*
polio	la polio(myélite)
pulling of a muscle	le claquage (musculaire)
rashes	les rougeurs *f*
respiratory difficulties	les troubles *m* respiratoires
rheumatism	le rhumatisme
ruptured tendon	la rupture de tendon
sciatica	la sciatique
septicemia	la septicémie
shivers	les frissons *m*
sinusitis	la sinusite
to sneeze	éternuer
sore throat	le mal de gorge
sprained	foulé
stomachache	les maux *m* d'estomac
stroke	l'embolie *f* cérébrale
sunburn	le coup de soleil
sunstroke	l'insolation *f*
swelling	l'enflure *f*
swelling, tumor	la grosseur, la tumeur
swollen	enflé
swollen tonsils	l'inflammation *f* des amygdales
tachycardia	la tachycardie
tetanus	le tétanos
typhoid	la typhoïde
ulcer	l'ulcère *m*
venereal disease	la maladie vénérienne
vertigo	le vertige
vision problems	les troubles *m* de la vue
a wound	la plaie
yellow fever	la fièvre jaune

Body—Doctor—Hospital

anesthesia	l'anesthésie *f*
ankle	la cheville
appendix	l'appendice *m*
back	le dos
bandage	le pansement
to bandage	faire un pansement
bladder	la vessie
to bleed	saigner
blood	le sang
blood pressure	*(elevated)* l'hypertension *f*
	(low) l'hypotension *f*
blood type	le groupe sanguin
bone	l'os *m*
bowel movement	les selles *f*
brain	le cerveau
to breathe	respirer
bronchia	les bronches *f*
bypass	le by-pass
cardiologist	le cardiologue
certificate	le certificat, l'attestation *f*
clavicle	la clavicule
consultation	la consultation
cough	la toux
diagnosis	le diagnostic
diet	le régime
digestion	la digestion
disinfect	désinfecter
esophagus	le tube digestif
examination	l'examen *m*, l'analyse *f*
face	le visage
gallbladder	la vésicule biliaire
genitals	les organes *m* génitaux
health insurance	la caisse d'assurance-maladie
hearing	l'ouïe *f*
heart	le cœur
hip	la hanche
hospital	l'hôpital *m*
intestine	l'instestin *m*
joint	l'articulation *f*
kidney	le rein
lip	la lèvre
liver	le foie
lower abdomen	le bas-ventre
lung	le poumon

medical Insurance Record Card	la feuille de maladie / de soins
menstruation	les règles f
muscle	le muscle
nerve	le nerf
nervous	nerveux
nurse (f.)	l'infirmière
nurse (m.)	l'infirmier
office hours	les heures f de visites
operation	l'opération f
pacemaker	le stimulateur cardiaque
pregnancy	la grossesse
to prescribe	prescrire
prosthesis	la prothèse
pulse	le pouls
pus	le pus
radiology	la radio(graphie)
rib	la côte
scar	la cicatrice
shot	la piqûre
sick	malade
skin	la peau
spinal column	la colonne vertébrale
splint	l'attelle f
station	le service
stitch	la piqûre
to stitch	recoudre
stomach	l'estomac m
surgeon	le chirurgien
to sweat	transpirer
to take an X-ray	faire une radio(graphie)
toe	l'orteil m
tongue	la langue
tonsils	les amygdales f
transfusion	la perfusion
tympanum	le tympan
ultrasound test	l'échographie f
unconscious	sans connaissance, évanoui
urine	l'urine f
vaccination	la vaccination
vaccination record	le carnet de vaccinations
virus	le virus
to vomit	vomir
waiting room	la salle d'attente

HEALTH

At the Dentist's

I have a bad toothache.
J'ai (très) mal aux dents.

It's this tooth (top / bottom / front / back) that hurts.
C'est cette dent-là (en haut / en bas / devant / derrière) qui me fait mal.

I have lost a filling.
J'ai perdu un plombage.

I have broken a tooth.
Je me suis cassé une dent.

Give me a shot, please.
Faites-moi une piqûre, s'il vous plaît.

Don't give me a shot, please.
Ne me faites pas de piqûre, s'il vous plaît.

bridge . . . . le bridge
cavity . . . . la carie
crown . . . . la couronne
dentures . . . . la prothèse
filling . . . . le plombage
gums . . . . les gencives f
incisor . . . . l'incisive f
jaw . . . . la mâchoire
molar . . . . la molaire
to pull . . . . arracher
tooth . . . . la dent
toothache . . . . le mal de dents
wisdom tooth . . . . la dent de sagesse

The Essentials from A to Z

Bank

Can you please tell me where there's a bank around here?
Pouvez-vous me dire où il y a une banque ici, s'il vous plaît?

II would like to change ... dollars (Canadian dollars) into ...
Je voudrais changer ... dollars (dollars canadiens) en...

I would like to cash ...
Je voudrais encaisser ...

  this traveler's check.
  ... ce chèque de voyage.

What is the maximum amount I can withdraw?
Quelle est la somme maximale que je peux retirer?

Do you have ... please?
Vous avez ..., s'il vous plaît?

  your ID card
  une pièce d'identité

  your passport
  votre passeport

Sign here, please.
Vous pouvez signer ici, s'il vous plaît?

account	le compte
amount	le montant, la somme
ATM	le distributeur de billets
bank	la banque
bank card	la carte banquaire
bank fees	la commission, les frais bancaires
bill (money)	le billet
cash	les espèces f

cent	le cent
change	la monnaie
check	le chèque
to make out a check	faire un chèque
code number	le numéro de code
coin	la pièce de monnaie
credit card	la carte de crédit
currency	la monnaie
euro	l'euro *m*
to exchange	changer
exchange rate	le cours de change
foreign currency	les devises *f*
form	le formulaire
in cash	en espèces
money	l'argent *m*
money exchange	le change
money order	le mandat
to pay	payer
payment	le paiement
payment machine	la machine de paiement
receipt	le reçu
signature	la signature
smart card	la carte à puce
Swiss franc	le franc suisse
transfer	le virement
wire transfer	le mandat télégraphique
traveler's check	le chèque de voyage

Film and Photography

➤ also Photo Items

Could you please take a photo of us?
Vous pourriez faire une photo de nous, s'il vous plaît?

That's very kind.
C'est très gentil.

Push this button.
Vous appuyez sur ce bouton.

This is how you adjust the distance / aperture.
C'est comme ça qu'on règle la distance / l'ouverture.

May I take your photo?
Je pourrais vous prendre en photo?

Now we will have a nice reminder of our vacation.
Ainsi nous aurons un beau souvenir de nos vacances.

camera	l'appareil photo *m*
landscape format	le format horizontal
photo	la photo
to photograph	photographier
portrait format	le format en hauteur
snapshot	l'instantané *m*

Lost and Found

➢ also Police

Can you please tell me where the lost and found is?
Pouvez-vous me dire où est le bureau des objets trouvés, s'il vous plaît?

I have lost ...
J'ai perdu ...

I forgot my handbag on the train.
J'ai oublié mon sac à main dans le train.

Notify me if someone finds it.
Avertissez-moi si on devait le retrouver.

Here is the address of my hotel / my home address.
Voici l'adresse de mon hôtel / mon adresse personnelle.

Police

Could you please tell me where the nearest police station is?
Pourriez-vous me dire où est le commissariat de police le plus proche, s'il vous plaît?

I would like to report ...
Je voudrais faire une déclaration ...

  a robbery.
  ... de vol.

  a holdup.
  ... d'agression.

Someone stole …
On m'a volé …

  my handbag.
  mon sac à main.

  my wallet.
  mon portefeuille.

  my camera.
  mon appareil photo.

  my car / my bicycle.
  ma voiture / mon vélo.

Someone has broken into my car.
On a fracturé la porte de ma voiture.

Someone stole … from my car.
On a volé … dans ma voiture.

My son / my daughter has disappeared.
Mon fils / Ma fille a disparu.

This man is bothering me.
Cet homme m'importune.

Could you please help me?
Vous pouvez m'alder, s'il vous plaît?

Your name and your address, please.
Votre nom et votre adresse, s'il vous plaît.

Please consult with the American / Canadian consulate.
Adressez-vous au consulat des États-Unis / du Canada, s'il vous plaît.

to arrest	arrêter
to beat up	rouer de coups
to bother	importuner
to break in	fracturer
car radio	l'autoradio *m*
check	le chèque
check card	la carte (de chèque)
to confiscate	confisquer
court	le tribunal
credit card	la carte de crédit
crime	le crime
custody	la détention préventive
drugs	la drogue
fraud	la fraude
guilt	la culpabilité
holdup	*(person)* l'agression *f* ; *(bank)* le hold-up

ID card	la carte d'identité
judge	le juge
key	la clé
lawyer	l'avocat *m*
to lose	perdre
papers	les papiers *m*
passport	le passeport
pickpocket	le voleur à la tire, le pickpocket
police	la police

Don't confuse *à la poste* and *au poste*. In the first case (*Venez à la poste*) you can go along with your mind at ease, but if you hear *Venez au poste*, be careful, because that means "to the police station."

police car	la voiture de police
policeman	l'agent *m* de police
prison	la prison
purse	le porte-monnaie
rape	le viol
registration	la carte grise
to report	faire une déclaration
sexual harassment	le harcèlement sexuel
theft	le vol
thief	le voleur
wallet	le portefeuille
witness	le témoin

Post Office

Where is ..., please?
Où se trouve ..., s'il vous plaît?

the nearest post office
le bureau de poste le plus proche

the nearest mail box
la boîte aux lettres la plus proche

How much does a letter / a postcard ... cost?
C'est combien une lettre / une carte postale ...

to the United States
pour les États-Unis

to Canada
pour le Canada

for Australia
pour l'Australie

Three ...-cent stamps, please.
Trois timbres à ... centimes, s'il vous plaît.

I would like to send this letter ...
Je voudrais envoyer cette lettre ...

airmail.
par avion.

express.
en exprès.

by registered mail.
en recommandé.

I would like to withdraw ... euros from my savings account.
Je voudrais retirer ... euros de mon livret d'épargne.

➢ **also Bank**

address	l'adresse *f*
addressee	le destinataire
airmail	par avion
charge	la taxe, le tarif
customs declaration	la déclaration en douane
declaration of value	la déclaration de valeur
dispatch form	le bulletin d'expédition
express letter	la lettre exprès
fax	le fax
fax machine	le télécopieur
to fill out	remplir
form	le formulaire
to forward	faire suivre
general delivery	poste restante
letter	la lettre
mail box	la boîte aux lettres
main post office	la poste centrale
package	le colis
packet	le paquet
pickup	la levée
post office	le bureau de poste
postage	le port
postal code	le code postal
postcard	la carte postale

registered letter	la lettre recommandée
savings book	le livret d'épargne
sender	l'expéditeur *m*
special issue stamp	le timbre de collection
stamp	le timbre
to stamp	affranchir
stamp machine	le distributeur de timbres
telegram	le télégramme
telex	le télex
weight	le poids

Using the Telephone

Can you please tell me where the nearest phone booth is?
Pouvez-vous me dire où est la cabine téléphonique la plus proche, s'il vous plaît?

> You can receive phone calls in any phone booth. The number is posted on the right at the top.

I want a telephone card, please.
Je voudrais une carte de téléphone, s'il vous plaît.

> Telephone cards (with a chip or a PIN number) and stamps are available not only in the post office, but also in every tobacco shop (*café-tabac* with a sign that looks like a carrot).

What is the prefix for ..., please?
Quel est l'indicatif de ..., s'il vous plaît?

I would like to place a call to ..., please.
Je voudrais téléphoner à ..., s'il vous plaît.

I would like to make a collect call.
Je voudrais un numéro en P.C.V.

Booth number ...
Cabine numéro ...

A Phone Conversation

This is ...
Mme/Mlle/M. ... à l'appareil.

Hello; who is this?
Allô? Qui est à l'appareil?

Hello, my name is ...
Bonjour Madame/Monsieur, ... à l'appareil.

Could I please speak to Mr. / Mrs ... ?
Est-ce que je pourrais parler à Monsieur/Madame ..., s'il vous plaît?

I'm sorry he/ she is not here.
Je suis désolé, il/elle n'est pas là.

Would you like to leave a message?
Vous voulez laisser un message?

Please tell him that I called.
Dites-lui que j'ai téléphoné.

This number is not in service at this time.
Ce numéro n'est pas attribué pour le moment.

For several years French telephone numbers have contained just ten digits, for the area code is always dialed as part of them. France is divided into five areas: 01 for the Ile de France, 02 for the northwest, 03 for the northeast, 04 for the southeast and Corsica, and 05 for the southwest.

answering machine	le répondeur automatique
appointment	la communication avec préavis
area code	l'indicatif *m*
busy	occupé
call	le coup de téléphone
to call	appeler, téléphoner à
cell phone	le portable
charge	la taxe, le tarif
collect call	l'appel *m* en P.C.V.
connection	la communication
conversation	la communication, l'entretien *m* téléphonique
to dial	composer le numéro
information	les renseignements *m*

local call	la communication en ville
long distance	la communication interurbaine
overseas call	l'appel *m* pour l'étranger
phone book	l'annuaire *m*
phone booth	la cabine téléphonique
phone card	la télécarte
phone number	le numéro de téléphone
to pick up	décrocher
portable phone	le portable
receiver	le combiné
telephone	le téléphone
yellow pages	les pages *f* jaunes

Toilet and Bathroom

Where is the toilet, please?
Où sont les toilettes, s'il vous plaît?

May I please use your bathroom?
Je pourrais me permettre d'utiliser vos toilettes?

Would you please give me the key for the bathroom?
Vous pouvez me donner la clé pour les toilettes, s'il vous plaît?

clean	propre
dirty	sale
flushing	la chasse d'eau
hand towel	la serviette de toilette
Ladies	dames
Men	hommes
sanitary napkins	les serviettes *f* hygiéniques
sink	le lavabo
soap	le savon
tampon	le tampon
toilet paper	le papier hygiénique
urinal	l'urinoir *m*

Articles

Forms

		Definite Article		Indefinite Article	
Singular	masculine	**le** train	the train	**un** train	a train
	feminine	**la** ville	the city	**une** ville	a city
Plural	for both genders	**les** trains villes	the trains cities	**des** trains villes	trains cities

Before nouns that begin with a vowel or a mute *h*
   a) *le* and *la* change to *l'*:   l'avion the airplane, l'heure the hour
   b) *un* is linked to the next word: un avion
   c) *les* and *des* are also linked: les heures
                                        des avions

Prepositions (relationship words) + Definite Articles

The prepositions *à* and *de* combine with the following definite
articles *le* and *les* to form a single word:

à + le → au   de + le → du

Je vais **au** cinéma. I go to the movie.	La valise **du** touriste est lourde. The tourist's suitcase is heavy.

à + les → aux   de + les → des

J'écris **aux** copains. I write to friends.	Je viens **des** Etats-Unis. I come from the United States.

Partitive Articles

The partitive article consists of *de* + the definite article. It designates
an unspecified amount or number.

indefinite quantity/ number	Je mange **du** pain.	I eat (some) bread.
	Je bois **de l'**eau.	I drink water.
	Je prends **de la** confiture.	I take some jam.

De Used to Specify Quantities

Nouns that designate a specific quantity or number are linked to the following noun with the preposition *de*.

specific quantity/ number	**un litre de** vin	a liter of wine
	une tasse de café	a cup of coffee
	un kilo d'oranges	a kilo of oranges
	un million de francs	a million francs
as well as:	**beaucoup de** fruits	lots of fruit
	un peu de fromage	a little cheese
	trop de limonade	too much lemonade

Nouns

Plural

Nouns are usually made plural by adding an *–s* to the end (which is not pronounced).

le train	the train	la route	the street
les train**s**	the trains	les route**s**	the streets

Nouns that already end in *–x*, *-z*, or *–s* don't change in the plural.

le prix	the price	le nez	the nose	le cas	the case
les prix	the prices	les nez	the noses	les cas	the cases

Subject — Direct Object — Indirect Object — Possessive

Nouns used as subjects and direct objects have the same form. Indirect objects are expressed with the preposition *à*, and the possessive is formed with *de*.

Subject (Who? What?)	**Le** musée Rodin est fermé. The Rodin Museum is closed.
Direct Object (Who? What?)	Je cherche **le** musée Rodin. I am looking for the Rodin Museum.
Indirect Object (To/for whom?)	J'écris une lettre **à** mon père. I am writing a letter to my father.
Possessive (Whose?)	Où est le sac **de** Françoise? Where is Françoise's bag?

Adjectives

Agreement of Adjectives and Nouns

Adjectives always agree in gender and number with the nouns they modify.

The feminine form of an adjective is formed by adding an *–e* to the end of the masculine form. If the masculine form already ends in *–e*, the adjective doesn't change.

	Singular	Plural
masculine	**Le** livre est passionnant. The book is exciting.	**Les** livres sont passionnant**s**. The books are exciting.
feminine	**La** revue est intéressant**e**. The magazine is interesting.	**Les** revues sont intéressant**es**. The magazines are interesting.

Adjective Placement

The adjective usually comes **after** the noun. un film **passionnant** an exciting film un voyage **fatigant** a tiring trip une voiture **rouge** a red car

Some adjectives come **before** the noun. un **bon** restaurant a good restaurant un **petit** café a small café une **grande** maison a large house

Comparatives of Superiority, Inferiority, and Equality

grand   →   plus grand que   →   le plus grand
large   larger than   the largest

- The comparative is formed by adding *plus (more)* or *moins (less)*.

plus grand	Paris est **plus** grand **que** Lyon. Paris is larger than Lyon.
moins grand	Toutes les autres villes sont **moins** grandes. All other cities are less/not so large.

aussi grand	La Pologne est **aussi** grande **que** la Norvège. Poland is as large as Norway.

- The superlative is expressed by the comparative plus the definite article.

le plus grand	New York est **la plus** grande ville **du** monde.
	New York is the largest city in the world.

- Note the special forms of *bon*:

bon	→	**meilleur**	→	**le meilleur**
good		better		the best

Adverbs

Forms

Some words are adverbs by their nature:

beaucoup	**bien**	**mal**	**vite**
lots	well	poorly	quickly

In addition, there are constructed adverbs, which consist of *–ment* added to the feminine form of adjectives:

lent/e	Il marche lent**ment**.	He walks slowly.

With adjectives that end in *–e* and have just one form, the *–ment* ending is added to this form:

simple	Elle s'exprime simple**ment**.	She expresses herself simply.

Regular Comparative

Adverbs function like adjectives in the comparative:

vite	→	**plus vite**	→	**le plus vite**
quickly		more quickly		most quickly

Irregular Comparatives

bien	→	**mieux**	→	**le mieux**
well		better		best
beaucoup	→	**plus**	→	**le plus**
much		more		most
peu	→	**moins**	→	**le moins**
little		less		least

A conduit **mieux que** B.	C'est C qui conduit **le mieux** des trois.
A drives better than B.	C drives the best of all three.
Elle mange **plus que** son mari.	C'est leur fils qui mange **le plus**.
She eats more than her husband.	Their son eats the most.
Tu gagnes **moins qu'**elle.	C'est moi qui gagne **le moins**.
You earn less than she.	I earn the least.

Verbs (Action Words)

Present Tense

a) Avoir, être

avoir		to have	être		to be
j'	ai	I have	je	suis	I am
tu	as	you have	tu	es	you are
il/elle	a	he/she/it has	il/elle	est	he/she/it is
nous	avons	we have	nous	sommes	we are
vous	avez	you have	vous	êtes	you are
ils/elles	ont	they have	ils/elles	sont	they are

In French "we" can be expressed in two ways: *on* and *nous*. *On* is primarily spoken, and *nous* is mainly written. After *on*, the verb is in the third person singular.

> **On** va au cinéma.
> **Nous** allons au cinéma.   We are going to the movies.

b) Regular Verbs

French verbs are divided among three groups (conjugations) depending on the ending of their infinitive form.

-er	-ir		-re
parler to speak	finir to finish	partir to leave	vendre to sell
je parle	je finis	je pars	je vends
tu parles	tu finis	tu pars	tu vends
il parle	il finit	il part	il vend
elle parle	elle finit	elle part	elle vend
nous parlons	nous finissons	nous partons	nous vendons
vous parlez	vous finissez	vous partez	vous vendez
ils parlent	ils finissent	ils partent	ils vendent
elles parlent	elles finissent	elles partent	elles vendent

- The *–er* group is the largest one; most verbs belong to it.
- Most *–ir* verbs are formed like *finir*.
- Only a few verbs follow the pattern of *partir*:

dormir	to sleep	servir	to serve
sentir	to smell	sortir	to go out

Perfect Tense (Past or Passé composé)

As in English, the perfect tense is constructed using the helping verb *avoir* (to have) or *être* (to be) plus the past participle.

The past participle comes from the infinitive (basic form) of each verb as shown here:

parl**er**	fin**ir**	part**ir**	ven**dre**
parl**é** spoken	fin**i** finished	part**i** departed	ven**du** sold

Irregular forms include the following:

avoir	être	recevoir	faire	prendre
eu had	été been	reçu received	fait done	pris taken

Like English, most verbs form the perfect tense using the helping verb *avoir*. When the perfect is constructed with *être*, the perfect participle agrees in gender and number with the subject of the sentence.

Perfect with *avoir*			Perfect with *être*		
j'	**ai**	été	je	**suis**	parti/partie
tu	**as**	eu	tu	**es**	
il	**a**	parlé	il	**est**	parti
elle	**a**	fini	elle	**est**	partie
nous	**avons**	vendu	nous	**sommes**	partis/parties
vous	**avez**	reçu	vous	**êtes**	
ils	**ont**	fait	ils	**sont**	partis
elles	**ont**	pris	elles	**sont**	parties

- The perfect is constructed with *être* in the case of reflexive verbs:

    Il s'**est** lavé.　　He washed up.

- *Avoir* is used with *être* (to be) and *voyager* (to travel)

    Il **a** été ...　　He has been ...
    Il **a** voyagé ...　　He has traveled ...

Future and Conditional Tenses

Future	Conditional	Future	Conditional
je **parlerai** I shall speak tu **parleras** il **parlera** elle **parlera** nous **parlerons** vous **parlerez** ils **parleront** elles **parleront**	je **parlerais** I would speak tu **parlerais** il **parlerait** elle **parlerait** nous **parlerions** vous **parleriez** ils **parleraient** elles **parleraient**	je **partirai** I shall leave je **prendrai** I will take	je **partirais** I would leave je **prendrais** I would take

- In order to express the future, the irregular verb *aller* is often used in the present tense + an infinitive form.

je	vais	partir	I shall go
tu	vas	parler	you (familiar) shall speak
il	va	boire	he shall drink
nous	allons	voyager	we shall travel
vous	allez	sortir	you (pl. and formal) shall go out
ils	vont	payer	they shall pay

- The conditional can be used to express a request or a question politely:

Je **voudrais** louer une voiture.	I would like to rent a car.
Est-ce que je **pourrais** avoir le plan de la ville?	Could I have the city map?

Imperative (Command Form)

The imperative of verbs in the *–er* group end in *–e* for the second person singular (*tu* / you, familiar); for verbs of the other groups it ends in *–s*.

Request	parler		venir	
In the *tu* form:	**parle**	speak!	**viens**	come!
In the *vous* form:	**parlez**	speak!	**venez**	come!

Important Irregular Verbs

aller to go   –   **allé** gone

Present:	je vais I go, tu vas, il va, nous allons, vous allez, ils vont
Perfect:	je suis allé I went, tu es allé usw.
Future:	j'irai I shall go, tu iras, il ira, nous irons, vous irez, ils iront
Conditional:	j'irais I would go, tu irais, il irait, nous irions, vous iriez, ils iraient

avoir to have   –   **eu** had

Present:	j'ai I have, tu as, il a usw.
Perfect:	j'ai eu I had usw.
Future:	j'aurai I shall have, tu auras usw.
Conditional:	j'aurais I would have, tu aurais usw.

boire to drink   –   **bu** drunk

Present:	je bois I drink, tu bois, il boit, nous buvons, vous buvez, ils boivent
Perfect:	J'ai bu I drank, tu as bu, il a bu usw.
Future:	je boirai I shall drink, tu boiras usw.
Conditional:	je boirais I would drink, tu boirais usw.

devoir to have to   –   **dû** had to

Present:	je dois I have to, tu dois, il doit, nous devons, vous devez, ils doivent
Perfect:	j'ai dû I had to usw.
Future:	je devrai I shall have to, tu devras usw.
Conditional:	je devrais I would have to, tu devrais usw.

dire to say   –   **dit** said

Present:	je dis I say, tu dis, il dit, nous disons, vous dites, ils disent
Perfect:	j'ai dit I said usw.
Future:	je dirai I shall say, tu diras usw.
Conditional:	je dirais I would say, tu dirais usw.

être to be   –   **été** been

Present:	je suis I am, tu es, il est, nous sommes, vous êtes, ils sont
Perfect:	j'ai été I was usw.
Future:	je serai I shall be, tu seras usw.
Conditional:	je serais I would be, tu serais usw.

faire to do — fait done

Present	je fais I do, tu fais, il fait, nous faisons, vous faites, ils font
Perfect:	j'ai fait I did usw.
Future:	je ferai I shall do, tu feras usw.
Conditional:	je ferais I would do, tu ferais usw.

pouvoir to be able — pu been able

Present:	je peux I am able/can, tu peux, il peut, nous pouvons, vous pouvez, ils peuvent
Perfect:	j'ai pu I was able/could usw.
Future:	je pourrai I shall be able, tu pourras usw.
Conditional:	je pourrais I would be able/could, tu pourrais usw.

prendre to take — pris taken

Present:	je prends I take, tu prends, il prend, nous prenons, vous prenez, ils prennent
Perfect:	j'ai pris I took usw.
Future:	je prendrai I shall take, tu prendras usw.
Conditional:	je prendrais I would take, tu prendrais usw.

savoir to know — su known

Present:	je sais I know, tu sais, il sait, nous savons, vous savez, ils savent
Perfect:	j'ai su I knew usw.
Future:	je saurai I shall know, tu sauras usw.
Conditional:	je saurais I would know, tu saurais usw.

venir to come — venu come

Present:	je viens I come, tu viens, il vient, nous venons, vous venez, ils viennent
Perfect:	je suis venu I came usw.
Future:	je viendrai I shall come, tu viendras usw.
Conditional:	je viendrais I would come, tu viendrais usw.

voir to see — vu seen

Present:	je vois I see, tu vois, il voit, nous voyons, vous voyez, ils voient
Perfect:	j'ai vu I saw usw.
Future:	je verrai I shall see, tu verras usw.
Conditional:	je verrais I would see, tu verrais usw.

vouloir to want — voulu wanted

Present:	je veux I want, tu veux, il veut, nous voulons, vous voulez, ils veulent
Perfect:	j'ai voulu … I wanted usw.
Future:	je voudrai … I shall want, tu voudras usw.
Conditional:	je voudrais I would want, tu voudrais usw.

Verbs Plus Objects

1. Most French verbs take direct objects the same way as English verbs:

aider			to help
applaudir			to applaud
écouter	quelqu'un	someone	to listen (to)
remercier			to thank
rencontrer			to meet

2. Some French verbs use an indirect object construction where English uses no corresponding preposition:

demander			to ask
parler	à quelqu'un	someone	to speak (to)
téléphoner			to telephone

3. Verbs with direct and indirect objects:

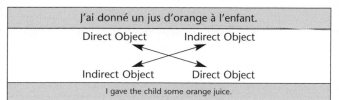

With verbs that have both a direct and an indirect object the direct (the thing) generally comes before the indirect (the person).

donner quelque chose à quelqu'un — to give something to someone
demander quelque chose à quelqu'un — to ask someone for something

4. Verbs with *de*:

avoir besoin **de** quelque chose — to need something
s'occuper **de** quelque chose — to occupy oneself with something
profiter **de** quelque chose — to take advantage of something
remercier quelqu'un **de** quelque chose — to thank someone for something

Word Order

The regular word order in a declarative sentence is as follows:

Subject	→	Predicate	→	Object
Paul Paul		prend takes		le train. the train.
Paul Paul		a pris took		le train. the train.

Interrogative (question) sentences take the following forms:

- Ton frère est venu? Did your brother come?
  (Same word order as in declarative sentence, but intonation rises.)
- Est-ce que ton frère est venu? Did your brother come?
  (Question using *est-ce que* + declarative sentence word order.)
- Où est ta voiture? Where is your car?
  (The subject comes after the verb. After an interrogative word the intonation often falls.)

Negation

Non   No

Encore une bière? – **Non,** merci.	Another beer? – No, thanks.

Ne ... pas   not

Il **ne** vient **pas.** Il **n'**est **pas** venu.	He is not coming. He didn't come.

Ne ... pas de   no/not any

Je **n'**ai **pas** d'argent.	I have no money.

Ne ... personne/rien/jamais/plus   Nobody/nothing/never/no more

Il **ne** connaît **personne.** Il **ne** veut **rien.** Il **ne** fume **jamais.** Il **ne** fume **plus.**	He knows no one. He doesn't want anything. He never smokes. He no longer smokes.

Pronouns

Personal Pronouns

1. Unstressed Personal Pronouns

		Subject (Who?)		Indirect Object (To/for whom?)		Direct Object (Whom?)	
Sing.	1. Pers.	je	I	me	to/for me	me	me
	2. Pers.	tu	you (s., fam.)	te	to/for you	te	you
	3. Pers.	il/elle	he/she/it	lui	to/for	le/la	him/her/it
				se	him/her/it	se	
Plural	1. Pers.	nous	we	nous	to/for us	nous	us
	2. Pers.	vous	you (pl., formal)	vous	to/for you	vous	you
	3. Pers.	ils/elles	they	leur	to/for them	les	them
				se		se	

Direct and indirect object pronouns come before the verb.
If they occur together before the verb, they are placed in the following order:

  ①   ②   ③
Indirect Object   Direct Object   Indirect Object

me				
te		le		
se	before	la	before	lui
nous		les		leur
vous				

  ①②
Je **te la** donne.   I give it to you.

  ② ③
Je **la leur** donne.   I give it to them.

2. Accentuated Personal Pronouns

	Singular		Plural	
1. Person	moi	I	nous	we
2. Person	toi	you	vous	you
3. Person	lui/elle	he/she	eux/elles	they

- **To emphasize the person**
  Moi, j'ai déjà mangé.   I have already eaten.
- **After prepositions**
  Nous partirons sans eux.   We will leave without them.
- **With an affirmative imperative**
  Donne-le-moi.   Give it to me.
  (*but:* Ne me le donne pas.   Don't give it to me.)

199

3. Y and en

y = there   *en* = some
These two pronouns are used like the personal pronouns.

Vous allez <u>à Paris/en France</u>?	Vous mangez <u>du poisson</u>?
– Oui, j'**y** vais demain.	– Oui, j'**en** mange quelquefois.
Are you going to Paris/to France?	Do you eat fish?
– Yes, I'm going (there) tomorrow.	– Yes, I eat (some) occasionally.

4. Reflexive Pronouns and Reflexive Verbs
(Pronouns and verbs that reflect back on the subject)

Reflexive pronouns come before the verb.
Reflexive verbs use *être* as a helping verb in the perfect tense.

Present			Perfect			
Je	**me**	souviens.	Je	**me**	**suis**	souvenu(e).
I remember.			I remembered.			
Tu	**te**	souviens.	Tu	**t'**	**es**	souvenu(e).
Il	**se**	souvient.	Il	**s'**	**est**	souvenu.
Elle	**se**	souvient.	Elle	**s'**	**est**	souvenue.
Nous	**nous**	souvenons.	Nous	**nous**	**sommes**	souvenu(e)s.
Vous	**vous**	souvenez.	Vous	**vous**	**êtes**	souvenu(e)s.
Ils	**se**	souviennent.	Ils	**se**	**sont**	souvenus.
Elles	**se**	souviennent.	Elles	**se**	**sont**	souvenues.

Possessive Pronouns

Possession / Possessor	Singular			Plural
	masculine	feminine		both genders
Singular	mon ton } sac son	ma ta } veste sa	my your his/her/its	mes tes } enfants ses
Plural	notre votre } sac leur } veste		our your their	nos vos } enfants leurs

* *Son/Sa* refers to a masculine or a feminine possessor.
  Leur refers to several possessors

sa	clé	his/her key
leur	clé	their key

Demonstrative Pronouns

	Singular		Plural	
masculine	**ce** livre	this book	**ces** enfants	these children
feminine	**cette** voiture	this car		

Ce changes to *cet* before masculine nouns that start with a vowel or a mute *h*: cet avion   this airplane

Relative Pronouns

Subject (Who? What?)	qui	le restaurant **qui** est fermé the restaurant that is closed
Direct Object (Whom? What?)	que	le crayon **que** j'ai perdu the pencil that I lost

Question Words

Who?	**Qui** est venu?	Who came?
Whom?	**Qui** as-tu vu?	Whom did you see?
To whom?	**A qui** écris-tu?	To whom are you writing?
About/from whom?	**De qui** parles-tu?	About whom are you speaking?
What?	**Qu'est-ce que** tu fais? **Que** fais-tu?	What are you doing?
Which?	**Quel** est ton livre? **Quelle** est sa voiture?	Which book is yours? Which car is theirs?
How much/how many?	**Combien de** kilomètres? Ça coûte **combien**?	How may kilometers? How much does that cost?
Where?	**Où** se trouve ...? **Où** vas-tu? **D'où** venez-vous?	Where is ...? Where are you going? Where are you from?
When?	**Quand** pars-tu?	When are you leaving?
At what time?	**A quelle heure** arrive-t-elle?	What time does she arrive?
How long?	**Combien de temps** a-t-il mis?	How long did he take?
How?	**Comment** vas-tu?	How are you?
Why?	**Pourquoi** est-il parti?	Why did he leave?

French – English Glossary

A

à *(time)* at; *(place)* in, at;
(direction) to
à cause de because of
à cette heure-ci at this time
à contre-cœur unwillingly
à court terme in the short term
à l'arrière to the rear
à l'étouffée braised
à l'extérieur outside
à l'intérieur inside, within
à l'occasion occasionally *adv*
à l'ouest de to the west of
à nous us
à point medium rare
à présent now
à travers through
à vous you
abbaye *f* abbey
abcès *m* abscess
abeille *f* bee
abîmé, e damaged, lousy
abréviation *f* abbreviation
abricot *m* apricot
absolument absolutely
accélérateur *m* accelerator
accepter to accept
accès sans marche *m* stair-free
access
accessibilité accessibility
accident *m* accident; avoir un
accident to experience an
accident
accompagnateur/accompa-
gnatrice *m/f* escort
accompagner to accompany
accueillir to welcome
acheter to buy
acte *m* act

acteur/actrice actor / actress
acteur/actrice de cinéma *m/f*
movie actor/actress
adaptateur *m* adapter
addition *f (in restaurant / café)*
check, bill
administration *f* administration
admirer to admire
adresse *f* address
adulte *m/f* adult
aérobic *m* aerobic
aéroglisseur *m* hovercraft
aéroport *m* airport
affectueux, -euse affectionate
affiche *f* poster
affirmer to affirm
affranchir to put postage on
affreux, -euse frightful
âge *m* age
agence *f* agency
agence de voyages *f* travel
agency
agent de police *m* police officer
agneau *m* lamb
agréable pleasant
agression *f* assault *(person)*;
holdup
aide *f* help
aider qn to help someone
aigre sour
aigreurs d'estomac *f pl*
heartburn
aiguille *f* needle
ail *m* garlic
aile *f* wing
ailleurs elsewhere
aimable likable, friendly
aimer to like/ love
air *m* air; air conditionné *m* air
conditioning

aire de jeux *f* playground
aire de repos *f* rest area
aire de service *f* service area
aisé, e easy
ajouter to add
album à colorier *m* coloring book
alcool à brûler *m* denatured alcohol
aller to go; **aller chercher** to pick up, get; **aller se coucher** to go to bed
allergie *f* allergy
allonger to lay down, to extend
allumage *m* ignition
allume-barbecue *m* barbecue lighter
allumer to light
allumette *f* match
alpinisme *m* mountain climbing
Alsace *f* Alsace
altitude *f* altitude
amande *f* almond
ambassade *f* embassy
ambulance *f* ambulance
améliorer to improve
aménagé/équipé pour handicapés handicap-/wheelchair-accessible
amende *f* fine
amer, -ère bitter
américain, e American; **Américain, e** the American person
ami, e friend; **être amis** to be friends
amour *m* love
amphithéâtre *m* amphitheater
ampoule *f* lightbulb
amusement *m* amusement, pleasure
amygdales *f pl* tonsils
an *m* year
analyse *f* analysis
ananas *m* pineapple

ancien, ne *(from early times)* old
âne *m* donkey, ass
anesthésie *f* anesthesia
angine *f* angina
anglais, e English
Anglais, e *f* Englishman/Englishwoman
Angleterre *f* England
anguille *f* eel
animal *m* animal; **animaux domestiques** *m pl* house pets
année *f* year; **année prochaine** next year
anniversaire *m* birthday
annonce *f* announcement; ad
annoncer to announce
annuaire *m* telephone book
annuel, le *adj* annual
annuler to cancel
anorak *m* parka
antibiotique *m* antibiotic
antigel *m* antifreeze
antique antique
antiseptique *m* antiseptic
août August
apogée *m* high point
appareil *m* device; **appareil photo** *m* camera; **appareil photo digital** *m* digital camera
appartement *m* apartment
appartenir to belong
appel en P.C.V. *m* collect call
appel pour l'étranger *m* overseas call
appeler to call; **s'appeler** to be named
appendicite *f* appendicitis
appétit *m* appetite
applaudissements *m pl* applause
apporter to bring
apprendre to learn
après *(time)* after
après-demain day after tomorrow (the)
après-midi *m* afternoon
aquarelle *f* watercolor

arbre *m* tree
arc *m* bow
archéologie *f* archeology
architecte *m/f* architect
architecture *f* architecture
arène *f* sand
arête *f* bone (fish)
argent *m* money; silver
argenté silver-colored
armoire *f* cupboard
arrêt *m* stop
arrêter to stop; **s'arrêter** to stop (oneself)
arrière, en ~ backwards
arrière-pays *m* back country
arrière-saison *f* late fall
arrivée *f* arrival
arrivée des bagages *f* baggage arrival
arriver to arrive; to happen
art *m* art
art graphique *m* graphic arts
Art nouveau Art nouveau
arte grise *f* car registration
artichaut *m* artichoke
articles de papeterie *m pl* stationery items
articles d'hygiène *m pl* drugstore items
articles ménagers *m pl* household goods
articulation *f* joint
arts décoratifs *m pl* decorative arts
ascenseur *m* elevator
asperge *f* asparagus
aspirine *f* aspirin
assaisonnement *m* seasoning
assaisonner to season
assez enough; quite; rather
assiette *f* plate; **assiette creuse** *f* soup bowl
assis, e, être ~ to be seated
association *f* association; **association de handicapés** *f* association for handicapped people

assurance *f* insurance; **assurance au tiers** *f* liability insurance; **assurance tous risques** *f* comprehensive insurance
asthme *m* asthma
atelier *m* workshop
athlétisme *m* track and field
Atlantique *m* Atlantic
attaque *f* attack
atteindre to achieve, reach
attelle *f* strap
attendre to wait, wait for; **s'attendre à** to expect
attention attention
attention! Attention! Be careful! Watch out!
atterrissage *m* landing
attestation *f* certificate
attester to certify
attraper to catch
au cas où in case
au chômage unemployed
au-dessous (de) below
au-dessus (de) above
au maximum at most
au niveau du sol at ground level
aubergine *f* eggplant
aucun, e no, none
augmenter to increase; *(prices)* to go up
aujourd'hui today
aussi also; **aussi ... que** as ... as
autel *m* altar
authentique authentic
automatique automatic
automne *m* autumn, fall
autoradio *m* car radio
autoriser to authorize, permit
autoroute *f* highway
autour de around
autre other; **d'autre part** on the other hand
autrefois formerly *(earlier)*
autrement *adv* otherwise
avance *f* advance; **par avance** in advance

avant before; **avant que** before; **en avant** forward
avant-dernier, -ière next-to-last
avant-hier the day before yesterday
avant-saison *f* early season
avantage *m* advantage
avec with
avenir *m* future
averse *f* rain shower
avertisseur d'incendie *m* fire alarm
aveugle *m/f* blind; blind person
avocat *m* avocado
avocat/e *m/f* lawyer
avoir to have
avoir besoin de to need
avoir le mal de mer to be seasick
avoir soif to be thirsty
avril April

babeurre *m* buttermilk
baby-sitter *m* babysitter
bac *m* ferry *(river)*
bac à sable *m* sandbox
badminton *m* badminton *(game)*
baffle *m* speaker *(stereo)*
bagages *m pl* baggage
bague *f* ring
baie *f* bay *(large)*
baignoire *f* bathtub
baiser to kiss
bal *m* ball *(party)*
balade *f* walk *(stroll)*
baladeur *m* portable CD player
balcon *m* balcony
balle *f* ball
ballet *m* ballet
ballon *m* balloon
banane *f* banana
banc *m* bench

bande élastique *f* rubber band
banlieue *f* outskirts
banque *f* bank
banquette-lit *f* sofa bed
barbe *f* beard
baroque *m* baroque
barque (à rames) *f* rowboat
barre de chocolat *f* chocolate bar
bas *m pl* stockings
bas, basse low; **en bas** below; **vers le bas** downward
bas-ventre *m* lower abdomen
basilic *m* basil
basket-ball *m* basketball
baskets *m pl* basketball shoes
bassin pour enfants *m* kiddy pool
bateau à voiles *m* sailboat
bâtiment *m* building
bâton stick
bâtons *m pl* ski poles
battre to beat, hit
beau, bel, belle handsome, beautiful
beau-frère *m* brother-in-law
beaucoup de lots of
bébé *m* baby
beige beige
belle-soeur *f* sister-in-law
bénéfice profit
béquille *f* crutch
besoin *m* need; **avoir besoin de** to need
bête dumb
beurre *m* butter
biberon *m* bottle (baby)
bicyclette *f* bicycle
bidon d'eau *m* water bottle
bidon d'essence *m* gas can
bien *m* well; **bien** *adv* good; though; **bien que** although
bien cuit well done
bien que although
bientôt soon
bienvenu, e Welcome!

bière *f* beer

bière sans alcool *f* non-alcoholic beer

bigoudis *m pl* hair curlers, rollers

bijouterie *f* jeweler's

bijoux *m pl* jewelry

bijoux fantaisie *m pl* costume jewelry

bikini *m* bikini

billet *m* ticket; billet aller-retour *m* bill *(money)* billet d'entrée *m* round-trip ticket billet enfants *m* children's ticket billet pour une journée *m* day pass

biscuit *m* cookie

bistrot *m* bar

blaireau *m* shaving brush

blanc white

blanchisserie *f* laundry

blazer *m* blazer

blessé, e *m/f* injured person

blesser to hurt, wound, injure

blessure *f* injury, wound

bleu blue

bloc *m* notepad

blond blonde

blues *m* blues *(music)*

body *m* body

bœuf *m* beef

boire to drink

bois *m* wood

boisson *f* drink

boîte *f* box; dance club

boîte à musique *f* music box

boîte automatique *f* automatic transmission

boîte aux lettres *f* mailbox

boîte de nuit *f* nightclub

boîte de vitesses *f* gearbox, transmission

bon *m* coupon

bon, bonne *adj* good; appropriate, right; bon marché cheap; être bon to taste good

bonbon *m* candy

bonnet de bain *m* bathing cap

bord *m* edge; *(ocean)* shore; sur les bords de la Seine on the banks of the Seine

botte *f* boot; bottes en caoutchouc *f pl* rubber boots

bouche *f* mouth

boucherie *f* butcher shop

boucle magnétique *f* magnetic loop

boucles *f pl* curls; boucles d'oreilles *f pl* earrings

boue *f* mud

bouée *f* flotation device; bouée de sauvetage *f* life saver

bougie *f* candle; bougie *f* spark plug

bouilli boiled

boulangerie *f* bakery

bouquet *m* bouquet

boussole *f* compass

bouteille *f* bottle

bouteille de gaz *f* gas cylinder

bouteille d'oxygène *f* oxygen bottle

bouteille thermos *f* Thermos© bottle

boutique *f* boutique

boutique hors-taxes *f* duty-free shop

bowling *m* bowling

bracelet *m* bracelet

bracelets *m pl* flotation wings

braille *m* Braille

brancher to plug in

bretelle *f* on-ramp / off-ramp

brocanteur *m* junk dealer

broche *f* brooch

broderie *f* embroidery

bronches *f pl* bronchi

bronchite *f* bronchitis

bronze *m* bronze

bronzé, e tanned *(brown)*

brosse *f* brush

brosse à chaussures *f* shoe-brush

brosse à dents *f* toothbrush

brosse pour la vaisselle *f* dishwashing brush

brouillard *m* fog

bruit *m* noise

brûler to burn

brûlure *f* burn

bruyant, e loud, noisy

buffet (de petit déjeuner) *m* breakfast buffet

buffet de salades *m* salad bar

buisson *m* bush

bulletin météo(rologique) *m* weather forecast

bungalow *m* bungalow

bureau *m* desk; office; bureau des objets trouvés *m* lost and found

bureau de change *m* change bureau

bureau de poste *m* post office

bureau de tabac *m* tobacco shop

bureau des objets trouvés *m* lost and found

bus *m* bus bus pour l'aéroport *m* airport bus

but *m* goal; *(soccer)* goal

by-pass *m* bypass

byzantin Byzantine

C

cabane *f* hut; shed

cabaret *m* cabaret

cabine *f* cabin

cabine équipée pour handicapés *f* handicap-accessible cabin *(ship)*

cabine téléphonique *f* phone booth

câble de démarrage *m* starter / jumper cable

câble de remorquage *m* tow rope

cachet *m* tablet

cachets contre la douleur *m pl* pain pills

cachets contre les maux de tête *m pl* headache pills

cadeau *m* gift

café *m* café

café *m* coffee

café-théâtre *m* theater café

caillouteux, -euse rocky

caisse *f* cash register; case

caisse d'assurance-maladie *f* health insurance

calcul rénal *m* kidney stone

calculatrice *f* calculator

calculer to calculate

caleçon *m* underpants

calme calm, quiet; peace *(quiet)*; lull *m*

caméra sous-marine *f* underwater camera

caméra vidéo *f* video camera

caméscope *m* camcorder

camion *m* truck

camper to camp

camping *m* camping; terrain de camping *m* campground

camping-car *m* camping vehicle

Canada *m* Canada

Canadien, ienne Canadian

canal *m* canal

cancer *m* cancer

canicule *f* heat wave

canne à pêche *f* fishing rod

canne d'aveugle *f* blind person's cane

canoë *m* canoe

canot (à rames) *m* rowboat

canot automobile *m* motorboat

canot de sauvetage *m* lifeboat

canot pneumatique *m* inflatable boat

capitaine *m* captain

capitale *f* capital

capot *m* hood *(of car)*

car for

car *m* tour bus

caractéristique (de) typical of
carafe *f* carafe
caravane *f* camper *(vehicle)*
carnaval *m* carnival
carnet de tickets *m* book of tickets
carnet de vaccinations *m* vaccination record
carotte *f* carrot
carrefour *m* intersection
carte *f* menu
carte à puce *f* chip card
carte bancaire *f* bank card
carte de crédit *f* credit card
carte de randonnées *f* hiking map
carte de téléphone *f* phone card
carte d'embarquement *f* boarding pass
carte d'identité *f* ID
carte d'invalidité *f* disabled person's ID
carte géographique *f* map
carte hebdomadaire *f* weekly pass
carte postale *f* postcard
carte routière *f* road map
carte verte *f* green insurance card
cartouche de gaz *f* gas cartridge
cas *m* case
cascade *f* waterfall
casino *m* casino
casque de moto *m* motorcycle helmet
casque de protection *m* bike helmet
casquette *f* cap
cassé broken
casse-croûte *m* snack
casser to break; **se casser** to get broken / torn
cassette *f* cassette
cathédrale *f* cathedral

cause *f* cause; **à cause de** because of
causer to cause
caution *f* caution
caverne *f* cave
CD *m* CD / compact disk
ce this
ce, cet, cette, ces *art* this
ce week-end this weekend
ceinture *f* belt
ceinture de moto *f* kidney belt
ceinture de sécurité *f* seat belt
célèbre famous
céleri *m* celery
célibataire single; *m* bachelor
celui-là, celle-là, ceux-là, celles-là that one / those
cendrier *m* ashtray
centimètre *m* centimeter
central, e central
centre *m* center
centre de gymnastique *m* fitness center
centre de soins *m* mobile care unit
centre social de soins *m* community care center
centre-ville *m* downtown
céramique *f* ceramics
cerises *f pl* cherries
certain, e *adj* certain, sure
certificat *m* certificate
cerveau *m* brain
ces *prn pl* these
c'est pourquoi that's why
chacun, e *prn* every one
chagrin *m* chagrin
chaîne *f* network *(television)*
chaise *f* chair
châlet *m* chalet
châlet *m* clubhouse
chaleur *f* heat
chambre *f* room
chambre à air *f* inner tube
chambre à coucher *f* bedroom

champ *m* field
champagne *m* champagne
chance *f* luck
change *m* (money) exchange office
changer to change; se changer to change clothes
chanson *f* song
chansonnier *m* cabaret artist
chanter to sing
chanteur/chanteuse (cantatrice) singer *(m. and f.)*
chantier *m* worksite
chapeau *m* hat
chapeau de soleil *m* sun hat
chapelle *f* chapel
chaque *adj* each
charbon de bois *m* charcoal
charcuterie *f* pork butcher's
charges *f pl* additional costs
chariot *m* baggage cart
chasse d'eau *f* flush
chat *m* cat
château *m* castle
château de sable *m* sand castle
chaud, e hot; warm
chauffage *m* heat
chauffage central *m* central heat
chauffe-biberon *m* bottle warmer
chauffer to heat
chauffeur/chauffeuse *m* driver, chauffeur
chauffeur/chauffeuse de taxi *m* taxi driver
chaussettes *f pl* socks
chaussure *f* shoe
chaussures de plage *f pl* beach shoes
chaussures de ski *f pl* ski boots
chaussures en plastique (pour la baignade) *f pl* bathing shoes
chef d'orchestre *m/f* conductor

chemin *m* road
chemin de fer à crémaillère *m* cog railway
chemin de randonnée *m* hiking trail
chemise *f* shirt
chemisier *m* blouse
chèque de voyage *m* traveler's check
cher, chère dear; expensive
chercher to look (for); aller chercher to pick up
chéri, e *m/f* dear
cheval *m* horse
cheveux *m pl* hair
cheville *f* ankle
chien *m* dog
chien d'aveugle *m* seeing-eye dog
chirurgien *m* surgeon
choc *m* shock
chocolat *m* chocolate
chœur *m* chorus
choisir to choose
choix *m* choice
choléra *m* cholera
chômage *m* unemployment
chose *f* thing
chou *m* cabbage
chou-fleur *m* cauliflower
christianisme *m* Christianity
cicatrice *f* scar
ciel *m* sky
cigare *m* cigar
cigarette *f* cigarette
cigarillo *m* cigarillo
cimetière *m* cemetery
cinéma *m* movie
cinéma en plein air *m* outdoor movie
cintre *m* clothes hanger
cirage *m* shoe polish
circuit *m* tour
circulation *f* traffic
cirque *m* circus

ciseaux *m pl* scissors
ciseaux à ongles *m pl* fingernail
  clippers
citoyen européen *m* European
  citizen
citron *m* lemon
clair, e clear; light
claquage (musculaire) *m*
  pulled muscle
classe *f* class
classicisme *m* classicism
classique *m* classic
clavicule *f* clavicle
clé *f* key
clé de contact *f* ignition key
client, e *m/f* client; customer
clignotant *m* blinker
climat *m* climate
clocher *m* church tower
cloître *m* cloister
clou de girofle *m* clove
club de golf *m* golf club
clubhouse *f* clubhouse
code *m* code
code postal *m* postal code
codes *m pl* low-beams
cœur *m* heart
coffre *m* trunk
coffre-fort *m* safe
coiffer to do someone's hair
coiffeur/coiffeuse *m/f*
  hairdresser / hairstylist
coiffure *f* hairstyle
coin *m* corner
coin-cuisine *m* kitchenette
coin-fenêtre *m* window seat
col *m* pass
colère *f* anger; en colère angry,
  mad
colique *f* colic
colis *m* parcel
collants *m pl* tights
collectionner to collect
collègue *m* colleague
collier *m* necklace
colline *f* hill

collision *f* collision
collyre *m* eye drops
colonne *f* column
colonne vertébrale *f* spinal
  column
combinaison de plongée *f*
  wetsuit
combiné *m* receiver (telephone)
comédie *f* comedy
comédie musicale *f* musical
  comedy
comédien/comédienne actor /
  actress
comestible edible
commande *f* order
commandes manuelles *f pl*
  manual controls (auto)
comme since; (comparison) as;
  comme ça like that
commencement *m* beginning
commencer to begin
comment how (question)
commission *f* commission
commotion cérébrale *f*
  concussion
commun, e *adj* common
communication *f*
  communication
communication avec préavis *f*
  appointment
communication en ville *f* local
  call
communication interurbaine *f*
  long-distance call
compagnie aérienne *f* airline
comparer to compare
compartiment *m* compartment
compartiment fumeurs *m*
  smoking section
compartiment non-fumeurs
  m non-smoking section
compatriote *m* compatriot
compensation *f* compensation
  (for damages)
compétent, e competent
compétition *f* competition

complet, -ète complete; entire; fully occupied; **complètement** *adv* completely, entirely

compliments, faire des ~ to praise

composer (un numéro) to dial a number *(telephone)*; **se composer de** to be composed of

compositeur/compositrice composer *(m. and f.)*

composter to date-stamp

composteur *m* ticket stamping / punching machine

comprendre to understand; **se faire comprendre** to make oneself understood

comprimé *m* tablet

compris, e included; understood

comptant, payer ~ to pay in cash

compte *m* account

compter to count

compteur *m* tachometer

concert *m* concert

concert symphonique *m* symphony concert

concierge *m/f* concierge

concombre *m* cucumber

condition *f* condition

conduire to lead; to drive

confiance *f* confidence

confirmer to confirm

confiserie *f* confectioner's shop

confisquer to confiscate

confiture *f* jelly

confondre to confuse

confortable comfortable

confrère *m* colleague

congé *m* vacation; **prendre congé** to take off

connaissance *f* knowledge; acquaintance; the acquaintance; **faire la connaissance (de)** to get to know / meet someone

connaître to know; **faire connaître** to introduce

connu, e known

conseil *m* advice; tip

conseiller to advise

consentir (à) to consent

conserver to conserve

conserves *f* preserves

consigne *f (bottles)* deposit

consigne automatique *f* baggage lockers

consommation *f* drink

consommation d'eau *f* water usage

constipation *f* constipation

consulat *m* consulate

consultation *f* consultation

contact *m* contact

contagieux contagious

contenir to contain

content, e happy, content; **être content de** to be happy about

contenu *m* contents

continent *m* continent

contraceptif *m* contraceptive

contraire *m* contrary, opposite

contrat *m* contract

contre against; **être contre** to be against

contre-indications counter-indications

contrôle de sécurité *m* security check

contrôle des passeports *m* passport inspection

contrôle-radar *m* radar control

contrôler to check / control

contrôleur/contrôleuse *m/f* conductor

contusion *f* bruise

convaincre to convince

convenir to fit; **convenir de** to acknowledge

conversation *f* conversation

convoyage *m* transport

copain/copine friend / pal

copain/copine (de jeux) playmate

copie f copy
coqueluche f whooping cough
coquillage m shellfish
corde f rope
corde à linge f clothesline
cordial, e cordial
cordonnier m shoemaker
coriace tough
cornichon m pickle
corps m body
correspondance f connection
cortège m procession
costume m suit; **costume régional/folklorique** m (folk) costume
côte f coast
côté m side; **à côté de** next to
côtelette f cutlet
coton m cotton
coton hydrophile m absorbent cotton
coton-tige m cotton swab
cou m neck
coucher spend the night; **aller se coucher** to go to bed
couches f pl diapers
couchette f berth
couler to flow
couloir m corridor
coup m blow; hit
coup de soleil m sunburn
coup de téléphone m telephone call
coupe de cheveux f haircut
coupe en dégradé f layer cut
couper to cut
couple m couple
coupole f cupola
coupure f a cut
cour f court
cour intérieur f inner courtyard
courant m current
courir to run
couronne f crown
courroie de transmission f drive belt

cours m course; **en cours de route** on the way
cours de change m exchange rate
cours de langue m language course
cours de natation m swimming lessons
cours de ski m pl ski instruction
courses, faire ses ~ to go shopping
court-circuit m short circuit
court, e short
court-métrage m short feature (film)
cousin/e m/f cousin
couteau m knife
couteau de poche m pocket knife
coûter to cut
couvent m convent
couvert m place setting
couverts m pl flatware, cutlery
couverture f blanket
couverture de laine f wool blanket
crabe m crab
craindre to fear; be afraid of
crampe f cramp
cravate f necktie
crayon de couleur m colored pencil
créatif, -ive creative
crème f cream
crème aigre f sour cream
crème chantilly f whipping cream
crème pour les mains f hand cream
crème solaire f suntan lotion
crevettes f pl shrimp
crevettes roses f prawns
cric m jack
crier to yell
crime m crime
crique f cove
crise cardiaque f heart attack
cristal m crystal
critiquer to criticize

crochet m hook
croire to believe
croisière f cruise
croisière à la voile f sailing cruise
croix f cross
crosse de golf f golf club
cru raw
cueillir to pick, gather
cuillère f spoon
cuillère à café f teaspoon
cuisine f kitchen; faire la cuisine to cook
cuisine diététique f special diet
cuisinier/cuisinière cook (m. and f.)
cuisinière f stove
cuisinière à gaz f gas stove
cuisinière électrique f electric stove
culture f culture
cumin m cumin
cure-dents m toothpick
curieux, -euse curious
curiosités f pl sights
curling m curling
cyclisme m cycling

D

d'abord first; at first
d'accord agreed!; se mettre d'accord to agree
dames Ladies
danger m danger
dangereux, -euse dangerous
dans in, into
dans la matinée in the morning
dans une semaine in a week
danse f dance
danser to dance
danseur/danseuse dancer (m. and f.)
date f date

date de naissance f date of birth
datte f date (fruit)
d'autre part on the other hand
de from (origin); of
de couleur colored
de longue conservation non-perishable
de passage on the trip
déambulateur m walker
debout, être ~ standing
décembre December
déchirer to tear up; se déchirer to get torn
décider to decide; décider (de) to decide on; se décider to resolve, determine
déclaration de valeur f declaration of value
déclaration en douane f customs declaration
déclarer to declare
déclencheur m shutter release
déclencheur automatique m automatic shutter release
décollage m takeoff
décommander to cancel, call off
découvrir to discover
décrire to describe
décrocher to pick up (phone)
déçu, e disappointed
dedans inside
défaut m fault, lack
définitif, -ive adj definitive; définitivement adv definitively
dehors outdoors
déjà already
déjeuner m lunch; petit déjeuner m breakfast
délicieux delicious
deltaplane m hang glider
demande f request
demander to request; demander qc à qn to ask someone for something
démanger to itch

213

démarreur *m* starter

demi, e *adj* half; une demi-heure a half-hour; faire demi-tour to turn around

demi-pension *f* half-pension

dent *f* tooth

dent de sagesse *f* wisdom tooth

dentifrice *m* toothpaste

déodorant *m* deodorant

dépanneuse *f* tow truck

départ *m* departure

dépasser to pass; exceed

dépenser to dispense

déposer to put down

depuis since

déranger to disturb

dernier, -ière last; en dernier lieu lastly

derrière behind

dès que possible as soon as possible

désagréable unpleasant

descendre to get off / out

désespéré, e hopeless, desperate

désignation *f* designation

désinfecter to disinfect

désirer to desire; want

dessert *m* dessert

dessin *m* drawing

dessin animé *m* cartoon

dessin sur modèle *m* drawing from a model

dessiner to sketch, draw

destinataire *m* addressee

destination *f* (travel) destination

détention préventive *f* custody

détour *m* detour

détruire to destroy

dette *f* debt

deux two

deuxième second; deuxièmement secondly

devant *(spatial relationship)* in front of

développer to develop

devenir to become

déviation detour

devises *f pl* currency

devoir to have to; must; duty *m*

dextrose *f* dextrose

diabète *m* diabetes

diabétique *m* diabetic

diagnostic *m* diagnostic

diarrhée *f* diarrhea

Dieu God

différence *f* difference

différer to differ; to postpone

difficile difficult

digestion *f* digestion

digue *f* dike

dimanche Sunday; on Sunday

dîner *m* dinner

diphtérie *f* diphtheria

dire to say

direct, e direct

directeur/directrice director; conductor *m/f*

direction *f* direction

direction du vent *f* wind direction

directive *f* directive / rule

discothèque *f* discotheque

disparaître to disappear

dispute *f* dispute

dissolvant *m* nail polish remover

distance *f* distance

distingué, e distinguished

distraction *f* entertainment

distributeur automatique *m* automatic dispensing machine

distributeur de billets *m* ATM; automatic ticket machine

distributeur de timbres *m* stamp machine

diviser to divide

documentaire *m* documentary

doigt *m* finger

domaine *m* region

dôme *m* dome

domicile *m* residence

dommage *m* damage; Quel dommage! What a shame!

donc thus

donner to give; se donner du mal to take the trouble

doré golden

dormir to sleep

dos *m* back

douane *f* customs

double double

doucement quietly; slowly

douche *f* shower

douche assise *f* seated shower

douleurs au dos *f pl* back pain

doux, douce sweet

doux/moelleux mellow *(wine)*

drame *m* drama

drap *m* sheet

draps *m pl* bed linens

droguerie *f* drugstore

droit *m* law; droits *m pl* duties

droit, e right; straight; à droite to the right

droits de douane *pl* customs duties

dur, e hard

durée *f* duration

durer to last

dynamo *f* generator

dynastie *f* dynasty

E

eau *f* water

eau chaude hot water

eau de refroidissement *f* cooling water

eau froide cold water

eau minérale *f* mineral water

eau potable *f* drinking water

échange *f* exchange

échanger to exchange

écharpe *f* scarf

éclair *m* lightning bolt

école *f* school

école d'équitation *f* riding school

écoliers/écolières *m/f pl* school children

écouter de la musique to listen to music

écouter (qn) to listen (to)

écouteurs *m pl* headphones

écrire to write; par écrit in writing

écriture *f* writing

édifice *m* building

éducation *f* education, upbringing

effrayer to frighten

église *f* church

éhonté, e shameless; brazen

élastique *m* elastic band

électricité *f* electricity

électrique *adj* electric

élévateur elevator

elle *f sing* she; elles *f pl* they

éloigné, e far, distant

emballage *m* packing

emballer to pack, wrap

emblème *m* emblem

embolie cérébrale *f* stroke

embouchure *f (river)* mouth

embouteillage *m* traffic jam

embrasser to kiss; to hug

embrayage *m* clutch

émission *f* broadcast

emmener to take

empêcher to prevent, hinder

empereur *m* emperor

emploi *m* usage; *(employment)* work, job

employer to employ, use

empoisonnement *m* poisoning

emporter to take

emprunter (a qn) to borrow *(from someone)*

en *(material)* of; en français in French

en arrière in reverse

en avant forward

en bas below

en daube braised

en dernier lieu lastly

en espèces in cash
en face de across from
en moyenne on average *adv*
en outre in addition
encore still; (ne ...) pas encore not yet
endive *f* endive
endommager to damage
endroit *m* place
enfant *m/f* child
enfin finally
enflé swollen
enflure *f* swelling
engagement *m* commitment; sans engagement not binding
ennuyeux, -euse boring
enregistrement des bagages *m* baggage registration
enroué hoarse
enseigner to show, teach
ensemble *adv* together
ensoleillé sunny
ensuite then
entendre to hear
enthousiasmé, e (par) excited *(about)*
entier, -ière entire, whole
entracte *m* intermission
entre between; among
entrée *f* entrance
entreprise *f* enterprise; company
entrer to enter; go in; Entrez. Come in!
enveloppe *f* envelope
envie *f* desire
environ around / approximately
environnement *m* environment
environs *pl* surroundings
envoyer to send
épaule *f* shoulder
épeler to spell
épice *f* spice
épicé spicy
épicerie *f* grocery store
épicerie fine *f* delicatessen *(international specialties)*

épilepsie epilepsy
épinards *m pl* spinach
épingle de sûreté *f* safety pin
épingles à cheveux *f pl* hairpins
époque *f* era; à l'époque at that time
épuisé, e exhausted
équipage *m (ship)* crew
équipe *f (sport)* team
équipement de plongée *m* diving equipment
erreur *f* error
escale *f* stopover
escalier *m* stair
escroc *m* swindler
escroquerie *f (swindling)* fraud
espace *f* space
espadon *m* swordfish
Espagne *f* Spain
Espagnol, e Spaniard (m. and f.); espagnol, e Spanish
espèces *f pl* cash
espérer to hope
espérons que let's hope that
essai *m* attempt, try
essayer to try / try on
essence *f* gasoline; prendre de l'essence to get some gas
essuie-glace *m* windshield wiper
Est *m* East; à l'est de east of
estimer to esteem, value
estomac *m* stomach
et and
étage *m* floor, story
Etat *m* state; état *m* condition
état de la mer *m* sea conditions
Etats-Unis *m pl* United States
été *m* summer
éteindre to turn off
étendue *f* extent, size
éternuer to sneeze
étoffe *f* fabric, cloth
étoile *f* star
étranger/étrangère foreigner *(m. and f.)*; stranger *(m. and f.)*

être *verb* to be; **être contre** to be against; **être pour** to be in favor of; **être humain** *m* a human being
être amis to be friends (with)
être assis, e to be seated, to sit
être bon to taste good
être content, e de to be happy about
être debout to stand
être originaire (de) to be (from)
être pressé, e to be in a hurry
étroit, e narrow, small
études *f pl* studies
euro *m* euro
Europe *f* Europe; **Européen, ne** *m/f* European person; **européen, ne** European
évanoui passed out / unconscious
évanouissement *m* fainting fit / blackout
événement *m* event
éviter to avoid
exact, e exact; **être exact** to be right
exagéré, e exaggerated
examen *m* examination
examiner to examine, investigate
excellent, e excellent
excursion *f* excursion
excursion à terre *f* land trip
excursion pour une journée *f* day trip
excuse *f* excuse; **(s')excuser** to excuse oneself
exemple *m* example; **par exemple** for example
exempt de droits de douane duty free
exercer to ply *(profession or trade)* **s'exercer** to practice
exercice *m* exercise
expéditeur *m* sender
exposition *f* exposition
expressément expressly
expression *f* expression

expressionnisme *m* Expressionism
extérieur *m* exterior; **à l'extérieur (de)** outside
externe external
extincteur *m* fire extinguisher
extraordinaire extraordinary

F

façade *f* façade
face, en ~ de across from
fâcheux, -euse annoying
facile easy
façon *f* type
facture *f* bill
faible weak
faim *f* hunger; **avoir faim** to be hungry
fair-play fair, sporting
faire to do; to make; *(to arrange for)* to have something done; **faire mal** to hurt; **faire la queue** to stand in line; **fait main** handmade
faire de la musique to play music
faire de la nage sous-marine to go snorkeling
faire de la plongée to dive
faire de la randonnée to hike
faire de l'auto-stop to hitchhike
faire des études to study
faire du canoë/ du kayak to go canoeing / kayaking
faire du cheval to ride horseback
faire du jogging to go jogging
faire du ski to ski
faire du surf to surf
faire du vélo to cycle
faire escale à to make a stopover in
faire le ménage to do the housework

faire les formalités d'embarquement *f* to check in

faire ses courses to go shopping

faire suivre to forward

faire un brushing to blow dry

faire un pansement to bandage

faire un rinçage to tint

faire une coloration to color

faire une déclaration to declare

faire une erreur de calcul to make an error in calculation

faire une radio(graphie) to X-ray

fait *m* fact; **en fait** *adv* in fact

fait maison homemade

falaise *f* cliff

famille *f* family

fanfare *f* fanfare

farci stuffed

farine *f* flour

fatigant, e tiring

fatigué, e tired

fausse-couche *f* miscarriage

faute *f* fault; mistake

fauteuil *m* armchair

fauteuil roulant *m* wheelchair

fauteuil roulant électrique *m* electric wheelchair

fauteuil roulant pliant *m* folding wheelchair

fauteuil transfert *m* wheelchair for boarding

faux, fausse false; phony

fax *m* fax

félicitations *f pl* congratulations

féliciter to congratulate

féminin, e feminine

femme *f* woman; married woman

femme de chambre *f* chambermaid

fenêtre *f* window

fenouil *m* fennel

ferme *f* farm

fermé, e closed

fermer to close; **fermer à clé** to lock

féroce ferocious; wild

ferry *m* ferry *(ocean)*

festival *m* festival

fête *f* celebration; party; name day

Fête-Dieu *f* Feast of Corpus Christi

fête foraine *f* fair; carnival

feu *m* fire

feu d'artifice *m* fireworks

feu (de circulation) *m* traffic light

feuille *f* sheet, page

feuille de maladie/ de soins *f* health record

feux arrière *m pl* backup lights

feux de détresse *m pl* warning signals, flashers

feux de position *m pl* parking lights

feux de route *m* high beams

février February

fiable reliable

fiancé, e *m/f* fiancé(e)

ficelle *f* string

fiche *f* plug

fidèle faithful

fièvre *f* fever

figues *f pl* gigs

fil de fer *m* wire

filet *m* net

fille *f* daughter; **jeune fille** *f* girl; **nom de jeune fille** *m* maiden name

film *m* film

film alimentaire *m* plastic wrap

film d'action *m* action film

film en noir et blanc *m* black-and-white film

film policier *m* detective film

film vidéo *m* video film

fils *m* son

fin *f* end

fin, e thin, fine

finalement finally

fixateur *m* hairspray

fixation *f* ski binding

flash *m* flash *(camera)*

fleur *f* flower
fleurir to bloom, blossom
fleuriste florist
fleuve *m* river
flocons d'avoine *m pl* oatmeal
foie *m* liver
foire à la brocante *f* flea market
fois *f* time
folklore *m* folklore
foncé dark
fonctionner to function
fontaine *f* fountain
football *m* soccer
force *f* force, strength
force du vent *f* wind speed
forcer to force
forêt *f* forest
forfait *m* pass
forfait électricité *m* flow rate
forfait-journée *m* day pass
forfait-semaine *m* week pass
forfait-weekend *m* weekend rate
format en hauteur *m* portrait format
format horizontal *m* landscape format
formation *f* training
forme *f* shape; condition; constitution; en forme fit
former to form
formulaire *m* form
fort, e strong; spicy
forteresse *f* fortress
fou, folle crazy
fouilles *f pl* excavations
foulard *m* headscarf
foulé sprained
fourchette *f* fork
fournir en to supply with
fracturer to break, fracture
frais *m pl* costs; expenses
frais bancaires *pl* bank fees
frais, fraîche fresh; cool
fraises *f pl* strawberries
franc suisse *m* Swiss franc

Français, e *m/f* French person; français, e French
France *f* France
frange *f* bangs
fraude *f* fraud
frein *m* brake
frein à main *m* handbrake
fréquemment *adv* frequently
frère *m* brother
friandises *f pl* sweets
frigo *m* refrigerator
frissons *m pl* chills
frit fried
froid, e cold; avoir froid to be cold
fromage *m* cheese
fromage à pâte molle *m* soft cheese
fromage blanc *m* white cheese
fromage de brebis *m* sheep's milk cheese
fromage de chèvre *m* goat cheese
frontière *f* border
fronton *m* gable
fruits *m pl* fruits
fumé smoked
fumer to smoke
fumeur *m* smoker
furieux, -euse furious
fusibles *m pl* fuses
futur, e future

G

gage *m* security deposit
gagner to earn, win
gai, e happy, merry
gain *m* profit; earnings
galerie (de peinture) *f* gallery
gant de toilette *m* washcloth
gants *m pl* gloves
garage *m* garage / repair shop
garantie *f* guarantee
garçon *m* boy

garçon/serveuse waiter / waitress
garde, mettre en ~ (contre) to warn (against)
garder to keep, store, watch
garderie f daycare
gardien de buts m goalie
gare f train station
gare principale f main railroad station
gare routière f bus station
gâteau m cake
gauche left; à gauche to the left
gaze f gauze
gel m frost
gel pour les cheveux m hair gel
gencives f pl gums
gêne, sans ~ carelessly, thoughtlessly, recklessly
genou m knee
gens m pl people
gentil, le nice
gilet m vest
gilet de sauvetage m life vest
glace f ice cream
glacière f cooler
golf m golf
gorge f gorge, ravine
gothique m gothic
gourde f flask
goût m taste
goûter (foods) to taste, try
gouttes f pl drops
gouttes pour les oreilles f pl eardrops
gouvernement m government
grabataire bedridden
grâce à through (means), by means of
gramme m gram
grand, e big, large
grand/e handicapé/e m/f severely handicapped person
grand magasin m department store
grand-mère f grandmother
grand-père m grandfather

grandir to grow
gras, grasse fat
gratiné au gratin
gratter to scratch
gratuit, e free, at no cost
grave bad; (illness) serious
gravillon m gravel
gravure à l'eau-forte f etching
gravure sur bois f woodcut
grec Greek
gril m grill
grille-pain m toaster
grippe f grippe
gris gray
gros, grosse fat
grossesse f pregnancy
grosseur f tumor, growth
grotte f grotto
groupe m group
groupe sanguin m blood type
groupe théâtral m theatrical troupe
guêpe f wasp
guichet m ticket window
guichet des bagages m baggage window
guide m guide, travel guide
guide de camping-caravaning m camping guide
gymnastique f gymnastics

H

habitant m inhabitant, resident
habiter to live
habits pour enfants m pl children's clothing
habituel, le customary, usual; habituellement adv customarily
hall m reception hall
hanche f hip
hand-ball m handball
handicap physique m physical handicap

handicapé en fauteuil roulant
m handicapped person in a
wheelchair
handicapé mental mentally
handicapped
harcèlement sexuel *m* sexual
harassment
hareng *m* herring
haricots *m pl* beans
haricots verts *m pl* green beans
hasard *m* chance
haut, e high; **en haut** above;
upward; **vers le haut** upward;
above
haut-parleur *m* speaker *(e.g.,
stereo)*
haute tension *f* high voltage
hauteur *f* height
hebdomadaire *adj* weekly
hébergement *m* lodging
herbes *f pl* herbs
hésiter to hesitate
heure *f* hour; **à l'heure** *adv* on
time, punctual
heure d'arrivée *f* arrival time
heure de départ *f* departure
time
heures de visites *f pl* visiting
hours
heures d'ouverture *f pl*
business hours
heureux, -euse happy; **(de)** to
be happy (about)
hier yesterday
histoire *f* history
hiver *m* winter
hockey sur glace *m* ice hockey
hold-up *m* hold-up *(bank)*
homme *m* man
hôpital *m* hospital
**horaire (de chemin de
fer/des bus/du métro/des
trolleys)** *m* schedule
horloger *m* wathcmaker
hors de outside
hors-jeu offside
hospitalité *f* hospitality

hôte/hôtesse host / hostess
hôtel de ville *m* town hall
(historical building)
hovercraft *m* hovercraft
huile *f* oil
huile d'olive *f* olive oil
huile solaire *f* suntan lotion
huîtres *f pl* oysters
humide damp
hydroglisseur *m* hydrofoil
hypertension *f* hypertension,
elevated blood pressure
hypotension *f* low blood
pressure

I

ici here
idée *f* idea; concept
identité *f* identity
il he, it
il y a there is / there are
il y a dix minutes ten minutes
ago
île *f* island
ils they *pl m*
impératrice *f* empress
imperméable *m* raincoat
importance *f* importance
important, e important;
significant
importuner to bother
impossible impossible
impression *f* impression
impressionnant impressive
impressionnisme *m*
Impressionism
impropre inappropriate
incendie *f* fire
incident *m* incident
inconnu, e unknown; a stranger
m/f
incroyable incredible,
unbelievable
indécent, e indecent

221

indécis, e undecided
indicatif *m* prefix, area code
indication *f* indication
indications *f* indications
indice de protection *m* sun block factor (SPF)
infarctus *m* heart attack
infection *f* infection
infirmier male nurse
infirmière nurse
inflammable flammable
inflammation *f* inflammation
inflammation des amygdales *f* swollen tonsils
information *f* information; **informations** news
informer to inform, instruct
infusion à la camomille *f* chamomile tea
inhabituel, le unaccustomed
innocent, e innocent
inquiet, -iète nervous
inscription *f* inscription; registration
insecte *m* insect
insignifiant, e insignificant
insister sur to insist on
insolation sunstroke
insomnie *f* insomnia
installation *f* installation
installations sanitaires *f pl* sanitary facilities
instant *m* instant, moment
instantané *m* snapshot
instestin *m* intestine
instruction *f* instruction
insuline *f* insulin
insupportable unbearable
intelligent, e intelligent
intention *f* intention
interdiction *f* prohibition
interdire to forbid
interdit, e forbidden
intéressant, e interesting
intérieur *m* interior
intermédiaire *m* intermediary
international, e international

interphone *m* intercom
Interrail Interrail
interroger to ask
interrompre to interrupt
interrupteur *m* light switch
intoxication alimentaire *f* food poisoning
inutile useless; **inutilement** in vain
inverse inverse
inversement inversely
invité, e *m/f* guest
inviter to invite
invraisemblable improbable
itinéraire *m* itinerary
ivre drunk

J

jamais ever; **ne (...) jamais** never
jambe *f* leg
jambon *m* ham
jambon cru *m* raw ham
jambon cuit/blanc/de Paris *m* cooked ham
janvier January
jardin *m* garden
jardin botanique *m* botanical garden
jaune yellow
jazz *m* jazz
je I
jean *m* jeans
jetée *f* pier
jeter to throw
jeu de boules *m* game of boules
jeu de quilles *m* game of skittles
jeudi Thursday
jeun empty stomach (on an)
jeune young; youth *(m. or f.)*; **jeune fille** *f* girl
jeûne *m* fasting
joie *f* joy
joli, e pretty
jouer to play

jouets *m pl* toys
jouir de to enjoy
jour *m* day; les jours ouvrables
  workdays
jour de l'arrivée *m* arrival day
jour ouvrable *m* workday
journal *m* newspaper
juge *m/f* judge
juillet July
juin June
jupe *f* skirt
jus d'orange *m* orange juice
jusqu'à until; jusqu'à
  maintenant so far
juste just; right
juteux juicy

K

kayak *m* kayak
kermesse *f* fair
ketchup *m* ketchup
kilo (gramme) *m* kilo
kilomètre *m* kilometer
kit de réparation des pneus *m*
  tire repair kit
kitsch kitschy
klaxon *m* horn

L

là there; là-bas over there
lac *m* lake
lacet *m* lace
laid, e ugly
laine *f* wood
laisser to leave
lait *m* milk
lait écrémé *m* skimmed milk
laiterie *f* dairy shop
laitue *f* lettuce
lames de rasoir *f pl* razor blades
lampe *f* lamp

lampe de chevet *f* bedside lamp
lande *f* field
langue *f* tongue; language
langue des signes *f* sign
  language
lapin *m* rabbit
large wide; *(clothing)* loose
largeur *f* width
largeur de la porte *f* width of
  the door
largeur du couloir *f* width of
  the corridor
laurier *m* laurel
l'autre the other
l'autre jour the other day
lavabo *m* sink
lavabos *m pl* lavatory
lave-vaisselle *m* dishwasher
laver to wash
laverie *f* laundromat
laxatif *m* laxative
leçons de ski *f pl* ski lessons
lecteur de cassettes *m* cassette
  player
lecteur de CD *m* CD player
léger, -ère light
légumes *m pl* vegetables
lent, e slow
lentement slowly *adv*
lentille *f* contact lens
lentilles *f pl* lenses
lessive *f* wash *(to be done)*;
  laundry soap
lettre *f* letter
lettre exprès *f* express letter
lettre recommandée *f*
  registered letter
leur *poss prn f* their
levée *f* lifting (of)
lever to pick up; lift; se lever to
  get up
lèvre *f* lip
librairie *f* bookstore
libre free
licence camping *f* camping
  permit

lieu *m* place; au lieu de instead of; avoir lieu to take place
lieu de naissance *m* place of birth
lieu de pèlerinage *m* pilgrimage site
ligne *f* line *(railroad, elec., tel.)*
lilas lilac
limonade *f* lemonade
lin *m* flax; linen
liquide liquid
liquide de frein *m* brake fluid
lire to read
liste *f* list
lit *m* bed
lit à étages *m* bunk bed
lit d'enfant *m* child's bed
litre *m* liter
livre *m* book
livre de cuisine *m* cookbook
livre de poche *m* pocket book
livret d'épargne *m* savings book
local, e local
localité *f* locality
location *f* advance booking
loge *f* box *(theater)*
loin far
long, longue long
longueur *f* length
Lorraine *f* Lorraine
lotion après-rasage *f* after-shave
louer to praise; to rent
lourd humid
lourd, e heavy
loyer *m* rent
luge *f* luge
lui he; him
lumbago *m* lumbago
lumière *f* light
lundi Monday
lundi de Pâques *m* Easter Monday
lundi de Pentecôte *m* Whit Monday
lune *f* moon

lunettes de plongée *f pl* diving goggles
lunettes de ski *f pl* ski goggles
luxueux, -euse luxurious

M

ma *poss prn* my
machine *f* machine
machine à café *f* coffee maker
machine à laver *f* washing machine
mâchoire *f* jaw
madame Madame *(direct address, before name)*
mademoiselle Miss
magasin d'antiquités *m* antique shop
magasin (d'articles) de sport sporting goods store
magasin de chaussures *m* shoe store
magasin de fruits et légumes *m* produce store
magasin de jouets *m* toy store
magasin de musique *m* music shop
magasin de photos *m* photo shop
magasin de produits diététiques *m* health food store
magasin de produits naturels *m* store for organic products
magasin de souvenirs *m* souvenir shop
magasin de vins *m* wine merchant
magasin de (vins et) spiritueux *m* liquor store
magasin d'électro-ménager *m* appliance store
magazine *m* magazine
magnétoscope *m* video recorder
magnifique wonderful
mai May

maigre thin

maillot de bain *m* bathing trunks

maillot de corps *m* undershirt

maillot une pièce *m* one-piece bathing suit

main *f* hand; fait main handmade

maintenant now

mairie *f* town hall *(government)*

mais but

maïs *m* corn

maison *f* house; à la maison at home

maison de vacances/de campagne *f* vacation / country house

maître-nageur *m* lifeguard

mal *adv* badly; faire mal to hurt; mal de dents *m* toothache; mal de gorge *m* sore throat

malade sick

maladie *f* sickness; maladie infantile *f* childhood disease

malentendant hearing impaired

malentendu *m* misunderstanding

malgré in spite of; malgré cela in spite of that

malheur *m* misfortune

malheureusement unfortunately

malvoyant visually impaired

malvoyant/e *m/f* visually impaired person; blind person

Manche *f* English Channel

manche *f* sleeve

mandarine *f* mandarin orange

mandat *m* money order; mandat télégraphique *m* wire transfer

manger to eat

manière *f* manner, way

manifestation *f* demonstration

manquer to lack; to miss

manteau *m* coat

maquereau *m* mackerel

marais *m* swamp

marchand de journaux *m* newspaper seller

marchand d'objets d'art *m* art dealer

marchander to haggle

marche *f* step, stair

marché *m* market

marche arrière *f* reverse

marché aux puces *m* flea market

marche-pied *m* step

marcher to go *(by foot)*; to walk

mardi Tuesday; mardi gras *m* Mardi Gras

marée basse *f* low tide

marée haute *f* high tide

margarine *f* margarine

mari *m* husband

mariage *m* marriage; wedding

marié, e (à) married (to)

maroquinerie *f* leather shop

marron brown

mars March

marteau *m* hammer

mascara *m* mascara

masculin, e masculine

massage *m* massage

match *m* match, game

match de football *m* soccer game

match nul tie game

matelas *m* mattress; matelas pneumatique *m* air mattress

matériel *m* material

matin *m* morning

matinée *f* matinée

mauvais, e bad

mauve mauve; lilac

maux de tête *m pl* headache

maux d'estomac *m pl* stomach pains

maximum, au ~ at the most

mayonnaise *f* mayonnaise

me me

méchant, e nasty, mean

mèches strands

médicament *m* medicine

médicament pour la circulation *m* circulation medication

Méditerranée, la ~ *f* Mediterranean

meilleur, e better, best

mélangé, e mixed

melon *m* melon

même same; even; **la même chose** *f* the same thing

mémorial *m* memorial

ménage, faire le ~ to do the housework

mensonge *m* lie

mensuel, le *adj* monthly

menu *m* menu; **menu enfants** *m* children's menu

mer *f* ocean; **la mer du Nord** North Sea

mercredi Wednesday; **mercredi des cendres** *m* Ash Wednesday

mère *f* mother

merveilleux, -euse wonderful

messe *f* mass

météo *f* weather report

mètre *m* meter; **mètre carré** *m* square meter

métro *m* subway

mettre to put, place, lay, put on; *(time)* to need; **se mettre en colère** to get angry

meuble *m* piece of furniture

micro-ondes *m* microwave

midi *m* noon

miel *m* honey

mieux *adv* better

migraine *f* migraine

milieu *m* middle

millimètre *m* millimeter

mince thin; slender

minibar *m* mini-bar

minigolf *m* miniature golf

minitel-dialogue *m* Minitel phone

minute *f* minute

miroir *m* mirror

mise en scène *f* direction; staging

mixte mixed

mode *f* fashion; **à la mode** fashionable

modèle *m* model

modern jazz *m* jazzercise

moderne modern

moi me; **à moi** to me

moins less; minus; **au moins** at least

mois *m* month

moitié *f* half; **à moitié** *adv* half

môle *m* breakwater; jetty

mon *poss prn* my

monastère *m* monastery

monde *m* world

moniteur/monitrice de ski ski instructor *(m. and f.)*

monnaie *f* change

monsieur Mister

Monsieur! Waiter! *(direct address)*

montagne *f* mountain

montant *m* sum, amount

monter to go up

montgolfière *f* hot-air balloon

montre-bracelet *f* wristwatch

montrer to show

monument *m* monument

mordre to bite

mort *f* death

mort, e dead

mosaïque *f* mosaic

mot *m* word

motel *m* motel

moteur *m* motor

mou, molle soft

mouche *f* fly

mouchoirs en papier *m pl* paper tissues

mouette *f* seagull

mouillé, e wet

moule *f* mussel

mourir to die

mousse à raser *f* shaving cream

mousse gel *f* shower gel

moustache f mustache
moustique m mosquito
moutarde f mustard
mouton m lamb
moyen m middle; **Moyen Age** m Middle Ages
moyen, ne adj average;
muet mute
multicolore multicolored
mur m wall
mûr, e ripe
mûres f pl blackberries
murs de la ville m pl city walls
muscle m muscle
musculation f bodybuilding
musée m museum
musée ethnologique m folklore museum
musique f music
musique classique f classical music
musique en direct f live music
musique folklorique f folk music
musli m muesli
mycose f mycosis

N

nager to swim
nageur/nageuse swimmer (m. and f.)
nappe f tablecloth
national, e national; domestic
nationalité f nationality
nature f nature; **nature morte** f still life
naturel, le adj natural; **naturellement** adv naturally
nausée f nausea
navette f shuttle bus
(ne ...) pas not; **(ne ...) pas du tout** not at all; **(ne ...) pas non plus** not ... either
né, e born

nécessaire necessary
négatif, -ive negative
neige f snow; **neige poudreuse** f powder snow
néphrite f nephritis
nerf m nerve
nerveux, -euse nervous
nettoyage de fin de séjour m final cleaning
nettoyer to clean; **nettoyer (à sec)** dry cleaning
neuf, neuve new
nez m nose
Noël Christmas
noir black
noix f nut; **noix de coco** f coconut
nom m name; **nom de famille** m last name
nombre m number
non-fumeur non-smoker
Nord m North; **au nord de** north of
normal, e normal; **normalement** normally
nos poss prn our
note f bill (in hotel); **notees** f notes
noter to write down
notre poss prn our
nouilles f pl noodles
nourisson m infant
nourriture f food
nourriture pour bébés f baby food
nous we; us
nouveau, nouvel, le new; **de nouveau** again
Nouvel An m New Year
nouvelle f novelty; news
novembre November
nu m nude
nu, e naked
nuage m cloud
nuageux cloudy
nuisible harmful
nuit f night

nulle part nowhere
numéro m number
numéro de code m PIN number
numéro de la maison/de l'immeuble m number on the house / building
numéro de la voiture m wagon number
numéro de téléphone m telephone number

O

objectif m objective lens
objet m object; **objets de valeur** m pl valuables
obligé, e, être ~ de to have to
observatoire m observatory
observer to observe
occasion f occasion
occupé, e busy; *(seat)* occupied
octobre October
odeur f odor
œuf m egg
offense f offense
office m *(workplace)* office; **office de tourisme** m tourist office
officiel, le official
offrir to offer; to give
oignon m onion
oiseau m bird
olive f olive
ombre f shadow
on one; we
opéra m opera
opération f operation
opérette f operetta
opinion f opinion
opposé, e opposite
opticien/ne m/f optician
or m gold
orage m storm
orange f orange
orange orange *(color)*
orchestre m orchestra

orchestre de danse m dance band
ordonnance f prescription
ordre m order
ordures f pl trash; garbage
oreille f ear
oreiller m pillow
oreillons m pl mumps
orfèvrerie f goldsmith's art
originaire native
original m original
orteil m toe
os m bone
oser to dare
otite f inflammation of the ear
ou or; **ou bien ... ou bien** either ... or
oublier to forget; to leave behind
Ouest m West; **à l'ouest de** west of
ouïe f hearing
outil m tool
outre, en ~ in addition
ouvert, e open
ouverture automatique des portes f automatic doors
ouvre-boîtes m can opener
ouvre-bouteilles m bottle opener
ouvrir to open

P

pages jaunes f pl yellow pages
paiement m payment
paille f straw
pain m bread; **pain blanc** m white bread; **pain noir** m dark bread; **pain de glace** m lunch bag cooler
paire f pair
palais m palace
pâle pale
palmes f pl swim fins
palourde f clam
pamplemousse m grapefruit

panier *m* basket

panne *f* breakdown; **en panne** out of order

panneau *m* sign

panorama *m* panorama

pansement *m* dressing

pantalon *m* pants; **pantalon de jogging** *m* jogging pants; **pantalon de ski** *m* ski pants

papeterie *f* stationery shop

papier *m* paper; **papier (d')alu** *m* aluminum foil; **papier à lettres** *m* stationery; **papier hygiénique** *m* toilet paper; **papiers** *m pl* papers

paprika *m* paprika

Pâques *f* Easter

paquet *m* package

par by; *(passive voice)* by; **par avance** in advance

par avion airmail

par hasard by chance

parachutisme *m* skydiving

paralysie *f* paralysis

parapente *m* hang glider

paraplégique paraplegic

parapluie *m* umbrella

parc *m* park; **parc animalier** *m* animal park; **parc de loisirs** *m* amusement park; **parc national** *m* national park; **parc ornithologique** *m* bird refuge

parce que because

pardessus *m* overcoat *(men's)*

pare-brise *m* windshield

pare-chocs *m* shock absorbers

pareil, le equal

parent, e relative

parents *m pl* parents

paresser to laze around

paresseux, -euse lazy

parfum *m* perfume

parfumerie *f* perfumery

parler to speak, talk

part *f* piece; **à part** separately

partager to share

parterre *m* orchestra *(theater)*

parti, e gone; away

partie *f* part

partir to depart; **partir (de)** to leave (from); **partir pour** to leave for; **partir en voyage** to leave on a trip; **à partir de** from; **partir (pour)** starting with

partout everywhere

passage *m* passage; **passage souterrain** *m* underground passage

passager/passagère passenger *(m. and f.)*

passe *f* pass

passé *m* past

passé, e over

passeport *m* passport

passer to pass; *(time)* to go by, to spend; **passer la nuit** to spend the night

passerelle *f* foot bridge

pastèque *f* watermelon

pastilles contre le mal de gorge *f pl* pills for a sore throat

pataugeoire *f* wading pool

pâté de foie *m* goose liver pâté

patience *f* patience

patin à roulette *m* roller skate

patinage *m* ice skating

patinoire *f* skating rink

patins à glace *m pl* ice skates

pâtisserie *f* pastry shop

pâtisseries *f pl* baked goods

patron *m* boss

pauvre poor

payer to pay; **payer comptant / en liquide** to pay in cash

pays *m* country; **pays natal** *m* native country

paysage *m* landscape

péage *m* toll

peau *f* skin

pêche *f* peach

pêcher to fish

pédalo *m* pedal boat

pédiatre *m/f* pediatrician

peigne *m* comb

peigner to comb
peignoir de bain *m* bathrobe
peindre to paint
peine *f* pain; **à peine** scarcely
peintre *m/f* painter
peinture *f* painting
peinture à l'huile *f* oil painting
peinture sur soie *f* silk screen
peinture sur verre *f* painting on glass
pellicules *f pl* dandruff
pelouse *f* lawn
pendant *prp* during; **pendant la journée** during the day; **pendant la semaine** during the week
pendentif *m* pendant
pénible painful
péniche *f* houseboat
penser to think
penser à to think about
pension complète *f* full pension
pension (de famille) *f* pension
pente *f* hill
Pentecôte *f* Pentecost
perche *f* perch
perdre to lose
père *m* father
perfusion *f* IV drip
période de fermeture de la pêche *f* closed fishing season
perle *f* pearl
permanente *f* permanent
permettre to permit
permis-bateau *m* boating license
permis de conduire *m* driver's license
permis de pêche *m* fishing license
permis, e allowed, permitted
permission *f* permission
perruque *f* wig
persil *m* parsley
personne *f* person; **ne personne** no one
personne à mobilité réduite *f* a person in a wheelchair
personnel *m* personnel

personnel, le personal
persuader to persuade
perte *f* loss
peser to weigh
pétanque *f* game of boules
petit, e little, small
petit-fils/petite-fille *m/f* grandson / granddaughter
petit pain *m pl* roll
petits pois *m pl* peas
pétrole *m* petroleum
peu little **à peu près** around; **un peu** a little; **un peu de** a little
peuple *m* people
peur *f* fear; **avoir peur de** to be afraid of
peut-être maybe, perhaps
phare *m* headlight; lighthouse
pharmacie *f* pharmacy
photo *f* photo, snapshot, picture
photographie *f* photography; photograph
photomètre *m* light meter
phrase *f* sentence
pickpocket *m* pickpocket
pièce *f* piece; room
pièce de monnaie *f* coin
pièce de théâtre *f* play
pièce populaire *f* popular piece
pied *m* foot; tripod
pierre *f* stone
pierreux, -euse stony
piéton *m* pedestrian
pile *f* battery
pillule (anticonceptionnelle) *f* pill *(contraceptive)*
pilote *m*/pilot
piment *m* hot pepper
pince à épiler *f* tweezers
pinces à linge *f pl* clothespins
ping-pong *m* ping-pong
piquer to sting
piquet de tente *m* tent peg
piqûre *f* shot, injection
piscine *f* swimming pool
piste cyclable *f* bicycle trail**

piste de ski de fond *f* cross-country ski trail

pitié *f* pity

place *f* place

place de stationnement *f* parking space

place de stationnement pour handicapés *f* handicap parking

plafond *m* ceiling

plage *f* beach

plage de nudistes *f* nudist beach

plaie *f* wound

plaine *f* plain

plaire to please

plaisanterie *f* joke

plaisir *m* pleasure, enjoyment

plan *m* plan; **plan de la ville** *m* city map

planche à roulettes *f* skateboard

plancher *m* floor

plante *f* plant

plaque de nationalité *f* country sticker

plaque d'immatriculation *f* number plate

plat *m* *(food)* course, food

plat du jour *m* daily special

plat, e flat, even

plat fait à la poêle *m* stir-fry

plat principal *m* main course

plate-forme *f* platform

plein, e full; occupied

pleine saison *f* busy season

pleurer to cry

plombage *m* filling

plombs *m pl* fuse

pluie *f* rain

plus more; plus; **plus de** more than; **plus que** more than; **au plus** at the most; **en plus** in addition

plus tard later

plus tôt earlier *(sooner)*

plutôt rather

pluvieux rainy

pneu *m* tire

pneu crevé *m* flat tire

pneu neige *m* snow tire

pneumonie *f* pneumonia

poche *f* pocket

poids *m* weight

poignée *f* handle

point d'arrivée du téléski *m* summit station

point de départ du téléski *m* overlook

point de vue *m* scenic outlook

point mort *m* neutral

pointe *f* point

pointure *f* size *(shoe)*

poireau *m* leek

poires *f pl* pears

pois chiches *m pl* chickpeas

poison *m* poison

poisson *m* fish

poissonnerie *f* fish market

poissonnier *m* fishmonger

poitrine *f* chest

poivre *m* pepper

poivron *m* sweet pepper

polaroïd *m* instant camera

poli, e polite

police *f* police

polio(myélite) *f* polio

pommade *f* pomade

pommade contre les brûlures *f* burn ointment

pomme *f* apple

pommes de terre *f pl* potatoes

pompe *f* air pump

pompe à essence *f* gas pump

pompiers *m pl* firemen

pont *m* bridge; deck

porc *m* pork

porcelaine *f* porcelain

port *m* harbor

port *m* port

portable *m* cell phone

portable *m* laptop computer

portail *m* portal

porte *f* door

porte automatique *f* automatic door

porte d'embarquement *f* gate

porte-monnaie *m* coin purse

portefeuille *m* wallet

porter to wear

portier *m* porter

portion *f* portion

portrait *m* portrait

posemètre *m* light meter

poser to set down

positif, -ive positive

possibilité *f* possibility

possible possible; rendre possible to make possible

poste *f* mail

poste frontière *m* border crossing

poste principale *f* main post office

poste restante general delivery

potage *m* soup

poteau des buts *f* goal post

poteau indicateur *m* signpost

poterie *f* pottery

potiron *m* pumpkin

poubelle *f* wastebasket

poudre *f* powder

poulet *m* chicken

pouls *m* pulse

poumon *m* lung

pour for; être pour to be in favor of; pour cent percent

pourboire *m* tip

pourquoi why

pourri, e rotten, lousy

pourtant however

pousser to push; *(plants)* to grow

poussière *f* dust

pouvoir to be able

pratique *adj* practical

pré *m* meadow

préférer to prefer

premier, -ière first; premiers secours *m pl* first aid

première *f* premiere; first time

prendre to take; to take away; *(transportation)* to use / take; prendre congé to go away; prendre part (à) to take part (in)

prendre de l'essence to get some gas

prendre son petit déjeuner to have breakfast

prénom *m* first name

préparer to prepare; *(food)* to cook

près near

près de near; à peu près nearly

prescrire to prescribe

présent, e present; à présent currently, now

présentation *f* presentation

présenter to present

préservatif *m* condom

presque almost, nearly

pressé, e hurried; être pressé, e to be in a hurry

pressing *m* dry cleaning

pression on tap

prêt, e ready; prepared

prêter to loan *(to someone)*

prêtre *m* priest

preuve *f* proof

prévenir qn to tell someone

prévisions météo(rologiques) *f pl* weather forecast

prier to beg

principal, e main

principalement mainly *adv*

printemps *m* springtime

priorité *f* priority; right of way

pris, e de vertige dizzy

prise de courant *f* wall socket; plug

prise multiple *f* multi-plug adaptor

prison *f* prison

privé, e private

prix *m* price; prix d'entrée *m* entry fee

prix au kilomètre *m* price per kilometer

prix du billet *m* ticket price
prix forfaitaire *m* all-inclusive price
probable probable *adj*
probablement probably *adv*
problème *m* problem
procession *f* procession
proche near
procurer to procure, provide
produire to produce; **se produire** to occur, happen
produit *m* product, result
produit pour laver la vaisselle *m* dishwashing soap
profession *f* profession
profond, e deep
programme *m* program
projet *m* plan *(intent)*
promenade *f* walk
promenade à cheval *f* horseback ride
promettre to promise
prononcer to pronounce
proposer to propose; to offer; to suggest
proposition *f* proposition
propre clean; tidy; decent
propriétaire *m* owner
propriétaire (de la maison) *m/f* home owner
propriété *f* property
prospectus *m* leaflet
protection des monuments *f* monument protection
protection solaire *f* sunscreen
protège-slips *m pl* panty liners
protester to protest
prothèse *f* prosthesis
provisions *f pl* provisions
provisoire *adj* temporary
prudent, e prudent, careful
prune *f* plum
public *m* public *(open to all)*
public, -ique public *(populace)*
pull-over *m* pullover
pus *m* pus

Q

quai *m* platform
qualité *f* quality; characteristic
quand *(time) (question)* when
quantité *f* quantity
quart *m* quarter
quartier *m* precinct
que *(interrog. prn)* what; *(comparison)* than; *(conj)* that; only
quel/le what
quelque chose something
quelquefois sometimes
quelques some, a few
quelqu'un someone
qu'est-ce que what
question *f* question
qui n'a plus faim full
quincaillerie *f* hardware store
quitter to leave; to take off

R

raccourci *m* short cut
raconter to tell
radiateur *m* radiator
radio *f* radio
radio(graphie) *f* X-ray, radiology
rafale *f* squall, gust of wind
rafraîchissement *m* refreshment
raide stiff
raie *f* part
raisins *m pl* grapes
raison *f* reason; **avoir raison** to be right
rallonge *f* extension cord
rame *f* oar
ramer to row
rampe *f* ramp, railing
rampe d'accès *f* access ramp
randonné, faire de la ~ pédestre to hike

randonnée cycliste *f* bicycle tour

randonnée (pour la journée) *f* excursion, day trip

rapide quick, fast

rappeler qc à qn to remind someone of something

rapporter to report; to bring back

raquette *f* racket

raquette de tennis *f* tennis racket

rare rare

rarement rarely *adv*

rasoir *m* razor

rater to fail

ravissant, e charming; ravishing

réception *f* reception

recevoir to receive

rechargeur *m* battery charger

réchaud *m* stove

réchaud à gaz *m* gas stove

récipient *m* container

réclamation *f* complaint; **faire une réclamation** to file a complaint

réclamer to ask for

récolte *f* harvest

recommander to recommend

récompense *f* reward

recoudre to sew up, stitch

reçu *m* receipt

réduction *f* reduction

réduction-enfants *f* children's discount

réfrigérateur *m* refrigerator

refuge *m* refuge

refuser to refuse

regard *m* look

regarder to look at

régime *m* diet

région *f* region

règlement *m* regulation

régler to settle, pay

règles *f pl* menstruation

regretter to regret

régulier, -ière *adj* regular; **régulièrement** *adv* regularly

réhausseur *m* child seat *(for car)*

rein *m* kidney

reine *f* queen

relation *f* relationship

relève de la garde *f* changing of the guard

religion *f* religion

remarquer to notice

remède *m* remedy

remercier (qn) to thank someone

remettre to remit; **remettre à plus tard** to put off until later

remise *f* discount

remise des clés *f* key return

remonte-pente *m* ski lift

remonte-pentes pour enfants *m* kiddy tow

remorquer to tow

remplacer to replace

remplir to fill (up)

Renaissance *f* Renaissance

rencontre *f* meeting

rencontrer to meet

rendez-vous *m* appointment

rendre to give back; *(money)* to return

renseignement *m* information

réparer to repair

repas *m* meal

repasser to iron

répéter to repeat

répondeur automatique *m* answering machine

répondre to answer; to reply; **répondre à** to answer; to meet

repos *m* rest

repousser *(time)* to postpone

représentation *f (theater)* performance

réservation *f* reservation; advance purchase

réserve naturelle *f* nature preserve

réserver to reserve; *(ticket)* to book

réservoir *m* gas tank

résoudre to resolve
respecter to respect
respirer to breathe
responsable responsible
ressembler to resemble
rester to stay; to be left over
restes *m pl* remains
restoroute *m* rest area
résultat *m* result
retard *m* delay
retenir to retain; to book *(seat)*;
   retenir qc to remember
retour *m* return; de retour back
retourner to return
rétroviseur *m* rearview mirror
rêve *m* dream
réveil *m* alarm clock
réveillé, e awake
réveiller to awaken; se réveiller
   to wake up
réveillon *m* Christmas Eve
revenir to come back, return
rez-de-chaussée *m* ground floor
rhumatisme *m* rheumatism
rhume *m* cold; rhume des foins
   m hay fever
riche rich
ridicule ridiculous
rien, (ne ...) ~ nothing
rire to laugh
risque *m* risk
rissolé browned, roasted
   (potatoes)
rivage *m* shore *(sea)*
rive *f* bank *(river)*
rivière *f* river
riz *m* rice
robe *f* dress
robinet *m* faucet
rocade *f* bypass; beltway
rocher *m* boulder; rock
roi *m* king
rôle principal *m* main role
roller *m* inline skate, roller blade
roman *m* novel
romarin *m* rosemary
rond, e round

ronfler to snore
rose pink
rôti roast
roue *f* wheel
roue de secours *f* spare tire
rouer de coups to beat up
rouge red
rouge à lèvres *m* lipstick
rougeole *f* measles
rougeurs *f pl* rash
route *f* route; street; en cours de
   route on the way
route départementale *f*
   secondary road
route secondaire *f* country road
rubéole *f* German measles
rue *f* street
rue adjacente *f* side road
rue principale *f* main street
ruelle *f* alley
ruine *f* ruin
rupture de tendon *f* ruptured
   tendon
rusé, e sly

S

sa *poss adj* his, her, its
sac *m* bag; sack; sac à dos *m*
   backpack; sac à main *m*
   handbag, pocketbook
sac de voyage *m* travel bag
sac en plastique *m* plastic bag
sac-poubelle *m* trash bag
s'acclimatiser to acclimatize
sachet *m* bag *(small)*
sachet de thé *m* teabag
sacoche *f* school bag
safran *m* saffron
saignement *m* bleeding
saignements de nez *m pl*
   nosebleed
saigner to bleed
saint, e holy
Saint-Sylvestre *f* New Year's Eve

saison *f* season
salade *f* salad
salami *m* salami
sale dirty
saleté *f* filth
salière *f* saltshaker
salle *f* hall, room
salle à manger *f* dining room
salle d'attente *f* waiting room
salle de bains *f* bathroom
salle de petit déjeuner *f* breakfast room
salle de séjour *f* living room
salle de télévision *f* television room
salon *m* living room
saluer to greet
samedi Saturday
s'amuser to have fun
sandales *f pl* sandals
sandwich *m* sandwich
sang *m* blood
sans without
sans alcool alcohol-free
sans connaissance unconscious
sans importance unimportant
sans obstacle barrier free
santé *f* health; en bonne santé healthy
s'approcher to approach
s'asseoir to sit down
sauce *f* sauce
saucisse *f* sausage
sauge *f* sage
sauna *m* sauna
saut à l'élastique *m* bungee jumping
sauter to jump
sauvage wild
sauver to save
savoir to know; knowledge *m*
savon *m* soap
savourer to savor
sciatique *f* sciatica
sculpteur *m* sculptor
sculpture *f* sculpture

sculpture sur bois *f* wood carving
se calmer to calm oneself
se dépêcher to hurry
se distraire to amuse oneself
se garer to park
se marier to get married
se méfier de to mistrust
se plaindre (de) to complain (about)
se promener to go for a walk
se réjouir to rejoice
se réjouir à l'avance de to look forward to
se renseigner to find out
se reposer to rest, relax
se rétablir to recover
se souvenir to remember
se taire to be quiet
sec, sèche dry
sèche-cheveux *m* hairdryer
sécher to dry
second, e second
seconde *f* second *(unit of time)*
secret, secrète *adj* secret; en secret *adv* in secret
sécurité *f* security, safety
s'efforcer de to force oneself to
s'égarer to get lost
seiche *f* cuttlefish
séjour *m* stay
séjourner to stay
sel *m* salt
sélectionner to select
self-service *m* self-service
selles *f pl* bowel movement
semaine *f* week; pendant la semaine during the week
semaine supplémentaire *f* extra week
semblable similar
semelle *f* sole
sens *m* sense
sensibilité *f* sensitivity
sentier *m* path
sentiment *m* feeling
sentir to feel; to smell

sentir mauvais to stink
s'entraîner to train
séparer to separate
septembre September
septicémie *f* blood poisoning
sérieux, -euse serious
serpent *m* snake
serrure *f* lock *(door)*
service *m* service
service (administratif) service (administrative); office
service auto-express *m* auto-express service *(daytime)*
service d'assistance *m* care-taking service
service de dépannage *m* breakdown assistance; tow service
service de transport (pour handicapés) *m* transportation (for the handicapped)
services d'aide sociale *m pl* social services
serviette *f* napkin
serviette de toilette *f* bath towel
serviettes en papier *f pl* paper towels
serviettes hygiéniques *f pl* sanitary napkins
servir to serve; se servir to use
s'étendre to stretch out, lie down
s'étonner (de) to be surprised (at)
seuil *m* threshold
seul, e alone; lonely
seulement only
sexe *m* sex
s'habituer à to get used to; être habitué, e to be used to
shampooing *m* shampoo
short *m* shorts
show *m* show
si if; whether; si! yes, indeed!
siècle *m* century
siège *m* seat
siège-enfants *m* child's seat
signal *m* signal

signal d'alarme *m* emergency brake
signature *f* signature
signe *m* sign; faire signe to wave
signer to sign
signification *f* meaning
simple simple
s'inquiéter to become nervous
s'intéresser (à) to take an interest (in)
sinusite *f* sinusitis
sirop contre la toux *m* cough syrup
situation *f* situation
ski *m* skiing
ski de fond *m* cross-country skiing
ski nautique *m* water skiing
skier to ski
slip *m* underpants
s'occuper de to take care of
socquettes *f pl* sockettes
sœur *f* sister
soie *f* silk
soif *f* thirst
soigner to treat
soir *m* evening
soirée *f* evening; party
soirée de danse folklorique *f* folk dance evening
sol *m* ground
solarium *m* solarium
soldes *m pl* sales
sole *f* sole *(fish)*
soleil *m* sun
solide solid
soliste *m/f* soloist
solitaire solitary
solution de réhydratation *f* electrolyte solution
sombre dark
somme *f* sum
sommet *m* summit
somnifères *m pl* sleeping pills
son *m* sound
son *poss adj* his, her, its
sonner to ring; *(clock)* to strike

sonnette f bell
sorte f type
sortie f exit
sortie (d'autoroute) f exit (highway)
sortie de secours f emergency exit
sortir to go out
souci m care; **se faire du souci pour** to worry about
soucoupe f saucer
soudain suddenly
soûl, e drunk
soulever to lift
soumis aux droits de douane subject to duty
soupe f soup
source f spring, source
sourd deaf
sourd/e-muet/te m/f deaf mute
sourd/sourde deaf person (m. and f.)
sous under
sous-titres m pl subtitles
sous-vêtements m pl underwear
soutien-gorge m bra
souvenir m souvenir
souvent often
sparadrap m Band-Aid
spécial, e special
spécialiste m/ specialist
spécialité f specialty
spectacle m performance, show
spectateur/spectatrice spectator (m. and f.)
sport m sport
sportif/sportive athletic
stade m stadium
station f station
station balnéaire f seaside resort
station de taxis f taxi stand
statue f statue
steward/hôtesse de l'air m/f steward/ess

stimulateur cardiaque m pacemaker
stop! Stop!
stops m pl brake lights
studio m studio, apartment
stupide stupid
style m style
stylo à bille m ballpoint pen
sucette (de caoutchouc) f pacifier
sucre m sugar
sucré, e sweet
sucrettes f pl sweetener
Sud m south; **au sud de** south of
suffire to suffice
suffisamment enough
Suisse f Switzerland; **Suissesse** Swiss person (m. and f.)
suivant, e following
suivre to follow
supermarché m supermarket
supplément m supplement
supplémentaire supplementary
supporter to bear; withstand
suppositoires m pl suppositories
sur on
sûr, e certain; reliable
sur le gril from the grill
sur les bords de la Seine banks of the Seine (on the)
surbaissé lowered
sûrement certainly
surf m surfboard
surface de réparation f penalty area / box
surpris, e surprised
surtout especially
surveiller to watch, keep an eye on
sympa pleasant (place)
sympathique nice
syncope f fainting fit
syndicat d'initiative m tourist office
système d'alarme m alarm system

ta your
table *f* table
table à langer *f* changing table
table de nuit *f* night table
tableau *m* painting
tache *f* spot
taille *f* size *(clothing)*
tailleur *m* suit
tailleur/couturière tailor /
  seamstress
talon *m* heel
tampon *m* stamp; tampon
tard late
tas, un ~ de a lot
tasse *f* cup
taux d'alcoolémie maximal *m*
  blood alcohol level
taxe de sécurité *f* security tax
taxes d'aéroport *m pl* airport
  duties
te you, to/for you
t(ee)-shirt *m* T-shirt
teinte *f* tint *(color)*
teinture d'iode *f* tincture of
  iodine
teinturerie *f* dry cleaner's
télécopieur *m* fax machine
télégramme *m* telegram
téléobjectif *m* objective lens
téléphérique *m* cable car
téléphone *m* telephone
téléphone (de la chambre) *m*
  telephone (room)
téléphone de secours *m*
  emergency phone
téléphoner to telephone, call
téléphoner à to call someone
télésiège *m* chairlift
téléski *m* ski tow
téléviseur *m* television
témoin *m/f* witness
température *f* temperature;
  fever
tempête *f* storm

temple *m* church; temple
temps *m* time; weather; à temps
  adv on time; en même temps at
  the same time
tendre tender
tendre to give; to hold out
tenir to hold; être tenu de to be
  obligated
tennis *m* tennis; tennis shoes *f pl*
tente *f* tent
terminal *m* terminal
terminer to end; se terminer to
  run out; end
terminus *m* endstation
terrain *m* terrain; land; terrain
  de sport *m* athletic field
terrain de football *m* soccer
  field
terrasse *f* terrace
terre *f* earth; land
terre cuite *f* terra-cotta
terre ferme *f* solid ground
tétanos *m* tetanus
tête head
tétine *f* pacifier
thé *m* tea
théâtre *m* theater
théâtre de la danse *m* dance
  theater
thermomètre *m* thermometer
thon *m* tuna
thym *m* thyme
tibia *m* tibia
tilleul lime flower tea
timbre *m* stamp
timbre de collection *m* special-
  issue stamp
timide timid
tire-bouchon *m* corkscrew
tirer to pull; to shoot
toast *m* toast
toi you; à toi to you
toile *f* linen
toilettes *f pl* toilets
toilettes pour handicapés *f pl*
  handicap toilets
toit *m* roof

toit ouvrant *m* sunroof
tomate *f* tomato
tombe *f* grave
tombeau *m* tomb
tomber to fall
ton *m* tone
ton *poss adj* your
torchon *m* dish towel
tôt early
toucher to touch
toujours always; still
tour *m* turn
tour de l'île *m* tour of the island
tour de reins *m* backache
touriste *m/f* tourist
tous all, everyone
tous les jours everyday
tous/toutes les deux both
tout *adv* totally; **tout à coup** suddenly; **tout de suite** right away
tout droit straight ahead
tout, toute all; **tous, toutes** all
toutes les heures every hour
toux *f* cough
toxique poisonous, toxic
traduire to translate
tragédie *f* tragedy
train *m* train
train autos-couchettes *m* car transport train *(overnight)*
train de banlieue *m* local train
traité sprayed
traiteur *m* delicatessen; *(homemade products)* caterer
trajet *m* journey; route
tram *m* streetcar
tranche *f* slice
tranches de charcuterie/de viande froide *f pl* cold cuts
tranquillisant *m* tranquilizer
transpirer to sweat
travail *m* work
travailler to work
travers, à ~ across
traverser to cross
très very

triangle de présignalisation *m* warning triangle
tribunal *m* court *(justice)*
triste sad
troisième third
tromper to deceive; **se tromper** to be mistaken
trop too much; too *(with adj.)*
trou *m* hole
trouble cloudy *(liquid)*
troubles cardiaques *m pl* heart trouble
troubles de la circulation *m pl* circulatory trouble
troubles digestifs *m pl* digestive trouble
troubles respiratoires *m pl* respiratory trouble
trouver to find; **se trouver** *(place)* to be located
tu you
tuba *m* snorkel
tube digestif *m* digestive tract
tumeur *f* tumor
tunnel *m* tunnel
turquoise turquoise
tuyau *m* hose; pipe; tip
tuyau d'échappement *m* exhaust pipe
tympan *m* eardrum
typhoïde *f* typhoid
typique (de) typical

U

ulcère *m* ulcer
un morceau de pain piece of bread
un quart d'heure quarter of an hour
un, une a, an, one
une fois once
uni single color
université *f* university
urgence emergency

urgent, e urgent
urine *f* urine
urinoir *m* urinal
usine *f* factory
usuel, le usual
utiliser to use

V

V.T.C. (vélo tout chemin) *m* touring bike
V.T.T. (vélo tout terrain) *m* mountain bike
vacances *f pl* vacation
vaccination *f* vaccination
vague de chaleur *f* heat wave
vaisselle *f* dishes
valable valid; être valable to be valid
valeur *f* value; sans valeur worthless
valise *f* suitcase
vallée *f* valley
vapeur *m* steamship
variable variable
varicelle *f* chicken pox
variétés *f pl* variety show
vase *m* vase
veau *m* veal
végétarien vegetarian
veille de Noël *f* Christmas Eve
vélo *m* bike
vélo de course *m* racing bike
vendre to sell
vendredi Friday
vendredi saint *m* Good Friday
venir to come
vent *m* wind
vente *f* sale
ventilateur *m* ventilator; fan
ventre *m* stomach
vents *m pl* flatulence
ver *m* worm
verglas *m* ice

véritable *adj* true
vernis à ongles *m* nail polish
verre *m* glass
verre à eau *m* water glass
verre à vin *m* wine glass
vers toward *(spatial relations)*; *(time)* around; vers le bas downward; vers le haut upward; vers midi around noon
version originale (la v.o.) *f* original version
vert green
vertige *m* dizziness
vésicule biliaire *f* gallbladder
vessie *f* bladder
veste *f* jacket
veste de cuir *f* leather jacket
veste de laine *f* wool jacket
vestiaire *m* coat room
vestiges *m pl* vestiges
vestiges archéologiques *m* archeological remains
vêtements *m pl* clothing
vêtements habillés *m pl* evening attire
veuf/veuve widower / widow
vexation *f* annoyance
viande *f* meat
viande hachée *f* hamburger
vidange *f* oil change
vide empty
vidéocassette *f* videocassette
vie *f* life
vieille ville *f* old city
vieux, vieil, vieille old
vif, vive lively
vigne *f* vine; vineyard
village *m* village
village de montagne *m* mountain town
village de pêcheurs *m* fishing village
village de vacances *m* vacation resort
ville *f* city
vin *m* wine

241

vin blanc *m* white wine; (vin) rosé *m* rosé; (vin) rouge *m* red wine

vinaigre *m* vinegar

viol *m* rape

violet violet

virage *m* curve

virement *m* transfer

virus *m* virus

vis *f* screw

visa *m* visa

visage *m* face

viseur *m* viewfinder

visite *f* visit; rendre visite à qn to visit someone

visite guidée *f* guided tour

visite guidée de la ville *f* guided city tour

visiter to visit

vite *adv* fast

vitesse *f* speed; gear *(auto)*, speed

vitrine *f* display window

vivre to live

voie *f* platform

voie rapide *f* fast lane

voir to see; view

voisin, e *m/f* neighbor

voiture *f* car

voiture-couchettes *f* sleeper car

voiture de police *f* police car

voix *f* voice

vol *m* flight

vol *m* theft

vol à voile *m* gliding

vol intérieur *m* domestic flight

vol international *m* international flight

volant *m* shuttlecock

volant mobile *m* steering wheel knob

volcan *m* volcano

voler to fly; to steal

voleur *m* thief

voleur à la tire *m* pickpocket

volley-ball *m* volleyball; volley-ball de plage *m* beach volleyball

volontiers gladly

volt *m* volt

voltage *m* voltage

votre your

vouloir to wish; want

vous you

voûte *f* vault

voyage *m* voyage, trip; voyage organisé *m* organized tour

voyager to travel

voyageur, -euse *m/f* traveler

vrai, e true; real; être vrai, e to be true; à vrai dire *adv* really; actually

vraiment *adv* truly, really

vue *f* view

W

wagon aménagé pour handicapés *m* handicap-accessible car

wagon-lits *m* sleeper car

wagon-restaurant *m* dining car

wagon sans compartiments *m* open car

watt *m* watt

western *m* western

Y

yaourt *m* yogurt

yeux *m pl* eyes

yoga *m* yoga

Z

zone piétonne *f* pedestrian crossing

zoo *m* zoo

English – French Glossary

A

A, an, one un, une
A few quelques
A little un peu de
Abbey l'abbaye *f*
Abbreviation l'abréviation *f*
About à peu près; environ
Above au-dessus (de)
Abscess l'abcès *m*
Absolutely *adv* absolument
Absorbent cotton le coton hydrophile
To accept *(invitation)* accepter
Access ramp la rampe d'accès
Accessibility l'accessibilité *f*
Accident l'accident *m*
To acclimatize s'acclimater
To accompany accompagner
Account le compte
Accustomed habituel, le;
Usually *adv* habituellement
Acquaintance *(person)* la connaissance
Acquaintanceship la connaissance
Across from en face de
Act l'acte *m*
Action film le film d'action
Actor/actress l'acteur/ l'actrice, le comédien/ la comédienne
Adapter l'adaptateur *m*
Adaptor plug la prise multiple
To add ajouter
Address l'adresse *f*
Addressee le destinataire
Administration l'administration *f*
Administrative service l'office *m*, le service (administratif)
Admission l'entrée *f*
Admission ticket le billet d'entrée
Adult l'adulte *m/f*
Advance reservation la communication avec préavis, la réservation
Advantage l'avantage *m*
Aerobic l'aérobic *m*
Affectionate affectueux, -euse, tendre
After après
After eating après le repas
After-shave la lotion après-rasage
Afternoon l'après-midi *m*
Again de nouveau
Against contre
Age l'âge *m*
Agency l'agence *f*
To agree convenir de
Air l'air *m*
Air conditioning l'air *m* conditionné
Air mattress le matelas pneumatique
Airline la compagnie aérienne
Airmail par avion
Airport l'aéroport *m*
Airport bus le bus pour l'aéroport
Airport taxes les taxes *m* d'aéroport
Alarm clock le réveil
Alarm system le système d'alarme
Alcohol-free sans alcool
Alcohol-free beer la bière sans alcool
All tous, toutes
Allergy l'allergie *f*
Alley la ruelle
Allowed permis, e

Almonds les amandes *f*
Almost presque
Alone seul, e, solitaire
Already déjà
Alsace l'Alsace *f*
Also aussi
Altar l'autel *m*
Although bien que
Aluminum foil le papier (d')alu
Always toujours
Ambulance l'ambulance *f*
American Américain, e
American (person) Américain, e
Amount le montant
Amphitheater l'amphithéâtre *m*
To amuse oneself s'amuser; se distraire
Amusement park le parc de loisirs
And et
Anesthesia l'anesthésie *f*
Angina l'angine *f*
Angry en colère
Animal l'animal *m*
Animal park le parc animalier
Animated film le dessin animé
Ankle la cheville
To announce annoncer
Announcement l'annonce
Annual annuel, le
To answer répondre *(respond)*; répondre à *(reply to)*
Answering machine le répondeur automatique
Antibiotic l'antibiotique *m*
Antifreeze l'antigel *m*
Antique antique
Antique shop le magasin d'antiquités
Apartment le studio; l'appartement *m*
Appendicitis l'appendicite *f*
Appetite l'appétit *m*
Appetizer l'entrée *f*
Applause les applaudissements *m pl*
Apples les pommes *f*

Appointment le rendez-vous
Apricots les abricots *m*
April avril
Arch l'arc *m*
Archeology l'archéologie *f*
Architect l'architecte *m/f*
Architecture l'architecture *f*
Arena l'arène *f*
Armchair le fauteuil
Around *(spatial relationship)* autour de; *(approximately)* à; *(time expressions)* vers
Around noon vers midi
To arrest arrêter
Arrival l'arrivée *f*
Arrival day le jour de l'arrivée
Arrival time l'heure *f* d'arrivée
To arrive arriver
Art l'art *m*
Art dealer le marchand d'objets d'art
Art nouveau l'Art nouveau
Artichokes les artichauts *m*
As ... as aussi ... que
Ash Wednesday le mercredi des cendres
Ashtray le cendrier
To ask interroger
To ask someone for something demander qc à qn
Asparagus l'asperge *f*
Aspirin l'aspirine *f*
Assistance service le service d'assistance
Association l'association *f*
Asthma l'asthme *m*
At first d'abord
At home à la maison
At least au moins
At most au plus, au maximum
At night la nuit
At that time à l'époque
At the same time en même temps
At this time à cette heure-ci
Athlete le sportif/ la sportive

Athletic field le terrain de sport, le stade
Atlantic l'Atlantique *m*
ATM le distributeur de billets
Attack l'attaque *f*
To attain atteindre
Attempt l'essai *m*
To attempt essayer
Attention attention
August août
Authentic authentique
Automatic automatique
Automatic door la porte automatique
Automatic door opener l'ouverture f automatique des portes
Automatic ticket puncher le composteur
Automatic transmission la boîte automatique
Automobile la voiture
Autumn l'automne *m*
Average *adj* moyen, ne; *(on the average)* adv en moyenne
Average le moyen
Avocado l'avocat *m*
Awake réveillé, e
To awaken réveiller

B

Baby le bébé
Baby food la nourriture pour bébés
Baby scale le pèse-bébés
Baby's bottle le biberon
Babysitter le baby-sitter
Bachelor le célibataire
Bachelor célibataire
Back le dos
Back country l'arrière-pays *m*
Back pain les douleurs *f* au dos
Backache le tour de reins, le lumbago

Backpack le sac à dos
Backup lights les feux *m* arrière
Backwards en arrière
Bad *adj* mauvais, e; ~ly *adv* mal
Badminton le badminton
Bag le sac; *(small)* le sachet
Baggage les bagages *m*
Baggage cart le chariot
Baggage locker la consigne automatique
Baggage pickup l'arrivée *f* des bagages
Baggage registration l'enregistrement *m* des bagages
Baggage window le guichet des bagages
Baked goods les pâtisseries *f*
Bakery la boulangerie
Balcony le balcon
Ball le ballon, la balle; *(party)* le bal
Ballet le ballet
Ballpoint pen le stylo à bille
Bananas les bananes *f*
Band le groupe
Band-Aid le sparadrap
Bandage le pansement
To bandage faire un pansement
Bangs la frange
Bank la banque
Bank *(river)* la rive; *(ocean)* le bord, le rivage
Bank book le livret d'épargne
Bank card la carte bancaire
Bank costs la commission, les frais bancaires
Banks of the Seine (on the) à sur les bords de la Seine
Baroque le baroque
Barrier free sans obstacle
Basil le basilic
Basket le panier
Basketball le basket-ball
Bathing cap le bonnet de bain
Bathing slippers les chaussures *f* en plastique (pour la baignade)

Bathing suit *(one piece)* le maillot une pièce
Bathing trunks le maillot de bain
Bathroom la salle de bains
Bathtub la baignoire
Battery la pile
Bay *(large)* la baie; *(small)* la crique
To be *(verb)* être; *(poss prn)* son, sa
To be able pouvoir
To be against être contre
To be called s'appeler
To be cold avoir froid
To be friends être amis
To be from être originaire (de)
To be happy about être content, e de
To be hungry avoir faim
To be in favor of être pour
To be lacking manquer
To be left over rester
To be located se trouver
To be mistaken se tromper
To be seasick avoir le mal de mer
To be thirsty avoir soif
Beach la plage
Beach robe le peignoir de bain
Beach shoes les chaussures *f* de plage
Beach volleyball le volley-ball de plage
Beans les haricots *m*
Beard la barbe
To beat up rouer de coups
Beautiful beau, bel, le
Because parce que
Because of à cause de
To become devenir
Bed le lit; to go to bed aller se coucher
Bed linen les draps *m*
Bedridden grabataire
Bedroom la chambre à coucher

Bedside lamp la lampe de chevet
Bee l'abeille *f*
Beef le bœuf
Beehive la ruche
Beer la bière
Before avant que
Before the meal avant les repas *m pl*
To begin commencer
Beginning/start le début/le commencement
Behind derrière
Beige beige
To believe croire
Bell la sonnette
To belong appartenir
Below au-dessous (de)
Belt la ceinture
Bench le banc
Best le/la meilleur, e
Better *adj* meilleur, e; *adv* mieux
Between entre
Bicycle le vélo, la bicyclette
Big grand, e
Bike helmet le casque de protection
Bike path la piste cyclable
Bike tour la randonnée cycliste
Bikini le bikini
Bill le billet *(money)*
Bill la facture; *(in restaurant, café)* l'addition *f*; *(in hotel)* la note
Bird l'oiseau *m*
Bird sanctuary le parc ornithologique
Birthday l'anniversaire *m*
Bistro le bistrot
To bite mordre
Bitter amer, -ère
Black noir
Black-and-white movie le film en noir et blanc
Blackberry les mûres *f*
Bladder la vessie

Blanket la couverture
Blazer le blazer
To bleed saigner
Bleeding le saignement
Blind aveugle; non-voyant/e
Blind person l'aveugle m/f; le/la non-voyant/e
Blind person's cane la canne d'aveugle
Blinker le clignotant
Blond blond
Blood le sang
Blood alcohol level le taux d'alcoolémie maximal
Blood poisoning la septicémie
Blood pressure *(high)* l'hypertension *f*; *(low)* l'hypotension *f*
Blood type le groupe sanguin
Blouse le chemisier
To blow dry faire un brushing
Blue bleu
Blues le blues
Boarding gate la porte *f* d'embarquement
Boarding pass la carte d'embarquement
Boarding wheelchair le fauteuil transport
Boating license le permis-bateau
Body le body; le corps
Bodybuilding la musculation
Boiled bouilli
Boiled ham le jambon cuit/ blanc/ de Paris
Bone l'os *m*
Book le livre
Booklet of tickets le carnet de tickets
Bookshop la librairie
Booth la cabine
Boots les bottes *f*
Border la frontière
Border crossing le poste frontière
Boring ennuyeux, -euse
Born né, e

To borrow emprunter
Boss le patron
Botanical garden le jardin botanique
Both les deux
To bother importuner
Bottle la bouteille
Bottle opener l'ouvre-bouteilles *m*
Bottle warmer le chauffe-biberon
Boulder le rocher
Boules le jeu de boules, la pétanque
Bouquet le bouquet
Bowel movement les selles *f*
Bowl l'assiette *f* creuse
Bowling le bowling
Box *(theater)* la loge
Boy le garçon
Bra le soutien-gorge
Bracelet le bracelet
Braille le braille
Brain le cerveau
Braised à l'étouffée; à l'étuvée
Brake le frein
Brake fluid le liquide de frein
Bread le pain
Breadth la largeur
To break fracturer
Break *(bone)* la fracture; Rupture *(groin)* hernie, f.
Breakdown la panne
Breakdown assistance le service de dépannage
Breakfast le petit déjeuner
Breakfast buffet le buffet (de petit déjeuner)
Breakfast room la salle de petit déjeuner
Breakwater le môle
To breathe respirer
Bridge le pont
To bring apporter
To bring back rapporter
Broadcast *(radio, television)* l'émission *f*

Broken cassé, e, en panne
Broken bone la fracture
Bronchi les bronches *f*
Bronchitis la bronchite
Bronze le bronze
Brooch la broche
Brother le frère
Brother-in-law le beau-frère
Brown marron; *(tanned)* bronzé/e
Browned *(potatoes)* rissolées
Bruise la contusion
Brush la brosse
Building le bâtiment *m*, l'édifice *m*
Bungalow le bungalow
Bungee jumping le saut à l'élastique
Bunk bed le lit à étages
Burn la brûlure
Burn ointment la pommade contre les brûlures
Bus le bus
Bus station la gare routière
Bush le buisson
Business hours les heures *f pl* d'ouverture
Busy season la pleine saison
But mais
Butcher shop la boucherie
Butter le beurre
Buttermilk le babeurre
To buy acheter
By *(passive voice)* de; par
By chance par hasard
Bypass le by-pass; la rocade
Byzantine byzantin

C

Cabaret le cabaret
Cabaret artist le chansonnier *m*
Cabbage le chou
Cable car le téléphérique
Café le café

Cake le gâteau
To calculate calculer
Calculator la calculatrice
Calling card la télécarte
Calm le calme
To calm oneself se calmer
Camcorder le caméscope
Camera l'appareil photo *m*
Campground le (terrain de) camping
Camping le camping
Camping guide le guide de camping-caravaning
Camping permit la licence camping
Camping vehicle le camping-car
Can, box la boîte
Can opener l'ouvre-boîtes *m*
Canada Canada
Canadian (person) Canadien, ienne
Canal le canal
To cancel *(room reservation)* décommander; *(travel tickets)* annuler
Cancer le cancer; le crabe
Candles les bougies *f*
Candy le bonbon
Canoe le canoë
Cap la casquette
Capital la capitale
Captain le capitaine
Car radio l'autoradio *m*
Carafe la carafe
Careful prudent, e
Carnival le carnaval
Carrots les carottes *f*
Case la caisse
Cash les espèces *f*
Cash register la caisse
Casino le casino
Casserole en daube
Cassette la cassette
Cassette recorder le lecteur de cassettes
Castle le château
Cat le chat

To catch attraper
Caterer le traiteur
Cathedral la cathédrale
Cauliflower le chou-fleur
To cause causer
Cave la caverne
CD/compact disk le CD
CD player le lecteur de CD
Ceiling le plafond
Celery le céleri
Cell phone le portable
Cemetery le cimetière
Center le centre
Centimeter le centimètre
Central central, e
Central heat le hauffage central
Central post office la poste
  principale
Century le siècle
Ceramics la céramique
Certain *adj* certain, e; *adv*
  sûrement
Certificate l'attestation *f*, le
  certificat
Chain *(jewelry)* le collier; *(auto)*
  la chaîne
Chair la chaise
Chairlift le télésiège
Chambermaid la femme de
  chambre
Chamomile tea l'infusion de
  camomille
Champagne le champagne
Change *(money)* la monnaie
To change changer
Change le change; Exchange
  l'échange *m*
To change clothes se changer
Change office le bureau de
  change
Changing of the guard la
  relève de la garde
Changing table la table à langer
Chapel la chapelle
Charcoal le charbon de bois
Charger le rechargeur

Charges les droits *m pl*; les
  charges *f*
Cheap bon marché
To check in faire les formalités *f*
  d'embarquement
Cheese le fromage
Cherries les cerises *f*
Chest la poitrine
Chewing gum le chewing-gum
Chicken le poulet
Chicken pox la varicelle
Chickpeas les pois *m* chiches
Child l'enfant *m/f*
Childcare la garderie
Childhood disease la maladie
  infantile
Children's clothing les habits *m*
  pour enfants
Children's discount la
  réduction-enfants
Children's menu le menu
  enfants
Children's ticket le billet
  enfants
Child's bed le lit d'enfant
Child's seat le siège-enfants
Child's seat *(for car)* le
  réhausseur
Chills les frissons *m*
Chocolate le chocolat
Chocolate bar la barre de
  chocolat
Choice le choix
Choir le chœur
Cholera le choléra
To choose choisir
Chop la côtelette
Christianity le christianisme
Christmas Noël
Christmas Eve la veille de Noël,
  le réveillon
Church *(Catholic)* l'église *f*;
  (Protestant) le temple
Church tower le clocher
Cigar le cigare
Cigarette la cigarette

Cigarillo le cigarillo
Circulatory troubles les troubles *m* de la circulation
Circus le cirque
City la ville
City bus le bus
City map le plan de la ville
City walls les murs *m* de la ville
Clams les palourdes *f*
Class la classe
Classic le classique
Classical music la musique classique
Classicism le classicisme
To clean nettoyer, faire le ménage
Clean propre *adj*
Clear clair, e
Clearance sale les soldes *m pl*
Client le client/la cliente
Cliff la falaise
Climate le climat
Cloister le cloître
To close fermer
Closed fermé, e
Closed season la période de fermeture de la pêche
Cloth le drap
Clothesline la corde à linge
Clothespins les pinces *f* à linge
Clothing les vêtements *m pl*
Cloud le nuage
Cloudy nuageux
Clove les clous *m* de girofle
Clubhouse le châlet, la clubhouse
Clutch l'embrayage *m*
Coach le car
Coast la côte
Coat le manteau; *(men's)* le pardessus
Coat hanger le cintre
Coat room le vestiaire
Coconut la noix de coco
Code le code
Coffee le café
Coffee machine la machine à café

Cog railway le chemin de fer à crémaillère
Coin la pièce de monnaie
Coin purse le porte-monnaie
Cold le rhume
Cold froid, e
Cold cuts les tranches *f* de charcuterie/ de viande froide
Cold water l'eau froide
Colic la colique
Collarbone la clavicule
Colleague le/ collègue, le/ confrère
To collect collectionner
Collect call l'appel *m* en P.C.V.
Collision le choc, la collision
To color faire une coloration
Colored de couleur
Colored pencil le crayon de couleur
Coloring book l'album *m* à colorier
Column la colonne
Comb le peigne
To comb peigner
To come venir
Come in! Entrez!
Comedy la comédie
Comfortable confortable
Common *adj* commun, e
Communication la communication
Companion l'accompagnateur *m*/l'accompagnatrice *f*
Company l'entreprise *f*
Compartment le compartiment
Compass la boussole
Compatriot le compatriote
Compensation la compensation
Competition la compétition
To complain about se plaindre de
Composer le compositeur/ la compositrice
Comprehensive insurance l'assurance tous risques

Concert le concert
Concussion la commotion cérébrale
Condom le préservatif
Conductor le contrôleur/la contrôleuse
Confectioner's shop la confiserie
Confidence la confiance
To confirm confirmer
To confiscate confisquer
To confuse confondre
To congratulate féliciter
Congratulations les félicitations *f pl*
Connection la correspondance
To consist of se composer de
Constipation la constipation
Construction site le chantier
Consulate le consulat
Consultation *(e.g., with doctor)* la consultation
Contact le contact
Contagious contagieux
Container le récipient
Contents le contenu
Continent le continent
Contraceptive le contraceptif
Contract le contrat
Contrary le contraire
Convent le couvent
Conversation la conversation
Cook le cuisinier/ la cuisinière
To cook faire la cuisine
Cookbook le livre de cuisine
Cookies les biscuits *m*
Cool frais, fraîche
Coolant l'eau *f* de refroidissement
Cooler la glacière
Copy la copie
Corkscrew le tire-bouchon
Corn le maïs
Corner le coin
Corpus Christi la Fête-Dieu
Corridor le couloir
Corridor width la largeur du couloir

To cost coûter
Costume jewelry les bijoux *m* fantaisie
Cotton le coton
Cotton swab le coton-tige
Couchette la couchette
Cough la toux
Cough syrup le sirop contre la toux
Count compter
Counter-indications la contre-indication
Country le pays
Country house la maison de vacances/ de campagne
Country sticker la plaque de nationalité
Couple le couple
Coupon le bon
Course le cours
Course *(food)* le plat
Court le tribunal
Courtyard la cour
Cousin le/la cousin/e
Cramp la crampe
Crazy fou, folle
Cream la crème
Creative créatif, -ive
Credit card la carte de crédit
Crew *(ship)* l'équipage *m*
Crime le crime
Cross la croix
Cross-country ski track la piste de ski de fond
Cross-country skiing le ski de fond
Crossing le passage
Crossroad le carrefour
Crown la couronne
Cruise la croisière
Crutch la béquille
To cry pleurer
Crystal le cristal
Cucumber le concombre; Pickle le cornichon
Culture la culture
Cumin le cumin

Cup la tasse
Cupboard l'armoire *f*
Cupola la coupole, le dôme
Curious curieux, -euse
Curlers les bigoudis *m*
Curling le curling
Curls les boucles *f*
Currency les devises *f*; la monnaie
Current *(elec.)* le courant
Curve le virage
Customs la douane
Customs declaration la déclaration en douane
Customs duties les droits de douane
Cut la coupure
To cut someone's hair coiffer
Cuttlefish la seiche
Cycling le cyclisme

D

Daily special le plat du jour
Dairy products store la laiterie
To damage endommager
Damaged abîmé, e; **Rotten** pourri, e
To dance danser
Dance band l'orchestre *m* de danse
Dance theater le théâtre de la danse
Dancer le danseur/ la danseuse
Dandruff les pellicules *f*
Danger le danger
Dangerous dangereux, -euse
Dark sombre
Dark bread le pain noir
Darkened foncé
Date la date
Date of birth la date de naissance
Daughter la fille
Day le jour

Day after tomorrow après-demain
Day before yesterday avant-hier
Day excursion l'excursion *f* pour une journée
Day pass le forfait-journée
Day ticket le billet pour une journée
Day trip la randonnée (pour la journée)
Deaf sourd
Deaf and dumb le/la sourd/e-muet/te
Deaf-mute sourd-muet
Deaf person le sourd/la sourde; le malentendant
Dear cher, chère *adj*
Dear le chéri, la chérie *m/f*
Debt la dette
December décembre
To decide décider (de)
Declaration of value la déclaration de valeur
To declare faire une déclaration; affirmer
Decorative arts les arts *m* décoratifs
Deep profond, e
Defect la panne
Definitive *adj* définitif, -ive; *adv* définitivement
Delay le retard
Delicatessen *(international specialties)* l'épicerie *f* fine
Delicious délicieux
Demonstration la manifestation
Denatured alcohol l'alcool *m* à brûler
Deodorant le déodorant
Department store le grand magasin
Departure le départ; la sortie
Departure time l'heure *f* de départ
Departure; takeoff le départ, le décollage

Deposit le gage; la caution; *(bottles and cans)* la consigne
To describe décrire
Dessert le dessert
Destination la destination
Detective movie le film policier
Detour la déviation; le détour
To develop développer
Device l'appareil *m*
Dextrose la dextrose
Diabetes le diabète
Diabetic le diabétique
Diagnosis le diagnostic
To dial *(phone number)* composer (un numéro)
Diapers les couches *f*
Diarrhea la diarrhée
Diet le régime
Difficult difficile
Digestion la digestion
Digestive track le tube digestif
Digestive trouble les troubles *m* digestifs
Digital camera l'appareil *m* photo digital
Dike la digue
Dining car le wagon-restaurant
Dining room la salle à manger
Dinner le dîner
Diphtheria la diphtérie
Direct direct, e
Direction la direction
Direction (theater) la mise en scène
Director le directeur/la directrice
Dirty sale
Disappointed déçu, e
Discotheque la discothèque
Discount la réduction; la remise
To discover découvrir
Dish le plat
Dish towel le torchon
Dishes la vaisselle
Dishwasher le lave-vaisselle
Dishwashing brush la brosse pour la vaisselle

Dishwashing soap le produit pour la vaisselle
To disinfect désinfecter
Disinfectant l'antiseptique *m*
To dispense dépenser
Display window la vitrine
Distance la distance *f*
Distant éloigné, e
Distinguished distingué, e
To disturb déranger
To dive faire de la plongée
Diving gear l'équipement *m* de plongée
Diving goggles les lunettes *f* de plongée
Dizziness le vertige
Dizzy pris, e de vertige
To do faire
Dock le quai
Documentary film le documentaire
Dog le chien
Domestic flight le vol intérieur
Door la porte
Dosage la posologie
Double le double
Downstairs en bas
Downtown le centre-ville
Drama le drame
To draw dessiner
Drawing le dessin
Drawing from a model le dessin sur modèle
Dream le rêve
Dress la robe
Drink la boisson, la consommation
To drink boire
Drinking water l'eau *f* potable
To drive conduire
Driver le chauffeur/la chauffeuse
Driver's license le permis de conduire
Drops les gouttes *f*
Drugstore la pharmacie; la droguerie

Drugstore item articles d'hygiène

Drunk soûl, e; ivre

To dry sécher

Dry cleaner le pressing

Dry cleaning nettoyer (à sec); la teinturerie

Dry hair les cheveux secs

Dry (wine) sec

Dryer le sèche-linge

Dual double

Dumb bête

During *prp* pendant

During the day pendant la journée

During the week pendant la semaine

Dust la poussière

Duty free exempt de droits de douane

Duty-free shop la boutique hors-taxes

Dynasty la dynastie

E

Each *adj* chaque; **Every one** *prn* chacun, e

Ear l'oreille *f*

Ear drops les gouttes *f* pour les oreilles

Ear infection l'otite *f*

Eardrum le tympan

Earlier plus tôt

Early tôt

Earrings les boucles *f* d'oreilles

Earth la terre

East l'Est *m*

East of à l'est de

Easter Pâques *f*

Easter Monday le lundi de Pâques

Easy facile

To eat breakfast prendre son petit déjeuner, déjeuner

Edible comestible

Eel l'anguille *f*

Eggplant les aubergines *f*

Eggs les œufs *m*

Either ... or ou ... ou, ou bien ... ou bien

Elastic band la bande élastique

Electric rate le forfait électicité

Electric stove la cuisinière électrique

Electric wheelchair le fauteuil roulant électrique

Electrical *adj* électrique

Electrical appliance store le magasin d'électro-ménager

Electrolyte solution la solution de réhydratation

Elevator l'ascenseur *m*; la plate-forme; l'élévateur

Elsewhere ailleurs

Embassy l'ambassade *f*

Emblem l'emblème *m*

Embroidery la broderie

Emergency l'urgence

Emergency brake le signal d'alarme

Emergency exit la sortie de secours

Emergency flashers les feux *m* de détresse

Emergency phone le téléphone de secours

Emperor/empress l'empereur *m*/ l'impératrice *f*

Empty vide

En route en cours de route

To encounter rencontrer

End la fin

Endive l'endive *f*

England Angleterre

English anglais, e

English Channel la Manche

English (person) Anglais, e

Enough assez, suffisamment

To enter entrer

Entertainment la distraction

Enthusiastic (about) enthousiasmé, e (par)
Entrance l'entrée *f*
Entry price le prix d'entrée
Envelope l'enveloppe *f*
Environment l'environnement *m*
Epilepsy l'épilepsie f
Epiphany la Fête des Rois, l'Epiphanie
Epoch l'époque *f*
Error l'erreur *f*
Especially surtout
Etching (la gravure à) l'eau-forte
Ethnological museum le musée ethnologique
EU citizen le/la citoyen européen/ne
euro l'euro *m*
Europe l'Europe *f*
European européen, ne
European person l'Européen *m*/l'Européenne *f*
Even même
Evening le soir, la soirée
Evening dress les vêtements *m* habillés
Every hour toutes les heures
Everyday tous les jours
Everything tout
Everywhere partout
Exact exact, e
Examination l'examen *m*, l'analyse *f*
Example l'exemple *m* ; For example par exemple
Excavations les fouilles *f*
Excellent excellent, e
Except for hors de
To exchange échanger
Exchange rate le cours de change
Excursion l'excursion *f*
Excuse l'excuse *f*
To excuse oneself s'excuser
To exercise s'exercer, s'entraîner
Exhaust pipe le tuyau d'échappement

Exhausted épuisé, e
Exhibit la pièce d'exposition
Exit la sortie
Exit ramp la sortie (d'autoroute)
Expenses les frais *m pl*
Expensive cher, chère
Exposition l'exposition *f*
Express letter la lettre exprès
Expression l'expression *f*
Expressionism l'expressionnisme *m*
Expressly expressément
Extension cord la rallonge
Extent l'étendue *f*
External *(use)* externe
Extra week la semaine supplémentaire
Extraordinary extraordinaire
Eye drops le collyre
Eyes les yeux *m*

F

Fabric l'étoffe *f*
Face le visage
Factory l'usine *f*
Fainting spell l'évanouissement *m*, la syncope
Fair (carnival) le fête foraine
Fair la kermesse
To fall tomber
False faux, fausse
Family la famille
Family name le nom de famille
Famous célèbre
Fan le ventilateur
Fan belt la courroie de transmission
Fanfare la fanfare
Far loin
Farm la ferme
Fashion la mode
Fast *adj* rapide; *adv* vite
Fast lane la voie rapide
Fasting jeûne

Fat gros, grosse
Fat-free milk le lait écrémé
Father le père
Fatty gras, grasse
Faucet le robinet
Fault la faute
Fax le fax
Fax machine le télécopieur
Façade la façade
To fear craindre; avoir peur de
February février
To feel sentir
Feeling le sentiment
Fennel le fenouil
Ferry *(river)* le bac, *(ocean)* le ferry
Festival le festival
Fever la fièvre; Temperature la température
Fiancé(e) le fiancé/la fiancée
Field le champ; la lande
Figs les figues *f*
To fill out remplir
Filling le plombage
Film le film
Final cleaning le nettoyage de fin de séjour
Finally enfin; finalement
To find trouver
To find (oneself) se trouver
Fine l'amende *f*
Finger le doigt
Fire le feu
Fire alarm l'avertisseur *m* d'incendie
Fire extinguisher l'extincteur *m*
Firemen les pompiers *m pl*
Fireworks le feu d'artifice
Firm ferme; Hard dur, e
First premier, -ière *adj*
First d'abord *adv*
First gear la première
First name le prénom
To fish pêcher
Fish le poisson
Fish bone l'arête *f*
Fish market la poissonnerie

Fish merchant le poissonnier
Fishing license le permis (de pêche)
Fishing rod la canne à pêche
Fishing village le village de pêcheurs
Fit en forme
To fit convenir
Fitness center le centre de gymnastique
Fixed price le prix forfaitaire
Flash attachment le flash
Flask la gourde
Flat plat, e
Flat tire le pneu crevé
Flatulence les vents *m*
Flea market la foire à la brocante, le marché aux puces
Flight le vol
Floor le plancher
Floor (story) l'étage *m*
Flotation ring la bouée
Flour la farine
Flower la fleur
Flower shop le/la fleuriste
Flush la chasse d'eau
To fly voler
Fly *(insect)* la mouche
Fog le brouillard
Fold-out couch la banquette-lit
Folding wheelchair le fauteuil roulant pliant
Folk play la musique folklorique
Folklore le folklore
Folklore evening la soirée folklorique
Following le suivant, la suivante
Food la nourriture
Food poisoning l'intoxication *f* alimentaire
Foot le pied
Footbridge la passerelle
For pour *prep*
For *conj* car
To force oneself s'efforcer de
Foreign étranger, -ère
Foreign country l'étranger *m*

Foreign person l'étranger/
l'étrangère
Forest la forêt
To forget oublier
Fork la fourchette
Form le formulaire
Formerly autrefois
Fortress la forteresse
To forward faire suivre
Forward en avant
Fountain la fontaine
France la France
Fraud l'escroquerie *f*; la fraude
Free libre; gratuit, e
Free gratuitement *adv*
Freeze le gel
French français, e
French woman la Française
Frenchman le Français
Fresh frais, fraîche
Friday vendredi
Fried frit
Friend l'ami/l'amie, le copain/
la copine
Friendly aimable
To frighten effrayer
Frightful affreux, -euse
From *(origin)* de
From the grill sur le gril
From time to time de temps en
temps
Fruit les fruits *m*
Fruit and vegetable shop le
magasin de fruits et légumes
Full qui n'a plus faim
Full plein, e; *(occupied)* complet,
-ète Complete entier, -ière
Full pension la pension complète
Fun l'amusement *m*
To function fonctionner
Furious furieux, -euse
Furniture (piece of) le meuble
Fuses les plombs *m pl*, les
fusibles *m pl*
Future l'avenir *m*
Future *(tense)* futur, e

G

Gallbladder la vésicule biliaire
Gallery la galerie (de peinture)
Game le match
Garage le garage
Garden le jardin
Garlic l'ail *m*
Gas bottle la bouteille de gaz
Gas can le bidon d'essence
Gas cylinder la cartouche de gaz
Gas pedal l'accélérateur *m*
Gas pump la pompe à essence
Gas range la cuisinière à gaz
Gas stove le réchaud à gaz
Gas tank le réservoir
Gauze la gaze
General delivery poste restante
Generator la dynamo
German measles la rubéole
To get angry over se mettre en
colère à cause de
To get gas prendre de l'essence
To get lost s'égarer
To get married se marier
To get off descendre
To get up se lever
Gift le cadeau
Girl la demoiselle; la (jeune) fille
To give donner
To give a gift offrir
To give back retourner
Gladly volontiers; Unwillingly à
contre-cœur
Glass le verre
Glass painting la peinture sur
verre
Gliding le vol à voile
Gloves les gants *m*
To go aller
To go back revenir
To go camping camper
To go hiking faire de la
randonnée
To go out sortir

To go shopping faire ses courses
To go up monter
Goal *(soccer)* le but *m*; Goalpost le poteau des buts
Goalie le gardien de buts
Goat cheese le fromage de chèvre
God Dieu
Gold l'or *m*
Golden doré
Goldsmith's art l'orfèvrerie *f*
Golf le golf
Golf club *(association)* le club de golf
Golf club *(implement)* la crosse de golf
Gone parti, e
Good *adj* bon, bonne; Well *adv* bien
Good Friday le vendredi saint
Gothic le gothique
Government le gouvernement
Gram le gramme
Grandfather le grand-père
Grandmother la grand-mère
Grandson le petit-fils; Granddaughter la petite-fille
Grapefruit le pamplemousse
Grapes les raisins *m*
Graphic art l'art *m* graphique
Gratiné gratiné
Grave la tombe
Gravel le gravillon
Gray gris
Gray card *(auto registration)* la carte grise
Greek grec
Green vert
Green beans les haricots *m* verts
Green card *(insurance card)* la carte verte
To greet saluer
To greet recevoir; To welcome accueillir
Grill le gril
Grippe la grippe

Grocery store l'épicerie *f*
Groin le bas-ventre
Grotto la grotte
Ground le sol; le terrain
Ground level le rez-de-chaussée
Ground level (at) au niveau du sol, surbaissé
Group le groupe
Guarantee la garantie
Guest l'hôte *m*, l'invité, e
Guide le/la guide
Guided tour la visite guidée
Guided tour of the city la visite guidée de la ville
Gums les gencives *f*
Gust of wind la rafale
Gymnastics la gymnastique

H

Hair les cheveux
Hair band l'élastique *m*
Hair dryer le sèche-cheveux
Hair gel le gel pour les cheveux
Hairdresser le coiffeur/la coiffeuse
Hairpins les épingles *f* à cheveux
Hairspray le fixateur
Hairstyle la coiffure, la coupe de cheveux
Half *adj* demi, e; *adv* à demi, à moitié; *n* la moitié
Half pension la demi-pension
Ham le jambon
Hamburger la viande hachée
Hammer le marteau
Hand la main
Hand brake le frein à main
Hand cream la crème pour les mains
Hand towel la serviette de toilette
Handbag le sac à main
Handball le hand-ball

Handicap-accessible aménagé/équipé pour handicapés

Handicap-accessible cabin (ship) la cabine équipée pour handicapés

Handicap-accessible car (train) le wagon aménagé pour handicapés

Handicap Association l'association *f* de handicapés

Handicap ID la carte d'invalidité

Handicap parking la place de stationnement pour handicapés

Handicap toilet les toilettes *f* pour handicapés

Handle la poignée

Handmade fait main

Handrail la rampe

Hang glider le deltaplane

Happy heureux, -euse; content, e

Happy (about) heureux, -euse (de)

Hard dur, e

Hardware store la quincaillerie

Hat le chapeau

To have avoir

To have an accident avoir un accident

To have to devoir

Hay fever le rhume des foins

He il, lui

Head tête

Headscarf le foulard

Headache pills les cachets *m* contre les maux de tête

Headaches les maux *m* de tête

Headlight le phare

Headphones les écouteurs *m*

Health and advice center le centre social de soins

Health food store le magasin de produits naturels

Health insurance la caisse d'assurance-maladie

Health insurance card la feuille de maladie/ de soins

Healthy en bonne santé

To hear entendre

Hearing l'ouïe *f*

Hearing impaired malentendant

Heart le cœur

Heart attack la crise cardiaque

Heart-felt cordial, e

Heart trouble les troubles *m* cardiaques

Heartburn les aigreurs *f* d'estomac

Heat le chauffage; la chaleur

Heat wave la canicule, la vague de chaleur

Heaven le ciel

Heavy lourd, e

To heed respecter

Heel le talon

Height la hauteur, l'altitude *f*

Help l'aide *f*; First aid les premiers secours

To help someone aider qn

Herbs les herbes *f*

Here ici

Hernia la hernie

Herring le hareng

High haut, e

High beams les feux *m* de route

High point le grand moment; *(fame, power)* l'apogée

High tide la marée haute

High voltage haute tension

Highway l'autoroute *f*

Hiking map la carte de randonnées

Hiking trail le chemin de randonnée

Hill la colline

Hip la hanche

His *poss prn* son, sa

History l'histoire *f*

Hitchhike faire de l'auto-stop

Hoarse enroué

To hold tenir

Holdup *(person)* l'agression *f*; Robbery *(bank)* le hold-up

Hole le trou

Holy saint, e
Homeland le pays natal
Homemade (fait) maison
Homeowner le/la propriétaire (de la maison)
Honey le miel
Hood le capot
Hook crochet; *(fishing)* le hameçon
Hopefully espérons que
Horn le klaxon
Horse le cheval
Horseback ride la promenade à cheval
Hospital l'hôpital *m*
Hospitality l'hospitalité *f*
Host/hostess l'hôte *m*/ l'hôtesse *f*
Hot chaud, e
Hot air balloon la montgolfière
Hot pepper le piment
Hot water l'eau chaude
Hour l'heure *f*; le cours; A half hour une demi-heure; A quarter hour un quart d'heure
House la maison
House/building number le numéro de la maison/ de l'immeuble
Houseboat la péniche
Household goods les articles *m* ménagers
Hovercraft l'hovercraft *m*, l'aéroglisseur *m*
How comment; As *(comparison)* comme
However pourtant
Human l'homme *m*; l'être *m* humain
Humid lourd
Hurried pressé, e; To be in a hurry être pressé, e
To hurry se dépêcher
To hurt faire mal
Husband le mari
Hut *(alpine)* le châlet
Hydroplane l'hydroglisseur *m*

I je, moi
Ice le verglas
Ice cream la glace
Ice hockey le hockey sur glace
Ice skates les patins *m* à glace
Idea l'idée *f*
If si
If you wish si tu veux/ si vous voulez
Ignition l'allumage *m*
Ignition key la clé de contact
Illness la maladie
Immediately tout de suite
Impaired vision malvoyant
Important important, e
Impossible impossible
Impressionism l'impressionnisme *m*
Impressive impressionnant
Improbable invraisemblable
In dans, en
In addition d'autre part, en outre
In advance par avance
In case au cas où
In cash en espèces
In French en français
In front of devant; Before avant
In-line roller skate le roller
In one week dans une semaine
In the afternoon à l'après-midi
In the evening le soir
In the morning dans la matinée; le matin
In the short term à court terme
In writing par écrit
Inappropriate impropre
Incident l'incident *m*
Incline la pente
Included compris, e
Indications indications *f*
Infant le nourisson
Infarction l'infarctus *m*
Infection l'infection *f*
Inflammable inflammable

Inflammation l'inflammation *f*
Inflatable boat le canot
  pneumatique
To inform informer
Information le renseignement;
  l'information *f*
Inhabitant l'habitant/e *m/f*
Injured person le blessé/la
  blessée
Inner courtyard la cour
  intérieur
Inner tube la chambre à air
Inscription l'inscription *f*
Insect l'insecte *m*
Insect repellant produit contre
  les insectes
Inside à l'intérieur, dedans
Insignificant insignifiant, e, sans
  importance
Insomnia l'insomnie *f*
To inspect contrôler
Inspector le contrôleur
Instead of au lieu de
Instruction l'instruction *f*;
  Training la formation
Insulin l'insuline *f*
Insult l'offense *f*, la vexation
Insurance l'assurance *f*
Intelligent intelligent, e
Interactions les interactions *f.pl*
Intercom l'interphone *m*
To interest s'intéresser (à)
Interesting intéressant, e
Intermission l'entracte *m*
International international, e
International call l'appel *m*
  pour l'étranger
International flight le vol
  international
Interrail Interrail
To interrupt interrompre
Intestine l'instestin *m*
Introduction la présentation
Investment *(money)* le
  placement
To invite inviter
To iron repasser

Island l'île *f*
Island tour le tour de l'île
To itch démanger, gratter
Itinerary l'itinéraire *m*

J

Jack (of a car) le cric
Jacket la veste
January janvier
Jaw la mâchoire
Jazz le jazz
Jazzercise le modern jazz
Jeans le jean
Jelly la confiture
Jeweler la bijouterie
Jewelry les bijoux *m*
To jog faire du jogging
Jogging pants le pantalon de
  jogging
Joint l'articulation *f*
Joke la plaisanterie
Judge le/la juge
Juicy juteux
July juillet
Jumper cables le câble de
  démarrage
June juin
Just the same malgré cela

K

Kayak le kayak
To keep garder, conserver
Ketchup le ketchup
Key la clé
Key return la remise des clés
Kiddy pool le bassin pour enfants
Kiddy tow le remonte-pentes
  pour enfants
Kidney le rein
Kidney disease la néphrite
Kidney stone le calcul rénal

Kilo le kilogramme, le kilo
Kilometer le kilomètre
King le roi
Kiss le baiser
To kiss embrasser
Kitchen la cuisine
Kitchenette le coin-cuisine
Kitschy kitsch
Knee le genou
Knife le couteau
To know connaître; To make an acquaintance faire de connaissance; To meet faire la connaissance (de)
To know (how) savoir

L

Lace le lacet
Ladies dames
Lake le lac
Lamb l'agneau *m*
Lamp la lampe
Land la terre
Land trip l'excursion *f* à terre
Landing l'atterrissage *m*
Landscape le paysage
Landscape format le format horizontal
Language la langue
Language course le cours de langue
Laptop computer le portable
Last dernier, -ière
To last durer
Last Monday lundi dernier
Lastly en dernier lieu
Late tard
Late season l'arrière-saison *f*
Later plus tard
Laugh rire
Laundromat la laverie
Laundry la lessive
Laundry (place) la blanchisserie
Laundry soap la lessive

Laurel le laurier
Lawn la pelouse
Lawyer l'avocat/e *m/f*
Laxative le laxatif
Layer cut la coupe en dégradé
To laze around paresser
Lazy paresseux, -euse; Rotten abîmé
To learn apprendre
Leather goods les articles de maroquinerie
Leather jacket la veste de cuir
Leather shop la maroquinerie
To leave partir (de); quitter; partir
To leave (for) partir (pour)
To leave on a trip partir en voyage
Leek le poireau
Left gauche
Leg la jambe
Lemonade la limonade
Lemons les citrons *m*
Lens la lentille
Lenses les lentilles *f*
Letter la lettre
Lettuce la laitue
Life la vie
Life jacket le gilet de sauvetage
Lifeboat le canot de sauvetage
Lifeguard le maître-nageur
Lifesaver la bouée de sauvetage
Light clair; la lumière
Light *(weight)* léger, -ère
To light allumer
Light bulb l'ampoule *f*
Light meter le photomètre, le posemètre
Light switch l'interrupteur *m*
Lighter l'allume-barbecue *m*
Lighthouse le phare
Lightning l'éclair *m*
To like aimer
Line la ligne
Linen le lin; Canvas la toile
Lip la lèvre
Lipstick le rouge à lèvres
Liquid liquide

Liquor store le magasin de (vins et) spiritueux
To listen to music écouter de la musique
To listen to someone écouter (qn)
Liter le litre
Little peu; ~ un peu a
To live habiter
Live music la musique en direct
Lively vif, vive
Liver le foie
Liver pâté le pâté de foie
Living room la salle de séjour
Loading area for ski lift le point de départ du téléski
To loan prêter
Lobby le hall
Local local, e
Local call la communication en ville
Local train le train de banlieue
Locality la localité
To lock fermer à clé
Lock la serrure
To lodge a complaint faire une réclamation
Lodging l'hébergement *m*
Long long, longue
Long-distance call la communication interurbaine
Look le regard; View *(overlook)* la vue
To look at regarder
To look for chercher
To look forward to se réjouir à l'avance de
Lorraine la Lorraine
To lose perdre
Lost and found le bureau des objets perdus
Lots of beaucoup de
Loud bruyant, e
Lovable aimable
Love l'amour *m*
To love aimer
Low bas, basse

Low beams les codes *m*
Low tide la marée basse
Luck la chance
Luggage lockers la consigne
Lull l'accalmie *f*
Lunch le déjeuner
Lunch bag cooler le pain de glace
Lunchtime le midi
Lung le poumon
Luxurious luxueux, -euse

M

Machine la machine
Mackerel le maquereau
Madame *(direct address, before name)* madame
Magazine le magazine
Magnetic loop la boucle magnétique
Maiden name le nom de jeune fille
Mail box la boîte aux lettres
Main course le plat principal
Main role le rôle principal
Main street la rue principale
Main train station la gare principale
Mainly *adv* principalement
To make faire
To make an error in math faire une erreur de calcul
Male nurse l'infirmier
Man l'homme
Mandarin oranges les mandarines *f*
Manner la manière; Way la façon
Manual controls (auto) les commandes *f* manuelles
Map la carte (géographique)
March mars
Mardi gras le mardi gras
Margarine la margarine

Market le marché
Marriage le mariage
Married marié
Mascara le mascara
Mass *(religion)* la messe
Massage le massage
Match l'allumette *f*
Material le matériel
Mattress le matelas
Mauve lilas, mauve
May mai
Mayonnaise la mayonnaise
Me me, moi
Meadow le pré
Meal le repas
Meaning la signification
Means (way of doing)
  le moyen
Measles la rougeole
Meat la viande
**Medication for the
  circulatory system** le
  médicament pour la circulation
Medicine le médicament
Mediterranean la Méditerranée
Medium rare à point
To meet rencontrer
Meeting la rencontre
Mellow *(wine)* doux/moelleux
Melon *(honey-dew)* le melon;
  (watermelon) la pastèque
Memorial le mémorial
Menstruation les règles *f*
Mentally handicapped
  handicapé mental
Menu le menu; la carte
Merry gai, e
Meter le mètre
Metro le métro
Microwave le micro-ondes
Middle le milieu
Middle Ages le Moyen Age
Migraine la migraine
Mild doux, douce
Milk le lait
Millimeter le millimètre
Mineral water l'eau *f* minérale

Mini-bar la vente ambulante
Miniature golf le minigolf
Minitel dialogue le minitel-
  dialogue
Minute la minute
Mirror le miroir
Miscarriage la fausse-couche
Misfortune le malheur
To miss manquer, rater
Miss *(direct address, before
  name)* mademoiselle
Mistake la faute; **Fault** le défaut
Misunderstanding le
  malentendu
Mixed mixte, mélangé, e
Mobile care unit le centre de
  soins
Model le modèle
Modern moderne; **Fashionable**
  à la mode
Moist humide
Moment l'instant *m*
Monastery le monastère
Monday lundi
Money l'argent *m*
Money order le mandat
Month le mois
Monthly mensuel, le
Monument le monument
Monument protection la
  protection des monuments
Moon la lune
More plus; ~ than plus que, plus
  de
Morning le matin
Mosaic la mosaïque
Mosquito le moustique
Motel le motel
Mother la mère
Motor le moteur
Motorail train *(night)* le train
  autos-couchettes, *(day)* le
  service auto-express
Motorboat le canot automobile
Motorcycle belt la ceinture de
  moto

Motorcycle helmet le casque de moto

Mountain la montagne

Mountain bike le V.T.T. (vélo tout terrain)

Mountain climbing l'alpinisme *m*

Mountain village le village de montagne

Mountains la montagne

Mouth la bouche

Mouth (of river) l'embouchure *f*

Movie le cinéma

Movie actor/actress l'acteur/l'actrice de cinéma

Mr. monsieur

Muesli le musli

Multicolored multicolore

Mumps l'inflammation *f* des amygdales; les oreillons *m*

Muscle le muscle

Muscle pull le claquage (musculaire)

Museum le musée

Music la musique

Music box la boîte à musique

Music shop le magasin de musique

Musical comedy la comédie musicale

Mussels les moules *f*

Mustache la moustache

Mustard la moutarde

Mute muet

Mutton le mouton

My mon, ma

Mycosis la mycose

N

Nail clippers les ciseaux *m* à ongles

Nail polish le vernis à ongles

Nail polish remover le dissolvant

Naked nu, e

Name le nom

Napkin la serviette

Narrow étroit, e

Nasty méchant, e

National national, e

National park le parc national

Nationality la nationalité

Natural *adj* naturel, le; ~ly *adv* naturellement

Nature la nature

Nature preserve la réserve naturelle

Nausea la nausée

Near proche *adj*; près de *adv*

Nearby près

Necessary nécessaire

Neck le cou

Necktie la cravate

To need avoir besoin de

Needle l'aiguille *f*

Negative négatif, -ive

Neighbor le voisin/la voisine

Neighboring street la rue adjacente

Nerve le nerf

Nervous nerveux, -euse

Net le filet

Network la chaîne

Neutral le point mort

Never (ne ...) jamais

New nouveau, nouvel, nouvelle; *(brand new)* neuf, neuve

New Year le Nouvel An

New Year's Eve la Saint-Sylvestre

News la nouvelle

Newspaper le journal

Newspaper merchant le marchand de journaux

Next to à côté de

Next to last avant-dernier, -ière

Next year l'année prochaine

Nice gentil, le; sympathique

Night la nuit
Night table la table de nuit
Nightclub la boîte de nuit
Ninepins le jeu de quilles
No, not any aucun, e
No one (ne ...) personne
Nobody personne
Noise le bruit
Non-binding sans engagement
Non-perishable de longue
  conservation
Non-smoker non-fumeur
Non-smoking section le
  compartiment non-fumeurs
Noodles les nouilles *f*
Noon midi *m*
Normal normal, e
Normally normalement
North le Nord
North of au nord de
North Sea la mer du Nord
Nose le nez
Nose hemorrhage les
  saignements *m* de nez
Not (ne ...) pas; ~ **at all** (ne ...)
  pas du tout
Note pad le bloc
Nothing (ne ...) rien
To notice remarquer
Not much un peu
Novel le roman
November novembre
Now maintenant, à présent
Nowhere nulle part
Nude le nu
Nudist beach la plage de
  nudistes
Number le numéro; le nombre
Number plate la plaque
  d'immatriculation
Nurse l'infirmière
Nutmeg la noix de muscade
Nuts les noix *f*

O

Oar la rame
Oatmeal les flocons *m* d'avoine
Object l'objet *m*
Objective lens l'objectif *m*
Observatory l'observatoire *m*
Occasionally *adv* à l'occasion
Occupied occupé, e
Ocean la mer
October octobre
Of *(material)* en
To offer offrir
Office le bureau
Official officiel, le
Offside hors-jeu
Often *adv* fréquemment; souvent
Oil l'huile *f*
Oil change la vidange
Oil painting la peinture à l'huile
Old vieux, vieil, le; *(from earlier
  times)* ancien/ne
Old city la vieille ville
Olive oil l'huile *f* d'olive
Olives les olives *f*
On sur
On an empty stomach à jeun
On/off ramp la bretelle
On Sunday dimanche
On tap pression
On the right à droite
On the weekend ce week-end
On time *adv* à temps, à l'heure
Once une fois
One *(indefinite pronoun)* on
Onions les oignons *m*
Only seulement, ne ... que
Open ouvert, e
To open ouvrir
Open car le wagon sans
  compartiments
Opera l'opéra *m*
Operation l'opération *f*
Operetta l'opérette *f*
Opinion l'opinion *f*
Opposite opposé, e

Optician l'opticien *m*
Or ou
Orange orange
Orange juice le jus d'orange
Oranges les oranges *f*
Orchestra l'orchestre *m*;
    (theater) le parterre
Orchestra conductor le/la chef
    d'orchestre
Order la commande
Organized trip le voyage
    organisé
Original l'original *m*
Original version la version
    originale (la v.o.)
Other (the) l'autre
Otherwise *adv* autrement
Our notre, nos
Outdoor movie le cinéma en
    plein air
Outdoors à l'extérieur; dehors
Outside à l'extérieur (de)
Over there là-bas
Overnight la nuit
Own propre
Owner le propriétaire
Oxygen cylinder la bouteille
    d'oxygène
Oysters les huîtres *f*

P

Pacemaker le stimulateur
    cardiaque
Pacifier la tétine; la sucette (de
    caoutchouc)
Package le paquet
Packing l'emballage
Paddle faire du canoë/ du kayak
Pain pills les cachets *m* contre la
    douleur
Painful pénible
To paint peindre
Painter le/la peintre
Painting la peinture, le tableau

Pair la paire
Palace le palais
Pants le pantalon
Panty liners les protège-slips *m*
Paper napkins les serviettes *f* en
    papier
Papers les papiers *m*
Paprika le paprika
Paraglider le parapente
Paralysis la paralysie
Paraplegic paraplégique
Parcel le colis
Parents les parents *m pl*
Park le parc
To park se garer
Parka l'anorak *m*
Parking lights les feux *m* de
    position
Parking space la place de
    stationnement
Parsley le persil
Part la raie; la partie
Particulars l'identité *f*
Party la soirée, la fête
Pass la passe; le col
To pass dépasser
Passenger le passager / la
    passagère
Passing through de passage
Passport le passeport
Passport control le contrôle des
    passeports
Past le passé *n*
Past passé, e *adj*
Pastry shop la pâtisserie
Patience la patience
To pay payer
To pay in cash payer comptant,
    payer en liquide
Payment le paiement
Peaches les pêches *f*
Pearl la perle
Pears les poires *f*
Peas les petits pois *m*
Pedal boat le pédalo
Pedestrian le/ piéton

Pedestrian area la zone piétonne

Pediatrician le/la pédiatre

Pediment le fronton

Penalty la peine; **Fine** l'amende *f*

Penalty box la surface de réparation

Pendant *(jewelry)* le pendentif

Pension la pension (de famille)

Pentecost la Pentecôte

Pentecost Monday le lundi de Pentecôte

People les gens *m pl*; le peuple

Pepper le poivre

Pepper mill le moulin à poivre

Percent pour cent

Perch la perche

Performance la représentation; le spectacle

Perfume le parfum

Perfume shop la parfumerie

Perhaps peut-être

Permanent (hair) la permanente

Person la personne

Person in a wheelchair la personne en fauteuil roulant

Person with reduced mobility la personne à mobilité réduite

Personal personnel, le

Personal ID card la carte d'identité

Petroleum le pétrole

Pets les animaux *m* domestiques

Phone book l'annuaire *m*

Phone booth la cabine téléphonique

Phone call le coup de téléphone

Phone number le numéro de téléphone

Photo la photo

Photograph la photographie

To photograph photographier

Photography shop le magasin de photos

Physical handicap le handicap physique

To pick up aller chercher

To pick up *(telephone)* décrocher

Pickpocket le voleur à la tire, le pickpocket

Pickup la levée

Piece la pièce; **A piece of bread** un morceau de pain

Pilgrimage site le lieu de pèlerinage

Pill *(contraceptive)* la pillule (anticonceptionnelle)

Pillow l'oreiller *m*

Pilot le/la pilote

PIN (personal identification number) le numéro de code

Pineapple l'ananas *m*

Ping-pong le ping-pong

Pink rose

Place le lieu; la place

Place of birth le lieu de naissance

Place settings les couverts *m*

Plain la plaine

Plant la plante

Plastic bag le sac en plastique

Plastic wrap le film alimentaire

Plate l'assiette *f*

Platform le quai

To play jouer

Play la pièce de théâtre

To play music faire de la musique

Playground l'aire *f* de jeux

Playmate le copain/ la copine (de jeux)

Pleasant agréable; sympa

To please plaire

Pleasure le plaisir

Plug la fiche

To plug in brancher

Plums les prunes *f*

Pneumonia la pneumonie

Pocket la poche

Pocket knife le couteau de poche
Pocketbook le livre de poche
Poison le poison
Poisoning l'empoisonnement *m*
Poisonous toxique
Polaroid camera le polaroïd
Police la police
Police car la voiture de police
Policeman l'agent *m* de police
Polio la polio(myélite)
Polite poli, e
Poor pauvre
Popular play la pièce populaire
Porcelain la porcelaine
Pork le porc
Pork sausage la charcuterie
Port le port
Portable CD player le baladeur
Portal le portail
Porter le portier, le/la concierge
Portion la portion
Portrait le portrait
Portrait format le format en hauteur
Possible possible
Post office le bureau de poste
Postal code le code postal
Postcard la carte postale
Poster l'affiche *f*
To postpone remettre à plus tard, repousser
Potatoes les pommes *f* de terre
Pots and pans la poterie
Pottery la poterie
Pound la livre
Powder la poudre
Powder snow la (neige) poudreuse
Practical pratique
Prawn les crevettes *f* roses
To pray prier
Pre-season l'avant-saison *f*
Precinct le quartier
Prefix l'indicatif *m*
Pregnancy la grossesse

Premiere la première
To prepare préparer
To prescribe prescrire
Prescription l'ordonnance *f*
Preserves les conserves
Pretty joli, e
To prevent empêcher
Previously avant
Price le prix
Price per kilometer le prix au kilomètre
Priest le prêtre
Prison la prison
Private privé, e
Probably *adv* probablement
Problem le problème
Procession la procession; le cortège
Product le produit
Profession la profession
Profit le bénéfice; Enrichment l'enrichissement *m*
Program *(theater)* le programme
Program booklet le programme
Prohibited interdit, e
To pronounce prononcer
Property la propriété, le domaine
Proposition la proposition
Prospectus le prospectus
Prosthesis la prothèse
Protective custody la détention préventive
Provisions les provisions *f pl*
Public public, -ique
To pull tirer
Pullover le pull-over
Pulse le pouls
Pump la pompe
Pumpkin le potiron
To punch *(ticket)* composter
Punctual à l'heure
Pus le pus
To put down déposer
To put on *(clothing)* mettre

Q

Quality la qualité
Queen la reine
Question la question

R

Rabbit le lapin
Racing bike le vélo de course
Racket la raquette
Radar control le contrôle radar
Radiator le radiateur
Radio la radio
Rag le torchon
Railroad station la gare
Rain la pluie
Rain shower l'averse *f*
Raincoat l'imperméable *m*
Rainy pluvieux
Ramp la rampe
Ramp access l'accès *m* sans
  marche
Rape le viol
Rare *adj* rare; ~ly *adv* rarement
Rash les rougeurs *f*
Rather assez
Ravishing ravissant, e
Raw cru
Razor le rasoir
Razorblades les lames *f* de rasoir
To read lire
Ready prêt, e
Real *adj* véritable
Really *adv* en fait, à vrai dire; *adv*
  vraiment
Rearview mirror le rétroviseur
Reason la raison
Receipt le reçu
To receive recevoir
Receiver le combiné
Reception la réception
To recommend recommander
To recover se rétablir

Red rouge
Red wine le (vin) rouge
Refreshments les
  rafraîchissements
Refrigerator le réfrigérateur, le
  frigo
Refuge le refuge
To refuse refuser
Region la région
Regional costume le costume
  régional/folklorique
To register inscrire
Registered letter la lettre
  recommandée
Registration l'inscription
To regret regretter
Regular *adj* régulier, -ière; ~ly
  adv régulièrement
Regular customer habitué, e
Regulation la directive, le
  règlement
Relationship la relation
Relative parent, e
Religion la religion
To remain rester
Remains les vestiges *m*, les
  restes *m*
To remark remarquer
Remedy le remède
To remember retenir qc; se
  souvenir
**To remind someone about
  something** rappeler qc à qn
Renaissance la Renaissance
Rent le loyer
To rent louer
To repair réparer
To repair *(damage)* réparer
To repeat répéter
To replace remplacer
Request la demande
Reservation la location, la
  réservation
To reserve retenir, réserver
Residence le domicile
Respiratory difficulties les
  troubles *m* respiratoires

Responsible compétent, e, responsable
To rest se reposer
Rest le repos
Rest area l'aire f de repos, l'aire f de service
To return rendre, remettre
Return le retour
Return trip le retour
Reverse la marche arrière
Reward la récompense
Rheumatism le rhumatisme
Rice le riz
Rich riche
To ride a bicycle faire du vélo
To ride horseback faire du cheval
Ridiculous ridicule
Riding school l'école f d'équitation
Right droit, e n
Right juste adj; (appropriate) bon, bonne
Right away tout de suite
Ring la bague
Ripe mûr, e
River la rivière; le fleuve
Road le chemin
Road map la carte routière
Roast rôti
Roll le petit pain
Roller blades les rollers
Roller skate le patin à roulette
Roof le toit
Room la pièce; la salle; la chambre
Room telephone le téléphone (de la chambre)
Rope la corde
Rosemary le romarin
Rosé wine le (vin) rosé
Round rond, e
Round-trip ticket le billet aller-retour
To row ramer
Rowboat la barque le canot (à rames)

Rubber boots les bottes f en caoutchouc
Ruin la ruine
Ruins les vestiges m archéologiques
To run courir
Ruptured tendon la rupture de tendon

S

Sad triste
Safe le coffre-fort
Safety pin l'épingle f de sûreté
Saffron le safran
Sage la sauge
To sail faire de la voile
Sailboat le bateau à voiles
Sailing cruise la croisière à la voile
Salad la salade
Salad bar le buffet de salades
Salami le salami
Salt le sel
Saltshaker la salière
Salve la pommade
Sand castle le château de sable
Sandals les sandales f
Sandbox le bac à sable
Sandwich le sandwich
Sanitary facilities les installations f sanitaires
Sanitary napkins les serviettes f hygiéniques
Saturday samedi
Sauce la sauce
Saucer la soucoupe
Sauna le sauna
Sausage la saucisse
To savor jouir de, savourer
To say dire
Scar la cicatrice
Scarcely à peine
Scarf l'écharpe f

Schedule l'horaire *m* (de chemin de fer/des bus/ du métro/ des trolleys)
School l'école *f*
School bag la sacoche
School children les écoliers/les écolières
Sciatica la sciatique
Scissors les ciseaux *m*
Screw la vis
To scuba dive faire de la nage sous-marine
Sculptor le sculpteur
Sculpture la sculpture
Sea conditions l'état *m* de la mer
Seagull la mouette
Seaside resort la station balnéaire
Season la saison
To season assaisonner *(with spices)*
Seasoning l'assaisonnement *m*
Seat le siège
Seatbelt la ceinture de sécurité
Second la seconde; deuxième
Second-hand dealer le brocanteur
Secondary road la route secondaire, la route départementale
Secondly deuxièmement
Security check le contrôle de sécurité
Security tax la taxe de sécurité
To see voir
To see to it that procurer
Seeing-eye dog le chien d'aveugle
To select sélectionner
Self-service le self-service
To sell vendre
Seminar le seminaire
To send envoyer
Sender l'expéditeur *m*
Sensitivity la sensibilité
Sentence la phrase

Separately à part
September septembre
Serious sérieux, -euse
To serve servir
Service le service
Service area le restoroute
To set mettre
Severely handicapped person le/la grand/e handicapé/e
To sew up recoudre
Sexual harassment le harcèlement sexuel
Shadow l'ombre *f*
Shame; pity le dommage
Shameless éhonté, e
Shampoo le shampooing
Shape la forme
Shaving brush le blaireau
Shaving cream la mousse à raser
She *f* elle
Sheep's milk cheese le fromage de brebis
Sheet la feuille
Shellfish le coquillage; Mussel la moule
Shinbone le tibia
Shirt la chemise
Shock absorber le pare-chocs
Shoe la chaussure
Shoe brush la brosse à chaussures
Shoe polish le cirage
Shoe store le magasin de chaussures
Shoemaker le cordonnier
Shop la boutique
Short *(measurement)* court, e
Short circuit le court-circuit
Short feature le court-métrage
Shortcut *(travel)* le raccourci
Shorts le short
Shot la piqûre
Shoulder l'épaule *f*
Show le show
To show montrer
Shower la douche
Shower gel la mousse gel

Shower seat la douche assise
Shrimp les crevettes *f*
Shutter release le déclencheur
Shuttle bus la navette
Shuttlecock le volant
Sick malade
Side le côté
Side effects les effets secondaires
Sideburns les pattes *f*
Sights les curiosités *f*
To sign signer
Sign le signe; *(notice)* le panneau
Sign language la langue des signes
Signature la signature
Signpost le poteau indicateur
Silk la soie
Silk painting la peinture sur soie
Silver l'argent *m*
Silvery argenté
Similar semblable; pareil, le
Simple simple
Since depuis
To sing chanter
Singer le chanteur/ la chanteuse
Single le simple
Single color uni
Sink le lavabo; l'évier
Sinus infection la sinusite
Sister la sœur
Sister-in-law la belle-soeur
To sit être assis, e
Situation la situation
Size *(clothing)* la taille; *(shoes)* la pointure
Skateboard la planche à roulettes
Skating le patinage
Skating rink la patinoire
To ski skier, faire du ski
Ski le ski
Ski binding la fixation
Ski boots les chaussures *f* de ski
Ski goggles les lunettes *f* de ski
Ski instructor le moniteur/ monitrice de ski

Ski lessons les cours *m*/leçons *f* de ski
Ski lift le téléski, le remonte-pente
Ski pants le pantalon de ski
Ski poles les bâtons *m*
Skin la peau
Skirt la jupe
Sky diving le parachutisme
Sled la luge
To sleep dormir
Sleeper car la voiture-couchettes; le wagon-lit
Sleeping pills les somnifères *m*
Sleeve la manche
Slender mince
Slice la tranche
Slow *adj* lent, e; **Slowly** *adv* lentement
Small petit, e
Small children (up to age ...) les petits enfants (jusqu'à ... ans)
Smart card la carte à puce
Smell l'odeur *f*
To smell sentir
To smoke fumer
Smoked fumé
Smoker le fumeur
Smoking section le compartiment fumeurs
Snack le casse-croûte
Snake le serpent
Snapshot l'instantané *m*
To sneeze éternuer
To snore ronfler
Snorkel le tuba
Snow la neige
Soap le savon
Soccer le football
Soccer field le terrain de football
Soccer game le match de football
Social services les services m d'aide sociale
Sockettes les socquettes *f*
Socks les chaussettes *f*
Soft mou, molle

Soft cheese le fromage à pâte molle
Softly doucement
Solarium le solarium
Sole la sole
Sole (shoe) la semelle
Solid ground la terre ferme
Soloist le/la soliste
Some quelques
Someone quelqu'un
Something quelque chose
Sometimes quelquefois
Son le fils
Song la chanson
Soon bientôt; As soon as possible dès que possible
Sore throat le mal de gorge
Sore throat lozenges les pastilles *f* contre le mal de gorge
Soup la soupe, le potage
Sour aigre
Sour cream la crème aigre
South le Sud
South of au sud de
Souvenir le souvenir
Souvenir shop le magasin de souvenirs
Space l'espace *f*
Spain l'Espagne *f*
Spaniard l'Espagnol/e
Spanish espagnol, e
Spare tire la roue de secours
To speak parler
Speaker le haut-parleur; *(stereo system)* le baffle
Special spécial, e
Special diet la cuisine diététique
Special issue stamp le timbre de collection
Specialist le/la spécialiste
Specialty la spécialité
Spectator le spectateur
Speed la vitesse
To spell épeler
To spend the night coucher, passer la nuit
Spice l'épice *f*

Spicy épicé
Spinach les épinards *m*
Spinal column la colonne vertébrale
Splint l'attelle *f*
Spoon la cuillère
Sport le sport
Sporting goods store le magasin (d'articles) de sport
Spot la tache
Sprained foulé
Sprayed traité
Spring le printemps
Spring (of water) la source
Square meter le mètre carré
Stadium le stade
Staircase l'escalier *m*
Stamp le timbre; le tampon
To stamp affranchir
Stamp machine le distributeur de timbres
To stand être debout
Star l'étoile *f*
Starter le démarreur
Starting with à partir de
State l'Etat *m*
Stationery le papier à lettres
Stationery store la papeterie
Statue la statue
Stay le séjour
To stay séjourner
To steal voler
Steamer le vapeur
Steep raide
Steering wheel knob le volant mobile
Step le marche-pied
Step la marche
Steward/stewardess le steward/ l'hôtesse *f* de l'air
Stick le bâton
Still encore; calme; Not yet (ne ...) pas encore
Still life la nature morte
To sting piquer
To stink sentir mauvais
To stir fry le plat fait à la poêle

274

Stockings les bas *m*, les chaussettes *f*

Stomach le ventre; l'estomac *m*

Stomachache les maux *m* d'estomac

Stone la pierre

Stony pierreux, -euse

To stop arrêter; *(bus, streetcar, etc.)* s'arrêter

Stop! stop!

Stop lights les stops *m*

To stop over in faire escale à

Stop, station l'arrêt *m*, la station

Stopover l'escale *f*

Storm l'orage *m*; la tempête

Story *(of building)* l'étage *m*

Stove la cuisinière; le réchaud

Straight droit, e

Straight ahead tout droit

Strands les mèches

Stranger l'inconnu(e)

Straw la paille

Strawberries les fraises *f*

Street la rue; Route la route

Streetcar le tram

Strenuous fatigant, e

To stretch out s'étendre; allonger

String la ficelle

Stroke l'embolie *f* cérébrale

Strong fort, e

Studio le studio

To study faire des études

Stuffed farci

Stupid stupide

Style le style

Subject to customs duties soumis aux droits de douane

Subtitles les sous-titres *m*

Suburb la banlieue

Subway le métro

Suddenly soudain, tout à coup

Sugar le sucre

Suit le costume; le tailleur

Suitcase la valise

Sum la somme, le montant

Summer l'été *m*

Summit le sommet

Summit station le point d'arrivée du téléski

Sun le soleil

Sun hat le chapeau de soleil

Sun protection factor (SPF) l'indice *m* de protection

Sunburn le coup de soleil

Sunday dimanche

Sunny ensoleillé

Sunroof le toit ouvrant

Sunscreen la protection solaire

Sunstroke l'insolation *f*

Suntan lotion la crème solaire

Suntan oil l'huile *f* solaire

Supermarket le supermarché

Supplement le supplément

Supplementary supplémentaire, en plus

Suppositories les suppositoires *m*

Sure *adj* sûr, e; ~ly *adv* sûrement

To surf faire du surf

Surfboard le surf

Surgeon le/la chirurgien/ne

Surroundings les environs

Swamp le marais

To sweat transpirer

Sweet sucré, e

Sweet pepper le poivron

Sweeteners les sucrettes *f*

Sweets les friandises *f*

Swelling la grosseur; l'enflure *f*

To swim nager

Swim fins les palmes *f*

Swimmer le nageur/la nageuse

Swimming lessons le cours de natation

Swimming pool la piscine

Swiss franc le franc suisse

Swiss person le Suisse/la Suissesse

Switzerland la Suisse

Swollen enflé

Swordfish l'espadon *m*

Symphony concert le concert symphonique

T-shirt le t(ee)-shirt
Table la table
Tablecloth la nappe
Tablet le comprimé, le cachet
Tachometer le compteur
Tailor le tailleur; **Seamstress** la couturière
To take prendre; *(things)* emporter; *(people)* emmener
To take a walk se promener
To take an X-ray faire une radio(graphie)
To take care of s'occuper de
To take one's leave prendre congé
To take part (in) prendre part (à)
To take place avoir lieu
Tampons les tampons *m*; mini/normal/super/super plus
Taste le goût
To taste good être bon
Taxi driver le chauffeur/la chauffeuse de taxi
Taxi stand la station de taxis
Tea le thé
Teabag le sachet de thé
To teach enseigner
Team l'équipe *f*
Teaspoon la cuillère à café
Telegram le télégramme
Telephone le téléphone
To telephone, call appeler, téléphoner à
Telephoto lens le téléobjectif
Television le téléviseur
Television room la salle de télévision
Telex le télex
To tell raconter
Temperature la température
Temple le temple
Temporary *adj* provisoire

Ten minutes ago il y a dix minutes
Tender tendre
Tennis le tennis
Tennis racket la raquette de tennis
Tennis shoes les tennis *f*; *(higher)* **basketball sneakers** les baskets *m*
Tent la tente
Tent pole le piquet de tente
Terminal le terminal; le terminus
Terra cotta la terre cuite
Terrace la terrasse
To testify attester
Tetanus le tétanos
To thank (someone) remercier (qn)
That *(conjunction)* que
That one/those celui-là, celle-là, ceux-là, celles-là
That's why c'est pourquoi
To the left à gauche
The other day l'autre jour
The same thing la même chose
Theater le théâtre
Theater café le café-théâtre
Theater troupe le groupe théâtral
Theft le vol
Their leur
Then ensuite
There là
There is/are il y a
Thermometer le thermomètre
Thermos bottle la (bouteille) thermos
They *pl m* ils; *pl f* elles
Thief le voleur
Thin mince; fin, e; maigre
Thing la chose
To think penser
To think about penser à
Third le/la troisième
Third-party, fire and theft l'assurance *f* au tiers

This morning / evening ce matin/ce soir
This/these ce, cet, cette, ces
Threshold le seuil
Throat la gorge
Through *(direction)* à travers; *(by means of)* grâce à; **By** *(passive voice)* par
Thursday jeudi
Thus donc
Thyme le thym
Ticket le billet
Ticket cost le prix du billet
Ticket machine le distributeur de billets
Ticket window le guichet
Tied game match nul
Tights les collants *m*
Time le temps
Timed shutter release le déclencheur automatique
Timid timide
Tincture of iodine la teinture d'iode
To tint faire un rinçage
Tip *(information)* le tuyau, *(advice)* le conseil
Tip le pourboire
Tire le pneu
Tire repair kit le kit de réparation des pneus
Tired fatigué, e
Tissues les mouchoirs *m* en papier
To *(destination)* à
To the rear à l'arrière
Toast le toast
Toaster le grille-pain
Tobacco le tabac
Tobacco shop le bureau de tabac
Today aujourd'hui
Toe l'orteil *m*
Together ensemble
Toilet paper le papier hygiénique
Toilets les toilettes
Toll le péage
Tomatoes les tomates *f*

Tomb le tombeau
Tomorrow morning / evening demain matin/ soir
Tone le ton; **Shade** la teinte
Tongue la langue
Tonsils les amygdales *f*
Too bad! Dommage!
Too, too much trop
Tools les outils *m*
Tooth la dent
Toothache le mal de dents
Toothbrush la brosse à dents
Toothpaste le dentifrice
Toothpick le cure-dents
To touch toucher
Tough coriace
Tour le circuit; le tour
Touring bike le V.T.C. (vélo tout chemin)
Tourist le/la touriste
Tourist office l'office *m* de tourisme, le syndicat d'initiative
To tow remorquer
Tow truck la dépanneuse
Toward *(spatial, temporal)* vers
Tower la tour
Towing cable le câble de remorquage
Towing service le service de dépannage
Town hall *(government)* la mairie; *(historical building)* l'hôtel *m* de ville
Toy store le magasin de jouets
Toys les jouets *m*
Track la voie
Track and field l'athlétisme
Traffic la circulation
Traffic jam l'embouteillage *m*
Traffic light le feu (de circulation)
Tragedy la tragédie
Trailer la caravane; *(auto)* la remorque
Train le train
Tranquilizer le tranquillisant
Transfer le virement

Transfusion la perfusion
To translate traduire
Transmission *(auto)* la boîte de vitesses
Transport le convoyage
Transportation service le service de transport (pour handicapés)
Trash les ordures *f pl*
Trash can le sac-poubelle
To travel voyager
Travel agency l'agence *f* de voyages
Travel bag le sac de voyage
Travel guide le guide
Traveler's check le chèque de voyage
To treat soigner
Tree l'arbre *m*
Trip le voyage, le trajet
Tripod le pied
Truck le camion
True vrai, e
Trunk *(of car)* le coffre
To try *(food)* goûter
Tuesday mardi
Tumor la tumeur
Tuna fish le thon
Tunnel le tunnel
To turn around faire demi-tour
Turquoise *(mineral* and *color)* turquoise
Tweezers la pince à épiler
Type la sorte
Typhus la typhoïde
Typical (of) typique (de), caractéristique (de)

Ugly laid, e
Ulcer l'ulcère *m*
Umbrella le parapluie
Unaccustomed inhabituel, le
Unbearable insupportable

Unbelievable incroyable
Unconscious sans connaissance, évanoui
Uncooked ham le jambon cru
Under sous
Underpants le caleçon; le slip
Underpass le passage souterrain
Undershirt le maillot de corps
To understand comprendre
Underwater camera la caméra sous-marine
Underwear les sous-vêtements *m*
Unemployed au chômage
Unfortunately malheureusement
United States États-Unis
University l'université *f*
Unknown inconnu, e
Unpleasant désagréable
Until jusqu'à; So far jusqu'à maintenant
Upstairs en haut
Upwards en haut, vers le haut
Urgent urgent, e
Urinal l'urinoir *m*
Urine l'urine *f*
Us à nous
To use utiliser
Usual usuel/le, habituel, le; Common commun/e

Vacation les vacances *f pl*
Vacation village le village de vacances
Vaccination la vaccination
Vaccination record le carnet de vaccinations
Valid valable
Valley la vallée
Valuables les objets *m pl* de valeur
Variable variable
Variety show les variétés *f*

Vase le vase
Vault la voûte
Veal le veau
Vegetables les légumes *m*
Vegetarian végétarien
Vehicle identification number le numéro de la voiture
Vending machine le distributeur automatique
Very très
Vest le gilet
Vice-versa inversement
Video camera la caméra vidéo
Video cassette la vidéocassette
Video film le film vidéo
Video recorder le magnétoscope
View la vue
Viewfinder le viseur
Viewpoint le point de vue
Villa la villa
Village le village
Vinegar le vinaigre
Vineyard la vigne
Violet violet
Virus le virus
Visa le visa
Vision-impaired person le/la malvoyant/e
To visit visiter
Visit la visite
To visit someone rendre visite à qn
Visiting times les heures *f* de visites
Volcano le volcan
Volleyball le volley-ball
Voltage le voltage

W

Wading pool la pataugeoire
To wait attendre; **To expect** s'attendre à
To wait in line faire la queue

Waiter/waitress le garçon/ la serveuse; *(direct address)* Monsieur!
Waiting room la salle d'attente
To wake up se réveiller
Walk la promenade
To walk marcher
Walker le déambulateur
Wall le mur
Wall socket la prise de courant
Wallet le portefeuille
Warning triangle le triangle de présignalisation
To wash laver
Washcloth le gant de toilette
Washing machine la machine à laver
Washroom les lavabos *m*
Wasp la guêpe
Wastebasket la poubelle
Watch out! Attention!
To watch (over) surveiller
Watchmaker l'horloger *m*
Water l'eau *f*
Water bottle le bidon d'eau
Water consumption la consommation d'eau
Water glass le verre à eau
Water skiing le ski nautique
Water wings les bracelets *m*
Watercolor l'aquarelle *f*
Waterfall la cascade
We nous
Weak faible
To wear porter
Weather forecast les prévisions *f* météo(rologiques)
Weather report le bulletin météo(rologique), la météo
Wednesday mercredi
Week la semaine
Week-pass le forfait-semaine
Weekend rate le forfait-weekend
Weekly *adj* hebdomadaire
Weekly menu la carte hebdomadaire

Weight le poids
Welcome bienvenu, e
Well done bien cuit
West of à l'ouest de
Western le western
Wet mouillé, e
Wet suit la combinaison de plongée
What que, qu'est-ce que; What kind of …? quel/le
Wheel la roue
Wheelchair le fauteuil roulant
When *(time)* quand; Than *(comparative)* que
Whipping cream la crème chantilly
White blanc
White bread le pain blanc
White cheese le fromage blanc
White wine le (vin) blanc
Whooping cough la coqueluche
Wide large
Widowed *(man)* veuf; *(woman)* veuve
Width of the door la largeur de la porte
Wife la femme
Wig la perruque
Wild sauvage, féroce
To win gagner
Wind le vent
Wind direction la direction du vent
Wind speed la force du vent
Wind surfing faire de la planche à voile
Window la fenêtre
Window seat le coin-fenêtre
Windshield le pare-brise
Windshield wiper l'essuie-glace *m*
Wine le vin
Wine glass le verre à vin
Wine shop le magasin de vins
Wing l'aile *f*
Winter l'hiver *m*
Winter tires le pneu neige

Wire le fil de fer
Wire transfer le mandat télégraphique
Wisdom tooth la dent de sagesse
To wish désirer; vouloir
With avec
Without sans
Witness le/la témoin
Woman la femme
To wonder s'étonner (de)
Wonderful magnifique; merveilleux, -euse
Wood le bois
Wood sculpture la sculpture sur bois
Woodcut la gravure sur bois
Wool la laine
Wool blanket la couverture de laine
Wool jacket la veste de laine
Word le mot
Work le travail; Job *(employment)* l'emploi *m*
To work travailler
Workday le jour ouvrable
Workshop l'atelier *m*, le garage
Worm le ver
To worry s'inquiéter
To worry about se faire du souci pour
Worthless sans valeur
To wound blesser
Wound la blessure; la plaie
To wrap emballer
Wristwatch la montre-bracelet
To write écrire
To write down noter
Writing l'écriture
Writing supplies les articles *m* de papeterie

X

X-ray la radio(graphie)

Y

Year l'année *f*, l'an *m*
To yell crier
Yellow jaune
Yellow pages les pages *f* jaunes
Yes (indeed)! Si!
Yesterday hier
Yoga le yoga
Yogurt le yaourt
You (familiar) tu, toi, te

You (polite) vous, à vous
Young jeune
Young person le/la jeune
Your ton, ta
Your votre

Z

Zoo le zoo